The Dynamics of European Nuclear Disarmament

*Rudolf Bahro, Ken Coates, Johan Galtung,
Carl C. Jacobsen, Robert Havemann,
Fernando Moran, Alva Myrdal,
Raimo Väyrynen*

Spokesman
for European Nuclear Disarmament
and the Bertrand Russell Peace Foundation

First published in 1981 by:
Spokesman
Bertrand Russell House
Gamble Street
Nottingham
for the Bertrand Russell Peace Foundation,
European Nuclear Disarmament

Cloth ISBN 0 85124 320 7
Paper ISBN 0 85124 321 5

Printed by the Russell Press Ltd., Nottingham

Foreword

As this book entered the printing press, a group of Scandinavian women set out on a long pilgrimage from Copenhagen to Paris. Their route was to take them through Germany, Holland and Belgium, touching the cities of Bremen, Eindhoven and Brussels along the way. Although many people joined in for parts of the journey, the central core of the marchers was composed of a small number of women from Norway, Sweden, Finland and Denmark, who walked the whole distance. These were the peace marchers.

Their goal was to secure the removal of all nuclear weapons, first from the Nordic areas, but also from the entire continent of Europe, East and West. They sought no advantages for either of the power blocs, and neither did they propose any disadvantage: their initiative was aimed against the fear of "limited" nuclear war in our area, which is the most intensively armed zone in a world full of murderous weaponry.

The contributors to this book make it their offering to the peace march. We hope it also helps carry the argument, and the cause, forward.

Contents

Glossary

Circular Error Probable. (CEP). A standard of accuracy in the delivery of nuclear warheads: the radius of that circle around any target within which half those missiles trained upon it would actually strike.

CND. Campaign for Nuclear Disarmament (in Great Britain).

Conference on Security & Co-operation in Europe. (CSCE). Thirty-two nation (Europe, plus USA and Canada) standing conference which began in 1972 in Helsinki and has reconvened at Belgrade and Madrid.

Cruise Missile. A guided missile which remains within the atmosphere, computerised to fly at low enough altitudes to avoid radar detection.

Comprehensive Test Ban. (CTB).

Department of Defence (United States) (DOD).

END. European Nuclear Disarmament.

Enhanced Radiation Warhead. (ERW) The so-called "neutron" bomb, with maximum radiation and minimum blast and heat.

Eurostrategic Missile. Those long- range nuclear missiles not covered in SALT agreements, but able to target on Europe. Soviet missile systems in this category are also called "grey area" systems, and are roughly equivalent to the United States' "forward based systems". The difference, of course, is that the former cannot reach the territory of the USA, but the latter can reach that of the USSR.

Flexible Response. The capacity to answer attack with a full range of options from conventional weaponry through to all-out nuclear war. This implies an interim level of combat in which "limited" use can be made of nuclear weapons.

FRG. Federal Republic of Germany.

Ground-launched Cruise Missile. (GLCM). A cruise missile launched from land emplacements or mobile launchers: in distinction from sea-launched cruise missiles (SLCM), which can be fired from submarines or surface vessels.

HLG (High-Level Group). A sub-group of NATO's Nuclear Planning Group, set up in 1977 to plan "modernisation" of theatre nuclear forces.

IISS. International Institute of Strategic Studies.

Initial Operating Capability. (IOC). The date by which a missile system is deployed ready for use in the field.

IRBM. Intermediate range ballistic missiles (2775-5550km) deployed by the USSR. Examples include SS5, SS20 missiles.

Kiloton (Kt). Explosive power of a nuclear bomb, measured in terms of its effective equivalence to a given weight of TNT. One kiloton = 1000 tons of TNT: one megaton = 1,000,000 tons of TNT.

LRTNF. Long-range Theatre Nuclear Forces: a general

description for the cruise and Pershing II missile programmes of the USA.

LTDP. Long-term Defence Programme.

MARV — see re-entry vehicles.

MIRV — see re-entry vehicles.

Mutual and Balanced Force Reductions. (MBFR) continuing talks at Vienna between the representatives of NATO and the Warsaw Treaty Organisation, aimed at limiting and reducing military confrontation in Central Europe.

NPT. Non-Proliferation Treaty.

Nuclear Planning Group. A NATO committee formed in 1966 for the briefing of its members, and a degree of participation in decisions. The USA, Great Britain, Italy and Federal Germany are permanent members. Others are chosen to serve by rotation.

Quick Reaction Alert. The readying of nuclear delivery systems to be fired at short notice.

Re-entry Vehicle. That part of a ballistic missile which contains a warhead, and which detaches itself to re-enter the atmosphere at the last stage of its rocket's trajectory. One missile can carry several such vehicles. Then it is described as MRV (Multiple Re-entry Vehicle). If the several warheads can be independently directed at different objectives, it will be called a MIRV, and if the warheads are carried in manoeuvrable vehicles, it is known as a MARV.

SACEUR. NATO's Supreme Allied Commander, Europe.

SALT. Strategic Arms Limitation Talks.

SAM. Surface-to-Air missile.

SLCM. Sea-launched Cruise Missile. See under "Ground-launched Cruise Missiles".

SLBM. Submarine-launched ballistic missile.

SAM. Surface-to-Air missile.

Tercom. Terrain Contour Matching: the guidance system which attempts to enable cruise missiles to follow map data and check their actual itinerary against their intended one.

Ken Coates is Reader in Adult Education at the University of Nottingham, and a Director of the Bertrand Russell Peace Foundation.

Introduction
Ken Coates

In 1980 we in Europe entered a new decade with all our diverse traditional celebrations. In Scotland people were first-footed, while in Italy they burnt the old year in their city squares, to the joyful noise of fireworks. Dancing, singing, embracing followed midnight all the way round the globe in the same annual ritual of renewal. Hope, we might all still hope, springs eternal.

Yet that same decade could all too easily be the last that most of us are allowed to join. War, and the talk of war, and the cost of war, were on the minds of all too many statesmen, and of all those citizens who remained alive to the movement of affairs. The uneasy détente between the two greatest military powers was in evident crisis. Economic collapse threatened lesser powers: slump was performing its purgative functions without always offering its former promise of ultimate recovery. Where possible, the rich exported their problems to the poor, which made the poor world more unstable than it had ever been. Political tension increased everywhere, and revolution or counter-revolution were not far away in many places. In Iran, in Salvador, in Poland, in Afghanistan, armies moved or threatened to move.

Military spending had reached the unprecedented annual figure of $500 billion, or 1.3 billion dollars each and every day. Fearsome new weapon systems were being installed, and others were actively being developed. New methods of chemical and biological warfare were designed and perfected.[1] It was to be a decade of confrontation, threat, and fear. It was also to be a decade of resistance, which is what this book is about.

But first, let us consider what it is that is feared by men and women who are not easily given to panic.

Kurt Vonnegut Jr., who has written the most powerful book we have about the Second World War,[2] was a prisoner of war in Dresden on the night that British and American bombers visited that city and killed 135,000 people. Like his hero, Billy Pilgrim, Vonnegut was locked into a slaughterhouse, which had been converted to prison use because there were too few pigs left to be converted into meat. On February 13th, 1945, Dresden was utterly destroyed, and the American prisoners, who, by in-advertence, had been fastened into the safest buildings in the city, emerged next morning to a moonscape, except that it was still burning. All those people had already burned. Many of them had melted. The largest bomb which fell during that night contained ten tons of TNT. Of course, a lot of such bombs were dropped.

The single bomb which obliterated Hiroshima, a little later in the year, had an explosive force equivalent to 13,000 tons of TNT. Soon men would know how to manufacture weapons vastly more powerful. A Minuteman III missile nowadays carries three independently targetable war-heads, each with a destructive force of 170,000 tons of TNT. These are not large war-heads by modern standards. But a single war-head of 100,000 tons of TNT equivalent would kill at least half the population of any middling city instantly, if it were detonated there. My own city is the centre of a built-up area housing half a million people. It would qualify for this kind of death-rate. Europe is full of such cities, many of them richer and more beautiful than mine, but all equally vulnerable. Such is the progress of civilisation that men have it in their power to eradicate Florence, and Athens, and Paris, and Rome, and Cambridge, and Leningrad, and New York, and London, and Moscow, and Belgrade, and Vienna and Stockholm in a single morning. Many more old buildings and venerable libraries could be cauterised in the following afternoon. The dead would then be uncountable. A ten megaton bomb, of which both the Russians and the Americans have large supplies, could destroy up to five million persons in any sufficiently densely populated conurbation.

After the Hiroshima explosion, the dead were enumerated as 71,379. But by 1950, within five years, this roll had increased by a further 200,000, as a result of radiation and other deferred effects. All this was achieved with 13 kilotons. Today the USSR has between one and two hundred war-heads of 25 megatons, or 25,000,000 tons of TNT equivalent. These have the capacity to flatten everything for 13 miles in every direction from their point of impact. As the Federation of American Scientists point out,

> "A five megaton bomb will do the same for cities with a radius of 7.5 miles. The Soviet Union is ready to deliver 400 such weapons. War-heads of about one megaton could level cities that are four miles in radius. The Soviet Union had 6,000 war-heads in that range. The US has only 2000 cities over the minimal size of 10,000 inhabitants. All of these could therefore easily be destroyed."[3]

No-one need doubt what is made plain below, that the Americans can repay with at least equal ferocity all this devastation.

The actual kill levels in American and Soviet territories would remain dissimilar because of disparities in the concentration of their populations. Even so, their finality is convincing, in both cases. Harold Brown, Secretary for Defence in the outgoing American administration, has provided the following official guesses of the death roll in an all-out nuclear exchange between the USA and USSR: between 20 and 55 million at the low end, and 155 to 165 million at the high end, in the United States; and from 23-34 million up to 64 or 100 million in the Soviet Union. "Beyond this" he added "secondary and indirect disruptions of the societies attacked, and longer-term fallout and other consequences to areas outside those attacked, would amplify the damage."[4]

This "damage" cannot easily be understood at the statistical level. Those who are not killed instantly can take a long time to die. Those who recover may die later. Those who live may not easily understand the shape of the mutilated world they have entered. Eleven-year-old Sakue Kawasaki, of Nagasaki, was in the shelter when the flash came. Hundreds of people, many already half-dead, swollen like pumpkins, and screaming, tumbled into the shelters afterwards. Sakue's father, who looked uninjured, came into the shelter at 5 o'clock, and took her out. They wandered in the smoke, trying to help the dying, while they searched for her mother. Mother was dead. Sakue's brother died before she had been found. Her big sister had also been killed. She and her father stayed about a week, and eventually cremated the bodies. Then they decided to go away from the ruins to the country. As they were deciding to leave, Sakue was later to report in a school composition,

"from somewhere a little girl about three years old appeared in front of us. When she saw me, she cried, "My big sister!" and hugged me. I was surprised and looked at the child's face but I couldn't recognize her. I'd never heard her name and didn't have the slightest idea where she was from. Though I explained to her many times that I was not her sister, she clung to me with a smile and insisted, "No. You're Sister! You are my sister." I'm sure she was the only survivor in her family. And she might have had a big sister who looked like me. She was a very cute little girl. We decided to raise her until somebody in her family could be found. The girl soon became attached to us. We had been lonesome because we had lost three of our own family. And our laughter returned to us as we welcomed a new member into our family. We were stirred to new energy because the innocent child made us laugh. We worked busily preparing to leave Nagasaki. After three days, on the day when we planned to leave, the little girl suddenly disappeared. We sent people to look for her, but we couldn't find that cute girl again. Finally we gave up looking and left for our home town.

Who on earth, who was that pretty girl who looked like an angel?"[5]

In 1945, two cities in Japan had been destroyed in this way, and much other destruction had been caused by conventional bombing. But Harold Brown is not wrong when he informs us that the nuclear war in the 'eighties is scheduled to count its dead in millions where thousands lay before. How many American, Russian, European children will not then know who their true sisters are, and where will they go? Which infirmaries will nurse all those who are sick, when nearly all are burnt? Dr. Hiatt, dean of the Harvard School of Public Health, has warned the American people that the next holocaust may well cause 25 million severe burn cases, at a time when half their nation's hospitals will have been incinerated and three-quarters of the competent medical personnel killed or incapacitated. "If the civil defence budget were in my hands, I would spend all $120 million on morphine" he has said.[6]

Of course, the civil defence budget of the United States, like that of many of her allies, is the merest placebo. Morphine would be a more sensible investment. Peace, a few dreamers think, might be more sensible still.

Having faced all these prospects more than twenty years ago, Bertrand Russell drew three rather evident conclusions: first, that any future large-scale war would bring disaster "not only to belligerents, but to mankind"; second, that little wars would always henceforward contain the risk of becoming great, and that the more of them there were, the more likely it would be that one or another of them might grow to encompass our general destruction; and third, that even were existing nuclear weapons all by agreement to be destroyed, the outbreak of any future major war would ensure that replacements would be used as soon as they could be manufactured.[7] So far more than a hundred "little" wars have raged since 1945, and two of them, those in Korea and Indo-China, involved the use of a firepower far more horrendously devastating than the totality of that available during the Second World War. In one sense, this fact does not contradict what Russell said: war in Afghanistan, or in Iran, or in Eritrea, or in Namibia, or who knows where next, does indeed carry the most fearful prospect of escalation, drawing in both active external sponsors and passive bystanders. In another sense, those who have preached the conventional doctrine of deterrence can be yielded (for what it is worth), their claim that ever-enlarging nuclear arsenals in both super-powers have up to now kept them apart from direct engage-ment one with another, and schooled them in exploring the delicate risks of proxy conflicts. The proxies will take no comfort from this.

This doctrine of deterrence has not stood still, however. One of its most loyal British proponents has been Mr Denis Healey, who informed us in the early 1950s that the best guide to the true state of the world was Thomas Hobbes, who understood power politics. For Hobbes, fear was an in-dispensable component of the impulse to statehood, upon which depended the public peace and the containment of the "war of each against all", which otherwise raged in the socie-ty of natural man. But if this doctrine had been true, Hiroshima would surely have generated sufficient fear to force us all to accept it as international polity. It did not. Deterrence theory, founded in one kind of technology, and within a given geo-political balance, has reiterated various rather primitively Hobbesian prescriptions to all who would listen, while both technologies and political realities have been borne along beneath it in a heaving flux of change. Hob-bes himself would have been infinitely wiser. He would never have ignored corporeal being because of a web of words. Order may once have been based on fear, but today fear has reached a point at which it imminently threatens to destroy what it has left of "order".

When Bertrand Russell sought to explain the confrontation of the nuclear superpowers, back in 1959, he offered a famous analogy:

"Since the nuclear stalemate became apparent, the Governments of East and West have adopted the policy which Mr Dulles calls 'brinkmanship'. This is a policy adapted from a sport which, I am told, is practised by the sons of very rich Americans. This sport is called 'Chicken!' It is played by choosing a long straight road with a white line down the middle and starting two very fast cars towards each other from opposite ends. Each car is expected to keep the wheels of one side on the white line. As they approach each other, mutual destruction becomes more and more imminent. If one of them swerves from the white line before the other, the other, as he passes, shouts 'Chicken!' , and the one who has swerved becomes an object of contempt. As played by youthful plutocrats, this game is considered decadent and immoral, though only the lives of the players are risked. But when the game is played by eminent statesmen, who risk not only their own lives but those of many hundreds of millions of human beings, it is thought on both sides that the statesmen on the other side are reprehensible. This, of course, is absurd. Both are to blame for playing such an incredibly dangerous game. The game may be played without misfortune a few times, but sooner or later it will come to be felt that loss of face is more dreadful than nuclear annihilation. The moment will come when neither side can face the derisive cry of 'Chicken!' from the other side. When that moment is come, the statesmen of both sides will plunge the world into destruction."[8]

We do not cite this passage out of piety. Russell's parable is no longer adequate. Various things have changed since 1959. Some were beginning to change, at any rate in minds like Mr Henry Kissinger's, even before that time.

Some changes were rather evident to ordinary people, more or less instantly. Others were not. Within the game of "chicken" itself, we had the Cuba crisis of 1962. Mr Khruschchev swerved. This persuaded certain shallow advocates of the game that deterrence actually worked. But rather more significantly, it also persuaded the more faithful Hobbesians among Mr Khrushchev's colleagues that considerably greater effort should be lavished on the perfection of a swerve-proof war machine. Consequently, the nuclear armament balance shifted, if not in the drastic manner announced by Washington alarmists, at any rate in the direction of something closer to effective parity.

In addition to this, proliferation of nuclear weaponry continued. This is discussed below, and all that we need say about it here is that it has complicated the rules of the game rather considerably. The French allowed if they did not actually encourage public speculation about the thought that their deterrent was more than unidirectional, if their putative defenders ever showed undue reluctance to perform, in time of need, the allotted role. The arrival of the Chinese as a growing nuclear force produced a new three-way "chicken", with both main camps holding out at least a possibility that, in appropriate circumstances, they might "play the China card". But here the metaphor is mixing itself. Staying within the rules Russell advanced, we would have to express it like this: the Chinese "deterrent" could, at least in theory, be set to intervene against either of the other participants in the joust, unpredictably, from any one of a bewildering number of side-entries to the main collision course.

As if this were not problem enough, the war-technology has itself evolved, so that:

a. military costs have escalated to the point where nuclear powers are quite apparently increasingly impotent if they are barred from using what has now become by far their most expensive weaponry; and

b. nuclear weapons technique aspires to (although it may very well fail to meet) infinitely greater precision in attack. This brings nearer the possibility of preemptive war, which is a perfectly possible abrupt reversal of standard detente presumptions.

To these facts we must add another, of powerful moment:

c. the stability of the world political economy, which seemed effectively unchallengeable in 1959, has been fiercely undermined by the collapse of the Keynesian world order, deep slump in the advanced capitalist countries, and growing social tension within the nations of the Soviet sphere of influence, who have not for the most part been able to evolve those democratic and consensual forms of administration which could resolve their political tensions in an orderly and rational manner.

In the interaction of these developments, we have seen the consolidation, amongst other delinquencies, of the doctrine of "limited" nuclear war. We can only reduce this veritable mutation in strategy to Russell's exemplary folk-tale if we imagine that each participant car in the game enfolds smaller subordinate vehicles, which can be launched down the white line at even greater speed than the velocity of approach of the main challengers. These lesser combatants can, it is apparently believed, be set loose on one another in order that their anticipated crashes may permit time for the principals to decide whether it might be wise themselves to swerve or not. Any desire of the small fry to change course is already taken care of, because they are already steered by remote control. Of course, the assumption is that those involved in the "lesser" combat will necessarily be destroyed. Maybe their destruction can save their mother vehicles from perishing, although careful analysts think it more likely not.

Stated in this way, the game has become even more whimsical than it was in Russell's original model. But stiffened up with precise and actual designations, it loses all traces of whimsy. The lesser vehicles in the developing game of "limited" war are all of Europe's nations. Whether or not their sacrifice makes free enterprise safer in New York, or allows Mr Brezhnev's successors time to build full communism (and we may well be agnostic on both scores) what is securely certain is that after it Europe will be entirely and poisonously dead, and that the civilisation of Leonardo and Galileo, Bacon and Hobbes, Spinoza and Descartes and, yes, Karl Marx, will have evaporated without trace.

Before we consider the project for limited nuclear war in a little more detail, it is necessary to unravel the conventional doctrine of deterrence somewhat further. Advocates of this schema will often repudiate the fable of the chicken game. "It is a malicious travesty", they will tell us. The vogue question which is then very commonly posed by such people is this: "you complain about the destruction of Hiroshima and Nagasaki: but would these events have taken place, if Japan then had the benefit of a possible nuclear response?" Let us worry this problem a little. First, some obvious points. Did the Japanese in this speculative argument possess an equivalence of weaponry or not? If they were nuclear-armed, but with a smaller number of war-heads, or inadequate delivery systems, it is possible that their retaliatory capacity could be evaluated and discounted, in which case the American attack would presumably have gone ahead. If, on the other hand, the American Government perceived that it might not avoid parity of destruction or worse, it would in all likelihood have drawn back. It might even have hesitated for fear of less than equal devastation. "Aha!" say the deterrent philosophers: "you have conceded our case". Well, hardly. We must first pursue it for a few steps, but not before pointing out that it has already become completely hypothetical, and already travesties many other known facts about the real Japanese war prospects in August 1945, quite apart from the then existing, real disposition of nuclear weapons. (There are some strong grounds for the assumption that the Japanese would actually have been brought to a very quick surrender if the nuclear bombardment had never taken place, or indeed, even had it not been possible). But for the sake of argument, we are temporarily conceding this special case of the deterrent argument. Let us then see what happens when we apply it further. In 1974, the Indian Government exploded a "peaceful" nuclear device. Subsequently Pakistan set in train the necessary work of preparation for an answering technology. Since partition, India and Pakistan have more than once been at war. There remain serious territorial claims at issue between them. The secession of Bangladesh inflicted serious humiliation on the Pakistan Government. What possible argument can be advanced against a Pakistan deterrent? We shall instantly be told that the present military rulers of that country are unsavoury to a remarkable degree, that they butchered their last constitutionally elected Prime Minister, and that they maintain a repressive and decidedly unpleasant administration. It is difficult, if not unfortunately impossible, to disagree with these complaints, all of which are founded in reason and justice. But as co-opted theorists of deterrence, we must dismiss them. Our adopted argument is, that if India and Pakistan are to be held apart from their next war, the deterrent is necessary to both sides. Their respective moral shortcomings, if any, or indeed, if all that have ever been alleged, have nothing to do with the case.

Late in April 1981, Mr F.W. De Klerk, the mineral and energy affairs minister of South Africa, publicly admitted that his country was producing a quantity of 45% enriched uranium, which announcement signified that South Africa had the capacity to manufacture its own nuclear armament. This news was scarcely electrifying, since a nuclear device had already apparently been detonated in the South Atlantic during the previous year, and it had therefore been assumed, almost universally, that the South African bomb already existed. What should the black African "front-line States" then do? Deterrence positively requires that Angola, Zimbabwe and Mozambique should instantly start work on procuring their opposing bombs. After all, South African troops have regularly been in action outside their own frontiers, and the very vulnerability of the Apartheid State make it perfectly possible that serious military contests could break out over the whole contiguous zone. To prevent such war, the Angolan or Zimbabwean bomb represents a prudent and uncontentious investment.

We can say the same thing about the States of the Middle East. To them we might add those of Central America. Would Cuba have been invaded during the Bay of Pigs episode, if she had deployed nuclear weapons? To cap it all, what about Japan? Her experience, surely, would seem to be the most convincing argument for developing an extensive arsenal of thermo-nuclear war-heads.

Strangely, these arguments are not heard in Japan. President Mugabe has not voiced them either. Japan's people have not escaped the customary scissions which are part of advanced industrial society, but if one thing binds them together, it is a virtually unanimous revulsion against nuclear weapons. African States repeatedly insist that they seek protection, not by deterrence, but by the creation of a nuclear-free zone. Clearly they have not yet learnt the lessons which are so monotonously preached in the Establishment newspapers of the allegedly advanced nations.

If we were to admit that all nation States had an intrinsic right to defend their institutions and interests by all the means available to any, then nuclear proliferation would not merely be unavoidable, but unimpeachable within the deterrent model. And it is this incontrovertible fact which reduces it to absurdity; and argues that Russell was in fact right to pose the question as he did. Very soon the chicken game will not only have a cluster of three nuclear States at one end of the white line, and a single super-State at the other, with the Chinese already able to intervene from a random number of side routes: but it will shortly have from twelve to twenty other possible contenders liable to dash, quite possibly unannounced, across the previously single axis of collision.*

*For those who still believe that this dreadful evolution will be prevented by the treaty on the Non-Proliferation of Nuclear Weapons, three warning notes. First, the Review Conference of August 1980, held in Geneva, failed to agree any "certificate of good health" for the operation of the treaty, because the nuclear powers had flouted all their solemn treaty promises to scale down their own nuclear stocks. Critics of the treaty said from the beginning that its weakness derived from the fact that under it the nuclear weapons-holding States were assuming the right to police the rest. This could only acquire moral validity if they began themselves to behave according to the same rules which they sought to impose on others. At Geneva, the Review Conference demonstrated that no such behaviour had materialised. Secondly, visible evidence of the collapse of the treaty's framework has come from the military relationship between the USA and Pakistan since the invasion of Afghanistan by the USSR. Vast conventional weapons shipments to Pakistan have

Deterrence, in short, was in the beginning, a bi-polar game, and it cannot be played in a multi-polar world. It is therefore collapsing, but the danger is that this collapse will result in universal destruction if alternative approaches are not speedily accepted. This danger arises because deterrence is a doctrine, a hitherto partially shared mythology, which may well lose all credibility before the material war potential which gave rise to it has even begun to be dismantled.

There was always, of course, a much simpler rebuttal of the doctrine. It is, was, and has always been, utterly immoral. Unfortunately, this argument, which is unanswerable, is not usually given even the slightest consideration in the world's war-rooms, although there is a fair deal of evidence that the people who staff these sometimes find it difficult to avoid traumatic neuroses about the effects of all their devilish labours.

However, the "lateral" proliferation of nuclear weapons to ever larger numbers of States, is by no means the most drastic process by which such weapons are multiplied. Lateral proliferation will provide more and more problems for the peace of the world, but the "vertical" proliferation of super-power arsenals is fearsome on an infinitely more dreadful scale. And it is the evolution of nuclear war-fighting doctrine, and the preparation for limited nuclear war, which provides the most serious threat we face in the 1980s, disturbed though rational men and women are bound to be by the prospects of the spawning of autonomously controlled atomic war-heads from one troubled region to the next. The "limited" nuclear exchange in Europe is likely to take place before one can be prepared on the Indian subcontinent, or, yet, in Africa. It is also scheduled to deploy as large a proportion of the firepower of the two great arsenals as may be needed.

---

already taken place, and vaster ones are contemplated, in spite of the previous US policy which had withheld arms supplies of all kinds from any State suspected of breaching the non-proliferation treaty. If breaches are now condoned by superpowers wherever their own perceived interests are at stake, then the treaty is not merely dead, but rotting away. Thirdly, as an augury, we have the Israeli bombardment of Iraq, which shows what we must expect now that proliferation is effectively uncontrolled. It was, coincidentally, Mr Ismat Kitani of Iraq who presided over the Geneva Review Conference, and who warned that "the failure of the talks would damage world peace".

How did we arrive at this mutation in strategic policy, which has begun to generate weapons designed to fight war rather than to "deter" it?

At the time when Bertrand Russell was campaigning for nuclear disarmament in Britain, there was an imbalance in the nuclear explosive stockpiles, although thermo-nuclear weapons already amply guaranteed the destruction of both superpowers, if they were to venture into war. According to Herbert York, the United States then had between twenty and forty million kilotons of explosives, "or the energy equivalent of some ten thousand World War II's".

> "We had reached" wrote York, "a level of supersaturation that some writers characterized by the word 'overkill', an understatement in my opinion. *Moreover, we possessed two different but reinforcing types of overkill. First, by 1960 we had many more bombs than they had urban targets, and second, with a very few exceptions such as Greater Moscow and Greater New York, the area of destruction and intense lethality that a single bomb could produce was very much larger than the area of the targets.* Since all, or practically all, strategic weapons were by then thermo-nuclear, it is safe to assume that those Soviet or Chinese cities which were equivalent in size and importance to Hiroshima and Nagasaki were, by that time, targets for weapons from one hundred to one thousand times as big as the bombs used in history's only two real demonstrations of what actually happens when large numbers of human beings and their works are hit by nuclear weapons."[9]

However, overkill has its limitations: bombs in the megaton class, York tells us, do not become proportionately more lethal as they become bigger. The size of the bomb "outruns the size of the target". This inevitably wastes much explosive power on "sparsely populated areas". Nonetheless, if the murderous effect of fallout is considered, even in the early 'sixties both superpowers could easily render the entirety of each other's territories intensely radioactive, and still have many unexpended bombs to spare.

The military doctrine which accompanied the perfection of this technology was one of the "massive retaliation", in the words of Secretary Dulles, or later, "Mutual Assured Destruction" as Defence Secretary MacNamara styled it. Although its advocates always insisted that this was a deterrent doctrine designed to prevent war, it did nonetheless, bear an undeniable relationship to Russell's game of "chicken", whenever conflict between the two powers entered the stage of open confrontation. But during MacNamara's own period, the seeds of the new doctrine of "flexible response" were already maturing. The assumption out of which this notion was to codify itself was that different levels of nuclear escalation could be defined, permitting an American President a power to move through a spectrum of lesser types of nuclear strike before all-out mutual destruction became unavoidable. In 1964, Mr MacNamara specifically mentioned the needs for "flexible capability" in nuclear forces. In 1969, Defence Secretary Clark Clifford called for weapons which could be "used effectively in a limited and controlled retaliation as well as for 'Assured Destruction' ".[10]

It was in March 1974 that the new Defence Secretary, James Schlesinger, announced a comprehensive justification for limited nuclear war. Since then, although United States spokesmen, including President Carter himself, have havered backwards and forwards on this question, "flexible targetting" has apparently gone remorselessly ahead, and the concomitant doctrines of limited war have become military orthodoxy. It is this fact which rendered the revelation, in August 1980, of the contents of Presidential Directive 59 so unsurprising to the specialists. It is also this fact which had previously provoked British military leaders and scientific planners, like Lord Mountbatten and Lord Zuckerman, to unrestrained protest.[11]

The burden of their complaint is simple. There is no way in which agreed rules can be established limiting either the size of weapons to be exchanged, or the nature of targets to be considered legitimate, or the quantity of devastation to be regarded as "acceptable". Nor is there any way in which thresholds can be determined, or infractions defined. What we know by inadvertence about targetting entirely reinforces this agnosticism. Neutral cities, military bases and even motorway junctions were among the targets specified in a plan which was stolen by a Soviet spy, and subsequently published.[12] Whatever damage was inflicted on communications in this model for attack, it is plain that enormous civilian casualties would be a necessary additional result. Europe, in particular, is closely packed with cities, and few of its military targets are quarantined away from large industrial or residential areas. Unlike Siberia, or parts of the continental United States, where there are big areas of sparse habitation, almost every nuclear explosion in our continent would produce vast civilian slaughter.

Of course, military doctrine is an arcane science, and while specialists debated these issues they were accorded a respectful if distant, albeit widespread, apathy. But, as the practical conclusions of their debates became plain, public moods began to change. First, the project for an enhanced radiation (or "neutron") bomb brought home to a wide audience the apparent truth that war-fighting, as opposed to "deterrent" weapons were far advanced in preparation. Then, the Soviet installation of SS20 missiles, which could strike European or Chinese targets, but not American ones, aroused concern not only among Governments. And finally, the NATO decision to "modernise" theatre nuclear forces in Western Europe, by installing Pershing II missiles and land-based cruise missiles throughout Western Europe, brought forth a storm of objections, and the beginning of a new approach to European disarmament.

Neither the Soviet, nor the American "modernisations" were uniquely responsible for this profound movement of opinion. Europeans had begun to perceive their intended role as victims: limited war in Europe meant that schedules were being evolved which made them prime targets. If any of them, on either side, were over-run, they could anticipate a double jeopardy: nuclear bombardment from the "enemy" while they were themselves a nuclear threat, followed by nuclear bombardment by their "allies" if anyone was left to hit. In this growing realisation, Europe began to generate a continental Resistance, from Scandinavia to Sicily, from Poland to Portugal. This epic movement is still in its earliest infancy, but already it demands attention. The papers which are published below are offered as ammunition in the struggle to preserve a continent, and a civilisation, from a threat more dire than apocalypse, after which there can be no renewal.

Footnotes

1, See the briefing prepared by the Russell Committee Against Chemical Weapons: *Oppose A New Chemical Arms Race,* Nottingham, Bertrand Russell House, February 1981.
2. *Slaughterhouse 5,* London, Panther 1972.

3. Federation of American Scientists: *FAS Public Interest Report,* Vol. 34, No. 2, Washington, February 1981.
4. Department of Defense: *Annual Report, Fiscal Year 1982,* Washington 1980.
5. Children of Nagasaki: *Living Beneath the Atomic Cloud,* Tokyo, San-Yu-Sha, 1949. p.32 *et sq.*
6. P.J. Hilts: *US Doctors Call Atom Defense Useless,* International Herald Tribune, 27th November 1980, p.10.
7. Bertrand Russell: *Commonsense and Nuclear Warfare,* London, Allen and Unwin, 1959, p.29.
8. Ibid, p.30.
9. Herbert York: *Race to Oblivion — A Participant's View of the Arms Race,* New York, Simon and Schuster, p.42.
10. See Jery Elmer: Presidential Directive 59 — America's Counter-force Strategy, Philadelphia, American Friends Service Committee, 1981.
11. *Apocalypse Now?* Spokesman, 1980.
12. See my essay in *Protest and Survive,* Penguin, 1980, for details of this bizarre story.

Part I
The Arms Race in Context

Carl G. Jacobsen is Professor at the University of Miami and Director of Soviet Studies in its Centre for Advanced International Studies.

The Nuclear Era: Its History; Its Implications

Carl G. Jacobsen

Thirty-five years ago the devastation of Hiroshima and Nagasaki brought Japan to her knees. The nuclear era had arrived. The atom would revolutionize world power calculations. Its profound, cataclysmic impact dwarfed even that earlier watershed, the introduction of gunpowder. The years following Hiroshima saw the inexorable spreading of nuclear technology, nuclear possession and nuclear capability.

By 1980 the world harboured over 60,000 nuclear warheads, many of a size that made the Hiroshima bomb look like a Chinese firecracker. By 1980 at least 6 countries possessed nuclear arsenals; the US, the USSR, China, Britain, France and India; two other countries, Israel and South Africa, were presumed (by Western intelligence agencies) to have at least some bombs; Pakistan was thought to be able to build a bomb within a matter of months; a number of States, including Brazil, Taiwan and South Korea were not far behind — 40 nations had the knowledge and expertise to acquire nuclear arms within the next ten years.

The world military budget has shot past the 500 billion (US) dollar mark. Knowledge of nuclear phenomena has become so widely available in the open literature that students at major universities have been able to come up with workable bomb designs. The fact, and the evident laxity of security as concerns both certain bomb depots and, most particularly, plutonium and nuclear "waste" storage and transportation methods (astounding amounts have been "lost" over the years — one might note that the C.I.A's estimate of current Israeli capabilities rests in part on the belief that one such shipment of plutonium ended up in Israel), all this makes it likely that non-governmental groups, even terrorists, may become "nuclear capable" in the future.

Increasing North-South disparities, increased resource competition (especially for dwindling energy resources), and the failure of the old economic order to fulfill expectations serves at the same time to heighten the potential for conflict. The possible causes for friction, antagonism, war, have multiplied. The dangers are made even more acute by public apathy, and widespread ignorance.

Today military budgets are still increasing, even faster than in recent years. And this at a time when even a small decrease could have a startling effect. Its been calculated that just five per cent of the world military budget could pay for vaccination against diseases presently killing more than five million children annually; and extend literacy by the end of this century to the 25 per cent of the world's adult population that is unable to read or write, and hence cut off from most sources of knowledge; and train health auxiliaries, barefoot doctors and midwives (these can take care of 85 per cent of a third world village's health needs), to service vast rural regions of the less developed world that presently have no access to professional medical services; one could also eradicate the malnutrition that today sees more than 500 million people eating less than the calories needed to sustain ordinary physical activity, and that condemns 200 million pre-school children to chronic hunger; by providing supplementary feeding to 60 million malnourished pregnant and lactating women infant mortality could be drastically reduced; and there would still be enough money to establish 100 million new school places (250 million new school places are needed by 1985 just to keep third world enrolment at the 50 per cent level), and to introduce hygienic water supply systems (today water-borne diseases kill 25,000 people every day; such diseases are the most common cause of death among children under 5!)

All this for just 5 per cent — yet military budgets keep going up, not down. Why? And how did we get here? That is what this endeavour hopes to explore.

Most people think of the immediate post-war world as one dominated by two superpowers, a "bi-polar world". Yet Moscow's superpower status was hollow. It rested on the West's fear of the unknown, on the images conjured up by Zhukov's conquest of Berlin . . . Alexander the First parading down the streets of Napoleon's Paris, cossacks, fables about "Asian hordes" . . . In economic terms the Soviet Union was no superpower. 70 per cent of her industrial capacity lay waste. The Nazi scorched earth policy had taken its toll. Even with a slashing of Armed Forces personnel and forced-pace reindustrialization it was not until 1949 that the USSR regained its industrial potential of 1939. In the military sphere her inferiority was even more startling. The US could obliterate Soviet society; the USSR could not inflict damage on the US homeland.

Why should it have mattered?

Western attitudes are relatively well-known: distrust and fear of the ideology championed by Moscow, unease and apprehension at Moscow's assertion of control in Eastern Europe, etc.

Soviet fear and suspicion is less well appreciated, or understood. A few points deserve mention: Bolshevik ideology had conditioned future Soviet leaders to expect that so-called capitalists would bend all efforts to destroy their revolution, to snuff out the dogma that proclaimed capitalism to be the enemy of more egalitarian hopes and designs. The allied interventions after the Revolution, when US, British, French, Canadian and Japanese troops landed on Russian soil, confirmed — indeed "proved" — the prejudice inculcated by ideology. Soviet leaders were also aware that final Allied withdrawal had reflected not goodwill, but rather resignation at the "white" armies' inability to secure sufficient popular support, together with a wave of mutinies in the French army, mass demonstrations in Britain, and a general war-weariness that made prosecution of a war effort in Russia and Siberia a political impossibility. Later depression hit the West. But there remained fear and conviction in Moscow that revived capitalism would try again. Nazi Germany was the first capitalist nation to revive, and true enough . . . The war had seen other capitalist nations aligned with Moscow, because they feared Berlin more. But the fall of the Third Reich would allow them to return their energies against their ideological nemesis. The post-war view from Moscow looked grim. US nuclear monopoly; US and allied bases around the perimeter of the Soviet Union. The map as seen from Moscow, a Moscow steeped in paranoia, pictured encirclement, danger. The view of Eastern Europe also differed. It was not just the Bolsheviks who saw control over Eastern Europe as necessary. Russian conservatives, moderates, liberals, agreed. East of the Tatra mountains in Western Czechoslovakia the ground is flat, all the way to Moscow, interrupted only by the Pripet marshes. Over twenty million dead in World War II, over 20 million in World War I, the Fuhrer, the Kaiser, Napoleon, Charles the Twelfth. What came to be known as the Iron Curtain closely paralleled the line Catherine The Great had drawn on the map of Europe, as the line east of which Russia could not afford to be weak, could not afford not to dominate. The Soviet Union had to strive for the power to ward off all possible enemies, or else renounce both her ideological and her nationalist aspirations. How could she pretend to leadership of an ideology that challenged the *status quo* if she resigned herself to perpetual inferiority? How could she attract allies if she could not help protect them? Britain and France could fall back on a powerful patron, they could rely on the US shield. Moscow saw herself as having no one to fall back on.*

While striving to secure off-setting power, Moscow found it necessary to hide her weakness. The drastic nature of post-war demobilization was not revealed. The first longer-range bombers, acquired in the 50s, would make fly-passes over Red Square, double back, and fly past again to give the appearance of greater numbers. When the first few missiles were developed in the late 50s Soviet leaders made fantastic claims as to their effectiveness, though the initial reality was that they were so primitive and so faulty that it is questionable whether any of them could have reached their target. The Soviet policy of deception encouraged Western over-reaction, and hence made their own task more difficult; but it did, perhaps, help keep the West "off balance".

By the end of the 40s a crash programme had given Moscow the nuclear bomb. But she still had no sure way of getting it to US soil. Even after she had developed some longer range bomber capacity, during the 50s, her ability to strike the US homeland remained questionable — in view of the efficiency of Western defence systems. The ICBM, intercontinental-range ballistic missile, was clearly the trump that was to release the USSR from the straight jacket of inferiority. But early limitations and faults were all too glaring.

This was probably the most dangerous period of post-war history. Herman Kahn thought it was an "accident that an accident did not happen". Some think it was a miracle. Soviet missile fuels of the time were as primitive as the missiles; they were liable to explode, and could not be stored in the missiles. Command and control procedures were equally uncertain. We now know it would have taken the Soviets one or two weeks to get their missiles aloft! What is more, they were above ground, and highly vulnerable to enemy bomber strikes. In a crisis Moscow knew that she would have to strike first if she was to have any chance at all of inflicting punishment on the US; Washington, on the other hand, knew that if American forces struck first then there might be no damage to US cities. A dangerous "temptation syndrome" affected calculations on both sides. Poor intelligence,

*Notwithstanding the real element of apprehension I fear, note also the domestic political utility that Stalin derived from Cold War tensions . . .

epitomised by the many occasions when flocks of Canadian geese were thought by radar scanners to be incoming Soviet bombers, did not improve matters.

The US proceeded with a massive missile programme. By 1966 she was to have over a thousand ICBMs, to go with her already established, and awesome intercontinental range bomber superiority. She would deter by demonstrating the ability to pulverise the Soviet Union.

Moscow, meanwhile, concentrated her efforts rather on ensuring the survivability of the limited forces at her disposal. She began experimenting with a crude Ballistic Missile Defence system, with the concept of mobile (and hence less easily targetable) missiles, and with satellite-based war-heads (the latter proved feasable, but also too vulnerable to hostile intercept). Soviet missiles were put to sea, on submarines, and into protective silos.

By the mid-60s Moscow could be said to have developed a secure "second strike force", a force that could with confidence be expected to survive an enemy strike, and be available for a retaliatory "second strike".

The "temptation syndrome" was no more. We had entered the age of Mutual Assured Destruction (some prefer the acronym, MAD). MAD — the guaranteed ability of either superpower to obliterate the other, even if the other attacks first — remains the essence of today's strategic balance, and it is likely to remain so for the foreseeable future.

The remainder of the 1960s, and early 70s saw a determined Soviet drive to catch up also with the wider panoply of US strategic power. The Strategic Arms Limitation Talks Treaty of 1972, SALT I, came to symbolise Soviet attainment of strategic parity. The treaty placed a ceiling on the number of missiles that each side was allowed, giving Moscow a sufficient edge to compensate for continuing American bomber superiority.

A couple of peculiarities of developments during the 60s need to be addressed. One relates to the increasing irrelevance of numbers. Already by the middle of the decade Washington had decided that qualitative improvement was far more cost effective than just adding to the number of existing missiles. Early 60s reports of Soviet ballistic missile defence efforts had led Washington to add decoys to her missiles, to confuse and saturate possible defence systems. Fears of Soviet radar progress, of Soviet ability to distinguish the real from the fake, led to ever more sophisticated decoys, and finally to multiple war-heads. Originally these were cluster war-heads that fell, free-fall. Then came technology that allowed earlier release of war-heads (thus guarding against longer range Soviet intercept missiles that might destroy the cluster before it separated), and multiple independently-targetable war-heads, MIRVs. These were war-heads that could be given independent thrust and direction, hitting widely dispersed targets — in fact, the target areas that could be hit by one multiple war-head missile, called the "footprint", emerged as an oblong some 1000km long and 300km wide. Targets a thousand kilometers apart could be "hit" by the same booster.

By the mid-60s, on the other hand, the Soviets had developed their pioneering missile defence efforts to the point where they had an effective capability against single war-head missiles, missiles employing decoys, and even missiles with cluster war-heads. But then existing defence technologies could not overcome the saturation potential of MIRV. US offensive technology had jumped ahead of Moscow's ability to come up with a counter or answer.

Early SALT negotiations about negotiations (1966-1967) had seen an American demand that one focus on limiting defences (in which Moscow had invested the greatest effort); the Soviet Union demanded limits on offensive forces (the area of American advantage). Formal negotations were put off for a while by the 1968 Soviet intervention in Czechoslovakia. When they got going Nixon was President, and positions had been reversed. Now Washington asked for offensive limits, Moscow for defensive.

Why the quick shift in attitudes? Well — 1966-7 saw the Washington Administration forced to give up its sole concentration on offensive capabilities. Domestic critics pointed to Soviet defence efforts, to the Adminstration's own evidence that the cost exchange ratio was beginning to look more favourable for defence aspirations. The cost exchange ratio measures the relative cost between a defence that might lessen casualty expectations by X per cent and the offence increases that the other side would need to bring casualty expectations back up to the old figure. Total defence schemes remained impossible, both technologically and economically, but more limited schemes (such as lowering fatality rates by 10 or 20 per cent) began to look cost effective; American strategists began to talk of a one-to-one relationship between defensive and offensive outlays, suggesting that "one dead Russian equals one live American", and that one was morally bound (in that case) to try for the latter, namely live Americans. The US began to deploy a limited defence system. In view of continued Soviet reliance on single war-head missiles, such a system held definite promise.

But on the other side of the coin the Soviet defence system, though more advanced, was as mentioned emasculated by emerging US multiple war-head technologies. Moscow therefore put her defence deployments on "hold" (though she continued to invest heavily into research, hoping that future technological breakthroughs might one day restore the viability of defence aspirations). In the meantime she geared up the assembly lines for a great jump in offensive missile numbers, and began focusing on the development of her own multiple war-head potential.

The change in SALT postures towards the end of the 60s merely reflected American recognition of the dynamism of the Soviet offensive procurement programme; and Soviet recognition of the fact that American defence efforts held extraordinary promise as long as she, Moscow, continued to be reliant on single war-head missiles.

The 1972 SALT I signing (the Treaty also limited defence deployments, originally to two sites, then just one) reflected American acceptance that Moscow now stood on the threshold of MIRV mastery, an event that ensured Soviet penetration capabilities. American defence technologies had been checkmated, as had Soviet defence technologies — at least temporarily. Both sides were forced to accept MAD, Mutual Assured Destruction, as an inevitable adjunct to then current super-power technologies. "Parity", though perhaps distasteful to one or the other, had become a fact of life.

Yet, while both sides had to accept MAD, *vis-a-vis* each other, as the inevitable (if perhaps distasteful) consequence of the character and limitations of existing technologies, they were not therefore resigned to conceding also other powers' penetration capabilities. The US may have felt scant reason to fear so-called Third powers at this time. But Moscow was looking at a vociferously hostile China and NATO-aligned Britain and France. These, and other prospective nuclear armed states, were not within reach of multiple war-head technologies. The Moscow defence system might hold a little promise against US means, but it retained significant promise against such penetration capabilities as could be mobilised by other challengers. The Moscow system provided a decisive degree of relative immunity against non-US challenges. Its survival, and continued extensive Soviet testing of evolving defence technologies, were predicated on Moscow's determination to retain this edge.

While the USSR had become a genuine superpower, however, she remained in essence a regional superpower. She was rapidly acquiring global economic interests (her worldwide fisheries and her krill harvesting off South-East Africa, for example, had become vital to the nation's protein requirements). But her ability to protect these interests and project power to distant arenas remained minimal. That was to change during the 70s.

The 1970s saw a three-pronged Soviet drive to truly match the global strategic and non-strategic option flexibility enjoyed by Washington. At the strategic level this took the form of "withholding"; the intercontinental range, Submarine Launched Ballistic Missile systems were assigned the role of strategic reserves (withheld from initial exchanges, they were to be used rather as inter-war bargaining and war termination leverage), supported by surface and air units designed to ensure the sanctity of home operating waters. To some extent the development reflected merely a new luxury of numbers, as suggested by the assumption that the US had long thought along similar lines. While means were limited they had to be targeted on cities, for maximum effect. Larger numbers allowed also for counter-force and counter-industry strategies. Once logical targets of possible immediate relevance were exhausted withholding strategies became the logical answer to mutterings of redundancy. Aside from the fact that overly cautious military planners operating on the basis of worse case calculations could not be expected to concede redundancy, however, there was the point that numbers do affect perceptions — a not immaterial point in peace time, since in the absence of war military potential is irrelevent except to the extent that it can be translated into political influence.

The second Soviet focus of the 1970s lay in a general effort to offset remaining US qualitative advantages. In the strategic arena two developments stood out. One was the conversion to MIRVs, multiple war-heads. By 1980 the USSR had still not caught up with US totals (the US lead in absolute numbers was in fact greater than it had been a decade earlier), but in a context of far higher figures on both sides the US percentage lead had been significantly eroded. The other trend related to missile accuracies. Moscow had long had to compensate for inferior accuracy technologies by increasing missile yields. Since a near ten-fold increase in yield only equates to a two-fold improvement in accuracy, this was less than ideal. By 1980 Moscow was finally able to test accuracies equal to those of the US Minuteman 3 force (deployed since the early 1970s). She could now face US planners with the same theoretical threat to land-based missile survivability that she had been forced to tolerate. Still, there was no rush to phase land missiles out, in favour of more survivable sea or air increments. Most analysts accepted that practical problems, of co-ordination and material and human imperfection, meant that a truly effective "take-out" strike remained the province of theory, not practice.

Major efforts were also devoted to up-grading Soviet conventional arms. In this area Moscow had long been advantaged quantitatively, though not as much as indicated by NATO brochures which would, for example, count Soviet reserve tanks in balance sheets which excluded US reserves (US forces in Germany alone had access to a reserve fleet of 5000 tanks). Moscow's disadvantage lay in inferior quality. Thus another point omitted from NATO tank balances was NATO's superior anti-tank means, both infantry carried and (especially) helicopter borne. So also in the field of airpower: Soviet planes tended to be short range interceptors, while the West could counter with more sophisticated multi-purpose planes capable also of deep interdiction and other missions for which the USSR had no counter. The 70s saw steady change in this pattern. By 1980 the newest Soviet fighter-bombers were much more comparable to those of NATO. A formidable fleet of Soviet anti-tank and anti-personnel helicopter gunships had been developed, and a profusion of transport helicopters were adding a new dimension to Soviet mobility. The US retained a numerical edge as concerns helicopters, but higher Soviet procurement rates were rapidly closing the gap.

The third area of major Soviet effort during the 1970s lay in the already mentioned emergency of theory and material relevant to distant force projection. The evidence can be traced from the build-up of Egyptian defences during the 1970 War of Attrition, through Angola in 1975 (when Soviet-Cuban aid helped the MPLA prevail against its South African supported opponents) and Ethiopia in 1978 (the repulse of Somalia's invasion of the Ogaden). The latter saw the simultaneous deployment, according to "reliable" US sources, of 225 transports, and a Soviet-Cuban ground operation that impressed both in its numbers and in its efficacy.

By 1980 the USSR could be said to have emerged as a truly global superpower. The US still retained greater interventionary potential (through her carrier forces), and more potential allies and proxies (French troops operated in as many African countries as did Cuban troops). But whereas US and Western interventionary designs in the Third World previously had been associated with military impunity, that was no longer the case. Soviet action and reaction capability had been proven credible. This also meant that Soviet protection, and therefore a Soviet alliance alternative had become credible. And that was a constellation that bespoke a significantly changed international environment.

Throughout history the emergence of a new actor able to project its power on the world arena has always led to a period of testing, for both old and new actors, before a new correlation of licence and limit evolves. This has always been a period of acute misunderstanding and apprehension; it is also worth noting that the historical norm is for communication to be undermined by perceptions of ideological adversity (such as between "popery" bent on world dominion, and "proddies" pictured as equally unrelenting). By 1978 the world had clearly entered another such period, and therein lay the main significance of "the Afghan Crisis"; it was one of history's ironies that the *pro forma* focal point of the crisis was to be found in the new boy's backyard rather than in more distant locales. Previous East-West crises, such as encapsulated by the term Cold-War, and the Cuban missile crisis in 1962, had in effect seen containment of a challenger by a *status quo* nation whose ultimate power to contain was unquestioned; the fact of relative strategic parity gave the 1980 confrontation a qualitatively different hue.

It was in this sense and in this sense only (as a symbolic test case), that the reaction to Moscow's extension of "full" control in Afghanistan acquired meaning. The Soviet action itself was little more than might have been expected. Ninety per cent of the country was controlled by fundamentalist rebels alienated by a Soviet "ally" who had expelled Soviet advisors of caution (including the Ambassador), persecuted those Soviet-supported members of his party who retained ties to the clergy and other traditional sectors of Afghan society, and sent feelers to Chinese and other (American) adversaries of Soviet power. It was a no-win situation for Moscow. She either had to accept the loss of her presence in Afghanistan, a presence dating from the early 19th Century, or extend it. As might have been expected she decided that one China and one Ayatollah facing her Moslem Central Asian republics was quite enough. "Imperialist" yes, but . . . . That same year saw a Chinese invasion of Vietnam that employed a far larger force and that saw perhaps greater ferocity and brutality (if once accepted reports of chemical biological warfare, reports that appeared better substantiated in the Chinese than in the later Soviet case). French and Moroccan paratroopers toppled two African governments during the second half of 1979 and "stabilised" others. The US had desisted from the use of large-scale military force since President Nixon's invasion of Cambodia, but it was open to charges that it had built a rich tradition prior to that event (and one is forced to note that this tradition had also encompassed a proclivity towards chemical-biological warfare; Agent Orange, used extensively throughout Indo-China, contained dioxin, a substance 100,000 times more potent than thalidomide). The Soviet intervention in Afghanistan was depressing to moralists, but drearily familiar.

As the first SALT Treaty of 1972 had come to symbolise the gradual flowering of detente that had preceded it, so the Afghanistan crisis took on symbolic meaning far beyond what might have been warranted by its content alone. It capped and symbolised the unravelling of detente aspirations. The possible disincentives to intervention had already fallen prey to the anti-Soviet mood of American domestic politics. NATO arms budgets had already been increased. Senate ratification of the 1979 SALT accord (signed by Presidents Carter and Brezhnev in Vienna) looked less and less likely. Hopes that Congress might yet ratify the Trades Agreement signed by President Nixon in 1972 were dashed by the announcement that China's application for Most Favoured Nation treatment would be decoupled from that of Moscow, and that China's would be granted (never mind that Beijing's human rights record appeared even more suspect than Moscow's). American high technology sales were increasingly subject to Administration embargoes. Soviet dissidents continued to find disproportionate fame on American lecture podiums, in American media. Andy Young, the Administration's most prominent proponent of the thesis that all the world's ills might not be caused by Moscow, but might sometimes owe something to local antagonisms, underdevelopment or different forms of exploitation, resigned his Ambassadorship to the US. Early 1979 saw Washington send its first Ambassador to Beijing while invading Chinese troops remained on the soil of Moscow's closest Asian ally; the end of the year saw preparation for the first visit to China of an American Secretary of Defence, amid "leaks" of military technological aid and defence policy co-ordination. The President seemed increasingly disinclined to accept the advice of the State Department and its Soviet specialists, choosing instead to rely on his National Security Advisor, Zbig Brezezinsky, a man whose views on occasion echoed the anti-Russian antipathies of his Polish ancestors.

Why? The answer is suggested by the previously referred to historical pattern, and the peculiarities of the Soviet interventions in Angola and Ethiopia. Moscow's demonstration of new found abilities in the Angolan crisis of 1975 might have provoked a crucial East-West test. The Soviet Union did indeed "probe". But the American challenge that Secretary of State Kissinger tried to orchestrate was hamstrung by Congressional opposition — perhaps fortuituously, in view of the fact that the Soviet client (the MPLA) enjoyed the legitimacy of widespread African sanction and support, while its more narrowly tribal based rivals were tainted by association with South Africa. The Ogaden War of 1978 suggested itself as the next most likely occasion for "eyeball to eyeball" confrontation. But Moscow's actions again enjoyed the advantage of considerable neutral support (after all, the *pro forma* objective of her intervention, support for Ethiopia's territorial integrity against Somali aggression, was a cause formally championed equally by Washington and its allies); again, effective US counter action would have entailed too heavy a diplomatic penalty. Moscow's cautious, judicious choice of time and place for the demonstration of new found capabilities, and the success with which she was able to associate her initiatives with moral imperatives ("anti-colonialism", "anti-apartheid", "anti-aggression") clearly frustrated American policy makers. The frustration grew apace with perceptions of Soviet success. It added an acute sense of urgency to the appeals of those who felt early confrontation to be required in order to prevent further slippage or erosion in the political authority of *status quo* power. To them, it became symbolically vital that an occasion to "stand up" be found. Afghanistan served the purpose. On the other side of the ledger, however, it should be said that the American "need" to be assertive on Afghanistan served also to cement Soviet resolve. It meant that compromise would not only undermine the security of their Afghan presence, but also unravel the global gains of two decades of military-political investment. Giving in to American pressure would turn the clock back to the time of the 1962 Cuban crisis. Soviet military-political investments since that date had been predicted precisely on their absolute determination to ensure that "never again", never again would they allow themselves to be so inferior in the military-strategic realm that their antagonist would feel able to dictate the terms of crisis resolution.

As Washington terminated the latest grain sales, cancelled scientific-cultural exchanges, tightened its technology embargo, and beefed up the American force presence in the Indian Ocean-Persian Gulf area; Moscow stood adamant. A quasi Cold War atmosphere of embittered tension spread. It became apparent not only that neither could concede to the imperatives and rationale of the other, but also that neither could force retreat on the other. A stand-off, rather than a single test producing decisive results, the Afghan confrontation began to take on the appearance of the opening volley of a more intense process of testing.

The most disturbing fact about the crisis was the fact that United States anti-Sovietism had been built on a solid foundation of perceived Soviet perfidy, while Soviet anti-American phobia rested on an equally convincing accumulation of perceived American villainy. The role played by misperception, real or feigned, was illustrated by the debate over the mobile multi-war-head SS20 missiles that Moscow began deploying in European Russia (and in the Far East) during the late 1970s. To Moscow, the SS20 finally redressed the imbalance caused by the potency of America's Forward Based Systems (FBS) of carrier and land-based aircraft with the range and sophistication to reach Soviet targets. Previous Soviet intermediate-range missiles had been both less accurate and more vulnerable (to hostile "take-out") than American systems. In an atmosphere of mutual suspicion, however, it was perhaps inevitable that NATO would ignore the fact that the SS20 did not negate continued FBS efficacy and focus instead on the indisputable point that SS20 accuracy and survivability entailed a greater threat to NATO territory than had previously existed. Hence the phenomenon of NATO defence budget increases amid Soviet protestations that these (and not the SS20) constituted the beginnings of a new arms race. Paranoia breeds paranoia; distrust finds its own motivating and indeed reinforcing rationale.

The state of the relationship was further illustrated when the US decided to proceed with the gigantic MX complex of multi-war-head missiles darting among multiple shelters — the military equivalent of the ultimate "shell game", now you see them, now you don't. Its rationale rested on the calculation that Soviet missile numbers and accuracy might threaten the survivability of fixed-location missiles such as the Minutemen. To some the logic of threat to silo-based missiles invited concentration rather than on less vulnerable air and seaborne forces, forces which in and of themselves possessed awesome overkill (especially since the old objection, that their once inferior accuracy precluded certain targeting options, has been large overtaken by technological advances), or on protected or mobile land alternatives. Others pointed out that practical problems of co-ordination, material and human imperfection, and the little-appreciated but vital "bias factor" (flight trajectories between the superpowers would encounter gravitational and atmospheric anomalies bound to detract from accuracy predictions based on frequent tests — accompanied by frequent adjustment of gyros and accelerometers — in different environments), continued to mock first strike spectres. Like the Soviets, who greeted the earlier appearance of US "take-out" accuracies with equanimity, they remained confident that in practice a significant portion of land forces would remain available for retaliation no matter the theoretical accuracy potential of the aggressor. The US Administration, however, chose the different path of conceding vulnerability, yet desisting from fundamental redeployment — probably because the possibility that such could be ascribed to Soviet prowess grated on too many sensibilities. Hence the MX, the viability of which was predicated on the SALT II treaty and its restrictions on Soviet (and American) war-head numbers, was in fact pushed with all the more vigour once it appeared that SALT II might not be ratified. The fact that a Moscow unrestrained by SALT obligations could deploy as many war-heads as required to dispose of all the "shells", whether filled or not, and the point that further Soviet war-head increments might be procured more cost effectively than any conceivable MX expansion scheme, seemed less relevant than the political imperative of facing down the Soviet challenge. Congressional willingness to fund the 60 billion dollar or more MX system at a time of budgetary restraints and cutbacks in social services was telling testimony to the depth and strength of this political imperative.

Another indicator of the prevailing mood lay in America's elaboration and institutionalising of what had once been known as the Schlesinger Doctrine — flexible strategic targeting practices designed to ensure that strategic weapons utilisation options not be restricted to "all or nothing", but allow also for limited attacks, "demonstration" strikes and the like. This might have been argued to reflect no more than simple acknowledgement of the logic inherent in the combination of new accuracy technologies and numerical redundancy (even the most pessimistic of worst case prognostications conceded overkill potential against traditional targets). The main argument for the not-so-new posture, however, was that the demonstration of a flexible war-fighting capability even in a "post-conventional" environment would buttress the credibility of America's determination not to squelch on commitments, and hence strengthen deterrence. Moscow had long emphasised "warfighting" (rather than "deterrence"), for both military and psychological reasons. The constellation sparked considerable fear on the part of critics, who were uneasy lest the conventional nuclear threshold was becoming dangerously diluted; they feared that a focus on the "tactical" utilisation of strategic weaponry obfuscated the reality of probable escalation. Still, the policy's consequences were bound to loom far larger at a time of possible implementation than they did when the matter at hand was restricted to the promulgation of theory: the victim of a "demonstration" strike could not be confident than an initially limited attack was not but the forerunner of more to come; and even if it was, was it really conceivable that it would not order a "counter demonstration" salvo; surely the psychology that would then begin to operate would mock most ivory tower discussions of crisis management . . . ? Some were so sceptical that they thought the whole exercise to be conscious or sub-conscious disinformation, a "Potemkin village", designed to divert attention from a *de facto* decision not to improve conventional war-fighting capabilities, a *de facto* decision to revert to a "massive retaliation" posture — the stand of the Eisenhower years.

The Soviet mood appeared equally intransigent. Moscow did harp more on the dangers and waste of an arms race, and she did take the public lead in championing arms control measures. But her actions often seemed calculated to convey the idea that she was taking up the gauntlet. Indeed, her actions sometimes appeared as if designed to goad US arms advocates. Thus while she appeared careful to keep within the written dictas of the signed but unratified SALT II treaty, she proceeded to take advantage of the treaty's loopholes and ambiguities. And when the nadir of the inter-state relationship set in in 1980 she even took action that suggested contravention of specific treaty terms as well (one thinks of American allegations that she was upgrading defences against aircraft so as to also give them a capability against missiles). More typically, she began demonstrating the ability to reload emptied silos. Officially only "rapid reload" was banned, and Soviet exercises were designed so as not to contravene the American "understanding" that this meant reloading accomplished within 24 hours of a missile's firing. Nevertheless, the fact that Moscow chose to exhibit a reloading capability at all, and hence also to suggest stockpiles of reserve missiles, was telling. Many were dubious of the military relevance of a Soviet ability to "lob salvos" (a concept consistent with Soviet artillery tradition), but its flaunting did not ease the task of American "arms controllers".

"Hardliners" appeared to be dominating decision making on both sides. In the US unrealistic exaggerations of the Soviet arms budget received the blessing of officialdom. In Moscow, the media gave great display to recently declassified US "war plans" of earlier decades — the purported forerunners of US aspirations today.

While the two superpowers continued to be mired in a perhaps cruicial adjusting and re-evaluation of the essence and portent of their offsetting military-political arsenals, outside observers often lost sight of how unique the superpower constellation still was. While the limits to superpower omnipotence dominated many headlines (as concerned their relative impotence to affect the course of some local crises, such as the Iran-Iraq war of 1980; as concerned their sometime inability to control erstwhile allies; and as concerned the very different, but fundamental, economic problems that continued to plague both nations), the fact remained that in the military sphere their pre-eminence could be argued to have increased rather than decreased.

China's superpower status rested largely on psychological factors. Hindsight scorned earlier projections of Chinese strategic forces for the 1970s and 80s. China's strategic force potential entering the decade of the 80s echoed that of the

USSR in the mid and late 1950s. China's supporting infrastructure was in fact less developed than was that of the USSR during those years. Beijing's military-technological inferiority *vis-a-vis* Moscow in 1980 was greater than that of Moscow *vis-a-vis* Washington two-and-a-half decades earlier. Then US then had possessed no missile defences and her arsenal of offensive strike means had lacked accuracy; this meant that crude Soviet missiles could hope to reach target areas when/if fired, and that silos and dispersal methods might otherwise ensure their invulnerability.

By 1980, on the other hand, the Soviet Union had deployed a ballistic missile defence system around Moscow (coupled with "testing facilities" at Sary Shagan in Central Asia, a location of some relevance to projected Chinese flight paths), that would likely ensure the sanctity of the heartland against Chinese attack through the 1980s. And she had established a defence research and investment programme designed to ensure that this advantage would be extended. The Soviet Union had furthermore, like the United States, developed missiles accurate enough to destroy an opponent's silos, and a general intelligence and fast reaction potential that must have looked daunting to Chinese strategic planners. It conjured up the possibility that Soviet reaction to Chinese missile firing preparation might be capable of ensuring that a preemptive strike arrived on target in time to abort the very process that had precipitated it.

Notwithstanding post-Mao advocacies (prioritising "traditional" force structures rather than "people's war" concepts), Mao's prescription for a limited "force de frappe" sufficient to inject an element of uncertainty into an opponent's calculations remained the optimum towards which short and medium-term Chinese defence planning could strive. Full superpower status appeared unattainable before the end of the century; and even that timescale was one that would demand an extraordinarily costly diversion of scarce skills and equipment. The extension of limited American military aid to Beijing in the aftermath of the Afghan crisis of December 1979 and 1980 suggested to some that the road to Chinese equivalence might be shortened. Even disregarding the fact that American policy ruled out sale of the most advanced technologies and hardware, however, such suggestions appeared facile. As in the civilian economic sphere, so also in the realm of defence: there are severe limits to how much new technology can be effectively absorbed by or integrated into a less developed infra-structure. The problem of digestibility is substantial indeed. Developmental short cuts are usually easier to implement on paper than in reality. Finally, one must note the possibility that Beijing might have concluded that offsetting power was less vital to Chinese aspirations than it might have been to Soviet aspirations. The world context was quite different. Whereas Moscow had perceived itself beseiged by forces united in their opposition to Soviet interests, with no existing or possible ally of substance, Beijing faced an outside world split by competing power alignments. China enjoyed more credible prospects for alliance manipulation, and greater scope for balancing perceived threats through the venues of diplomacy and alignment shifts. Moscow faced adverserial unity as concerned both military and economic power. Beijing faced a duality of military power, a multiplicity of economic (and perhaps political) power. In the former case it was a matter of zero-sum perception (what one side gained, the other lost); the latter case allowed also for mutual advantage, and less stark concepts of relativity.

But while Moscow and Washington might be able to ensure and perhaps perpetuate a degree of invulnerability to military threats from other quarters, the 1980 outlook was jeopardised by the emergency of new and different challenges. While the primary threat perceptions in Moscow and Washington continued to revolve around the status and prospects of established challenges, these were increasingly crowded by other threats that promised to have even greater long term potency.

On the one hand there was the evident fact that most previous restraints on nuclear proliferation had been eliminated. Knowledge concerning nuclear weaponry and simple delivery systems had become diffused, and widely available in the open literature. ''Terrorist'' access was looming as evermore likely.

More importantly, nations previously deterred not by the difficulty of procuring nuclear weaponry (this had long been surmountable), but rather by the far greater problems of designing or otherwise acquiring delivery systems that might make possession meaningful, now faced a world in which these latter problems appeared to constitute less and less of an obstacle. Ballistic missile concepts remained beyond the financial and technological reach of all but a few. By the late 70s, however, the knowledge to make simpler cruise missiles (essentially pilotless airplanes, drones) was becoming widely dispersed. As opposed to ballistic missiles they could be shot down; yet they were cheap, and hence suggestive of the possibility that defences (or at least non-superpower defences) might be saturated through sheer numbers. Furthermore, the same years saw an explosion in the sale to third world countries of sophisticated fighter bombers; where earlier sales focused on less advanced models, the emerging pattern saw the most modern designs sold and bartered.

There was the point that while superpower systems and superpower command and control were advanced and pretty secure, that would not be the case with emergent capabilities. These were likely to be primitive and vulnerable. The "temptation syndrome" associated with the limited Soviet capabilities of the late 50s promised to become a recurrent phenomenon, or nightmare. A multiplying of primate slow-reacting forces deployed in vulnerable above-ground configurations, forces that could be "taken out" by hostile strikes and that therefore had to be utilised in initiating salvos in order to be relevant or effective, guaranteed that even local crises would spark a degree of paranoia and a war-initiating logic and incentive that could only be destabilising. To make matters worse, although the madman spectre might not be valid as concerned the superpowers, many were less sanguine when contemplating current and foreseeable proliferation trends. The Idi Amin of the '70s could not "go nuclear"; one of the late '80s and'90s might well be able to do so . . .

Prospects were exacerbated by fear concerning the availability of resources. By 1980 there could be scant doubt that energy scares (and very real shortages, actual or potential), were but the harbinger of a rapidly approaching world of more intense competition for an ever-lengthening list of depleting or inadequate strategic resources.

Demographers suggested that India's population alone would reach a billion-and-a-half within perhaps forty years.

Throughout Africa, Asia and Latin America the continuing and rapidly accelerating population spiral promised to further increase the tensions, jealousies and antagonisms engendered by the long established fact of ever widening North-South disparities. Fewer and fewer observers remained confident about the ability of the existing world economic order(s) to rise to the challenge.

How many nuclear capable States would coming years bring? A 1980 Scientific American analysis concluded that 40 then non-nuclear States would (if they made that decision) be able to deploy nuclear arsenals by 1990. Some of these could be seen as cluster-States, sub-groups of nations whose ultimate decisions would depend more on those of other group members than they would on superpower or distant considerations. Thus India's explosion of a "peaceful nuclear device" obviously spurred Pakistan's efforts to develop a like capability; this in turn put pressure on India to proceed with the development of more significant nuclear force structures; both phenomena put pressure on Iran, Saudia Arabia and other neighbouring nations. Brazil, Argentina and perhaps Chile constitute another sub-group; a decision by either of these to "go nuclear" would clearly be a powerful, and probably decisive spur to those advocating a similar course in the other capitals. Japan, whose aversion to nuclear weaponry is basic to the national psyche, might feel obliged to reconsider if Taiwan and South Korea chose to pursue their acknowledged nuclear potential (relations between the three are clouded by a number of actual and potential areas of dispute). The assumption that Israel has acquired nuclear means obviously spurred Libya's financing of the Pakistani effort, as well as Iraq's purchases of French reactor and processing technology, etc. . . .

Even States not part of potentially friction-ridden sub-groups, such as Canada, Norway or Sweden might one day be forced to re-evaluate the premises that underline their nuclear arms abstinence. The expected jump in the number of *disaffected* nations able to target nuclear devices will lead to a very different international environment indeed. Canada, Norway and Sweden might thus also be affected by the prospect that State and inter-State combatants in areas that might attract UN peace-keeping forces would be evermore likely to have access to nuclear arms.

By 1980 projections coalesced around predictions of 20 to 50 nuclear states by the end of the century. The most eminent scientists spoke of a probability of nuclear war by the end of the century, not just a possibility. That did of course not necessarily mean Armageddon. The majority saw local nuclear wars that might not involve the superpowers, at least not directly, as more likely; yet all feared the dangers of escalation.

It should be noted that arms races, prospects for proliferation and escalation, and the like, are phenomena that cannot easily be turned on and off at the tap. Thus one of the factors that has fuelled (and still fuels) the Soviet-American arms race, and that promises to fuel and bedevil also the armament programme of "Nth" states, is the concept of "lead time". This is the time required to research and develop a new weapon system; the lead time for a modern weapons system averages out at ten or more years. This means that one must today plan (and lock oneself into) programmes designed to meet possible threats of ten-twenty years down the line. Since one does not always know what choices an opponent may make among the many options for weapons improvement and development that present themselves, and since one cannot know which technological "gleams in the eye" the opponent is able to master, and which prove elusive or illusory, there is always an inherent and very real "need" to allocate for efforts far out of proportion to what history may justify. An analagous factor, one of similar import, is that of "worst case planning". This means that you maximise the opponent's ability to overcome difficulties, while you minimise your own.

Two examples from the early 60s spring to mind. Secretary of Defence McNamara and his "whizz kids" were disdainful of then existing ballistic missile defence technologies and refused to budget for an American effort in the field; they were scathing in their comments on the primitive defence system that Moscow nevertheless persevered with. Yet, although personally extremely sceptical about the effectiveness of the Soviet endeavour, they nevertheless felt compelled to order counter-measures based on the assumption that their confidence was unjustified, on the assumption that the Soviet System might work after all. Immensely expensive programmes of "penetration aid", multiple war-heads and "MIRVing" developments were authorised to counter what was claimed to be ineffectual . . . . The other side to this coin was found in sometimes ludicrous extrapolations of what could go wrong with offensive missiles. Such early missiles were, as previously mentioned, primitive and faulty, afflicted by a number of so-called "degradation factors" (categories of faults, such as those due to design or production mistakes, those due to transport, storage, firing and in-flight inadequacies and phenomena, etc.). By maximising everything that could conceivably go wrong, one arrived at very limiting estimates of effectiveness. Since policy-planners at the time were unaware of the debilitating effects of "fratricide" (an in-flight or off-target explosion is itself likely to incapacitate follow-up war-heads intended to ensure against the failure of the first), the obvious answer appeared to lie in a compensatory quantum leap in numbers, the multiplying of missiles assigned to each target. Then came more perfect, later missile generations, and appreciation of "fratricide" and its implication. And we arrived at the (late 70s) scientific judgment that the arsenals amassed by the superpowers contained perhaps fifty times the "yield effect" theoretically necessary to destroy both societies.

1980: a world of some 60,000 nuclear war-heads, "tactical" and "strategic", many with a power a thousand times greater than that which devastated Hiroshima — looking to a future of continued escalation of numbers, and "fingers on the trigger".

The world scientific community (or at least that 50% not yet under contract to defence departments and defence related industries) tended increasingly to agree with the judgment of Lord Zuckerman, former British Government Science Advisor, that in the absence of extensive defence deployments, logic decreed that just one missile-armed submarine ought to suffice. One American Poseidon submarine for example, carried 160 independently targetable warheads — 160 extinct cities, perhaps 20 million dead — a scale of destruction equalling that suffered by the USSR during World War II. Many, indeed, felt with Lord Mountbatten, who had insisted that the belief that nuclear war could be contained and escalation avoided once an initial exchange had taken place was, militarily speaking, nonsense.

But while the inexorable pauperisation and alienation of an ever more nuclear capable Third World could be dramatically and fundamentally alleviated through programmes costing less than the 25 billion dollars that was 5 per cent of world arms expenditures (see introduction), even that appeared beyond the realms of practical politics.

The world's population had for too long been socialised to the view that nuclear arms were synonymous with power, and that one's numbers of nuclear weapons were synonymous with one's status of relative power. Whatever the military irrelevance, whatever the military redundancy of certain numbers, they had become sacrosanct due to the political fallout which they were believed to entail.

With the international political context not conducive to arms control advocacies, numbers redundancies were instead obfuscated through the promulgation of post-facto rationalisation doctrines suggesting tactical use of strategic missiles, "demonstration" strikes, "surgical' incisions and the like. American and other critics of such doctrines, who feared that the conventional nuclear threshold was becoming dangerously diluted, and that a focus on the "tactical" potential of strategic weaponry could blind one to the reality of probably escalation, might have become overly jittery. There were those who argued that the policies' consequences were bound to loom far larger at a time of possible implementation than they did when the matter at hand was restricted to the promulgation of theory. But, Mountbatten would have remained sceptical, and fearful.

Finally, one should perhaps return to the unquestionable fact of escalating conflict potential that lies inherent in ever-increasing North-South disparities, resource and energy scarcities, "stagflation", and the failure of traditional economic theory and management, of the old "economic order", and in the inter-relation and inter-dependence of so many of these phenomena. Thus the anti-apartheid, anti-racism and anti-colonial struggle which promises to continue to engulf Southern Africa may be seen as but one aspect of the more general problem of North-South tensions; yet the struggle rages in an area that harbours some of the world's rarest and most vital strategic minerals and it will therefore inevitably impact also on the immediate calculations of military planners in the US, the USSR, Europe and elsewhere. The problem of depleting resources, be it minerals, oil or protein, may well be the single most likely generator of future armed conflicts. Other traditional great power rivalries, be they derived from irredentist territorial aspirations, ideology, or whatnot, appeared more manageable.

The extent to which any aspect of the composite maelstrom of impending crises was manageable was open to doubt. Yet it was clear that apathy or resignation were emotions that could no longer be afforded.

Marek Thee is Editor of the Bulletin of Peace Proposals, of the Oslo International Peace Research Institute.

European Security in the Eighties

Marek Thee

Elements of crisis and conflict

As we enter the eighties, problems of security in Europe are becoming more precarious than at any time since World War II. In both the political and military domains, conflict situations are accumulating which may change entirely the parameters of peace and war. In particular, two processes stand out in the current crisis. On the one hand, there is the accelerated arms race. On the other, there is an upsurge of political pressures in Europe, challenging the post-World War II status, as apparent in the events in Poland. Unless the persistent structural and historical nature of these processes can be clearly apprehended and steps are taken to defuse the situation — to halt the arms race and creatively to integrate currents of change into the process of détente — these crisis phenomena may yet meet, with explosive effect.

A number of critical developments — both regional and global in nature — serve to worsen the situation by affecting the European scene, whether directly or indirectly. Among them are:

1. A profound crisis in détente. In the course of 1980 and the beginning of 1981 détente has largely given way to a tougher international climate reminiscent of the the Cold War. This has been characterised by a new rush to armaments, including nuclear weapons, as well as by an overall deterioration of East-West relations. In this context one should realise that, in the new political and military circumstances, a Cold War portends far greater dangers than ever in the past. The world is today saturated, as never before in history, with weapons and weapons systems that are new, both in a quantitative and a qualitative sense. Especially todays third and fourth generation of nuclear weapons have been refined for different tactical and strategic uses. They have also reached an operational utility which greatly increases the temptation to make use of them — a probability particularly dangerous in times of crisis and stress. One is reminded here of the warning given by President Carter in his farewell address:

"The risk of a nuclear conflagration has not lessened . . . The danger is becoming greater. As the arsenals of the superpowers grow in size and sophistication, and as other governments — perhaps even, in the future, dozens of governments — acquire these weapons, it may only be a matter of time before madness, desperation, greed and miscalculation lets loose the terrible force . . ."[1]

Coming from a position of high insight and influence, this warning should be taken seriously. One is reminded of the prophetic warning issued twenty years earlier by President Eisenhower in his farewell address, where he referred to possible "grave implications" stemming from the "rising power of military science" and the mushrooming growth of military R&D "in conjunction with an immense military establishment and a large arms industry".[2]

Increased dangers are also inherent in the new global political-military dynamics which have been accelerated by the shift from a bipolar East-West to a triangular US-Soviet-Chinese constellation. The more decision making centres and lines of confrontation, the stronger the arms race and greater the general unpredictability of the political-military process.

2. A deep-rooted crisis in arms control, with Europe the focal area of soaring armaments. The freeze of SALT II and the stalemate in other arms control negotiations reflect not only a hardening of political positions. They reflect a structural crisis which has resulted from the dynamics of an arms race driven by a technological momentum impervious to social and political control. Today's predicament stems from a growing inverse relation between politics and military technology. It is historically well established that there is a close structural relationship between military technology, institutions of government and the exercise of power. Today, with military technology undergoing a revolutionary upsurge and military R&D usurping a commanding position in science and technology generally, this relationship is becoming more and more twisted and errant. Not only does politics seem unable to keep military technology (i.e. the arms race) under control, politics has increasingly become hostage to the Frankenstein momentum in military technology[3] — as in fact predicted by a concerned President Eisenhower two decades ago. In the process, the military imperative tends to prevail over political considerations; and attitudes shaped by the availability of new military instrumentation rather than rational statesmanship tend to dictate politics. The problem then is how to regain the sovereignty of sound political thought over the dynamics of armaments, and how to make mature political determination effective.

3. Growing strains in North-South relations coupled with a trend towards the globalisation of conflicts. On the one hand Third World demands for a New International Economic Order and a new division of labour and resources are resisted by the North. On the other hand the energy crisis, very much linked to relations with the South, has led to a destabilisation of the international economy, with Europe one of the most sensitive links in the chain of crisis. In other words, international interdependence has come in conflict with rigidities in the North-South relation. One of the outcomes is recourse to the use of force; this is increasingly replacing sound political and economic responses to crisis situations. In the process, Europe is constantly exposed to pressures to become party to the use of force and is drawn into confrontations outside its borders. Obviously, the impact of this on European security will be both complex and serious.

The inter-relation of all the above issues — military and political, economic and social, internal and external — produces formidable challenges. Some of the dangers are acute indeed. One need only mention "the risk of a nuclear war which could be launched by accident, either because of technological failure or human error"[4] and which may cause the explosion of a substantial part of the more than 10,000 nuclear weapons deployed in Europe by the two military alliances. Nor can one exclude the possibility of rapid conflict escalation as a result of mounting East-West tension in the wake of political confrontations between the two superpowers or political processes in Eastern and Western Europe. Such dangers are sufficiently real to justify the growing sense of insecurity which now pervades Europe and the urgency to search for solutions to ease tension and improve the political climate in East-West relations. But Europeans need also look ahead beyond imminent dangers, to apprehend the dynamics of events which, in the long run, augur an almost unavoidable catastrophe for the old continent unless a change of direction can be undertaken in time.

This paper is mainly concerned with the growing dangers for European security as they present themselves today and may develop further during the eighties. It tries to analyse the factors behind the arms race and assess its dynamics, in the hope of casting a coherent framework for alternative security strategies.

The military horizons

Security in Europe, as it has evolved after World War II, has largely become a function of East-West relations, particularly of the confrontational relations between the United States and the Soviet Union. One of the effects of the US-Soviet arms race was a systematic military build-up in Europe on the dividing lines between the two military alliances, NATO and the Warsaw Pact. This process has gone ahead uninterrupted during the last 30 years, both in times of the Cold War and during the period of détente. From the end of the 1950s, as the doctrine of "massive retaliation" emerged, the military build-up was expanded to include also tactical nuclear weapons; short-, medium- and intermediate-range ballistic missiles, artillery shells, demolition mines, all kinds of miniaturised nuclear devices. Their deployment proceeded consistently as new tactical nuclear weapons left the production lines and as the doctrine of "flexible response" replaced "massive retaliation". But there was an element of irrationality and inconsiderate rush in this deployment, as the nuclear powers never had a credible theory of how to use these weapons in a densely populated Europe — barring the destruction of the continent.[5] Thus, Europe became a dumping ground for armaments by the two superpowers; it has accumulated the largest military stocks and the greatest concentration of nuclear weapons in the world. Projected into the future, if this process continues, one can hardly see how, if war should break out, Europe can avoid becoming the main battlefield between the giants.

The arms race and security

Can this process be halted? An obvious first precondition for alternative action is a better understanding of the arms race dynamics, of the fallacies of the dominant military doctrines and the depth of crisis in arms control.

It is now evident that the arms race of the recent decades, focused mainly on the race in military technology, has not enhanced but weakened the security of all concerned. It had an inverse effect on security. Even the superpowers have suffered. The growth of their strategic capabilities has made their homelands vulnerable to attack by ballistic missiles, with a very short warning time. A modern ballistic missile fired from the territory of one of the superpowers can reach the territory of the other within half an hour. And the faster the race — the more nuclear war-heads enter the arsenals and the more perfect the delivery vehicles — the greater one's vulnerability. This is even more true for other countries, especially those in Europe, who have to face an ever-increasing destructive power of the modern war machine.

If it can be historically proved that, as a rule, arms races have led to war, this should also hold for the nuclear age, characterised as it has been by the explosion of new military technology. As stated in the recent UN study: "History indictates that once a particular type of weapon has been developed past the testing stage it will generally be used".[6] Nuclear weapons are no exception. Their usability was built-in from their inception, and they were immediately put to use in Hiroshima and Nagasaki. The probability that they will be used again in moments of stress grows in direct proportion to their perfection. This understanding has long been blurred by the myth of "nuclear deterrence". However, the more the doctrine of deterrence evolves towards the war-fighting counterforce and countervailing strategies with the framework of "extended deterrence", the more clear does it become that by relying on a "balance of terror" nuclear deterrence has in reality stimulated armaments and has turned the arms race into constant war preparation.[7] We shall come back to this point later.

The action — reaction — overreaction fallacy

An important mechanism behind the arms race lies in the pattern of action and reaction. This, in the circumstances of technological rivalry, leads to overreaction and finally to autistic, internally driven and self-sustained impulses, reinforcing the race.

Both sides in the East-West arms race justify their armaments not as a policy willingly undertaken, but as a reaction to armament by the adversary. Earlier, when arms races were predominantly of a quantitative nature, one might conceivably argue that in responding with "measure for measure" the race could be at least blunted if not halted altogether. Responses of a quantitative nature could be kept on a moderate, proportionate level. In addition, as arsenals grew in size, became costly and began to reach quantitative saturation, one could expect a gradual lessening of the pace of armaments.

Both these assumptions have lost their validity today, when the centre of gravity of the arms race has decisively shifted

MAREK THEE

from quantity to quality. As anxiety in the arms race is mainly about new weapons and weapon systems, and as the gestation period for the production of such weapon systems is fairly long (from 10 to 15 years), reaction tends to aim far into
the future, with an eye not on existing arsenals but rather on
possible technological innovations. It thus tends to be programmed less in quantitative terms and more with a vision of
qualitative build-ups, a vision enhanced by the usual military
worst-case scenarios. The outcome is thus overreaction — a
response out of proportion to real challenges. Parallel to this,
the pace of technological change subdues restraint which
might be induced by high costs and by the growth of weapon
stocks.

Moreover, in an atmosphere of secrecy in military affairs,
without exact knowledge of programmes and achievements in
military research and developments of the adversary, contingency planning is largely based on the state of
technological advances in one's own military research. One's
own technological achievements thus become a stimulant for
further armaments. Coupled with the overreaction resulting
from the action-reaction impetus, we arrive at strong armaments dynamics driven by both external and internal impulses.

The more advanced the technological race, the greater the
role of internal stimulants.[8] The race assumes a life of its
own, perpetuating itself even when external pressures disappear. The intensification of the arms race in the 1970s despite
détente and various arms control agreements seems to confirm this.

Evidently, the action-reaction pattern serves the security
interest of no one. All parties become victims to the military
build-up. A rational approach, as far as the superpowers and
the military alliances East and West are concerned, would
rather dictate a strategy of independent judgement and
refusal to surrender to the action-reaction dynamics. In order
to restrain the arms race, ways must be found to break out of
the vicious circle of action-reaction-overreaction. Rather
than yield to pace-setters in armaments, each military alliance
could declare existing nuclear arsenals as being more than
enough for "minimum deterrence", and simply drop out
from the race. As unattractive as such a strategy may be for

military leaders, it might nonetheless prove effective in enhancing security. The whole international climate might undergo a radical change; under the pressure of public opinion, the arms race could be brought to a halt. Those who would like to continue the armaments build-up would be deprived of their allegation concerning external pressures, and in the long run also the autistic momentum would be weakened. However this may be, whenever armaments are justified today as a reaction to a build-up of armaments by the adversary, sound scepticism is in order. This is applicable to both the NATO and the Warsaw Pact military alliances.

The impact of military research and development (R&D)

Military R&D is evidently a key factor in contemporary armaments dynamics. It is generally estimated that on a global scale military R&D employs up to 500,000 of the best qualified scientists and engineers commanding a budget amounting to 10-15 per cent of military expenditures, i.e. US $60-80 billion annually at the current rate. This accounts for one-third to a half of the world's human and material resources devoted generally to research and development.[9] Since military R&D has usurped controlling positions in research and development in almost all natural and physical sciences as well as in many fields of social, behavioural and medical sciences, its impact reaches far beyond military affairs. It exerts a decisive influence on the course of the entire human scientific and technological endeavour, distorting priorities and amputating research that could be devoted to urgent human needs.[10]

In the military field the impact of military R&D is spectacular. Its effect pervades all domains, from the technological reorganisation of armies to the evolution in strategic thinking. Most striking is the recent emergence, in quick succession, of a series of new weapons and weapon systems which have revolutionised the art of modern warfare, conventional and nuclear. These include the proliferation of diverse new nuclear war-heads for tactical and strategic missions, one recent product being the neutron enhanced radiation bombs; parallel great advances have been made in the perfecting of nuclear delivery vehicles — range, speed, accuracy, guidance and reliability — as seen in MIRVS (independently targetable re-entry vehicles), MARVS (manoeuvrable re-entry vehicles) or cruise missiles; other feats include the introduction of precision guided munitions (PGMs) and feverish efforts to develop an entirely new generation of weapons based on the application of "direct energy transfer" such as laser and charged particle beams. It is symptomatic that budget appropriations for military R&D have been steadily rising in recent years, to a much larger degree than the growth of military budgets.[11]

However, it is not the size alone of investments that determines the role of military R&D. More significant is the structure and mode of operation which tend to sustain and perpetuate the armaments momentum. Some features are of special importance.

First is the competitive drive in military technology on the national and international level, engaging thousands of research centres and the various branches of the armed forces. This stimulating structured rivalry both fuels the race and enhances efficiency. On the one hand there is a race involving parallel projects. On the other hand there is a meeting of different technologies in breakthrough accomplishments. Individual and group ambitions, special interests and professional cravings, buttressed by high material incentives and special privileges, contribute to heighten the stakes. The cumulative effect of such structured competition within the huge empire of most advanced research, reinforced by political and ideological motivation, is to energise the armaments dynamics — which in itself, through other factors, has an enormous latent potential.

Second, complementary and in conjunction to the impulse to technological competition, come structural features which assure permanence and continuity for military R&D efforts. Decisive in this respect is the long gestation period required for invention and development of new weapons. Long lead-times, 10 years or more, in the research and development process involve initial conceptualisation, design, model production, testing, improvement, repeated testing, evaluation, prototype production, training and deployment, with many of the functions in the cycle performed again and again until perfection is reached. Such long lead-times have a double effect. Apart from assuring constancy and perpetuity (as well as being a stabilising factor in the work of military R&D), they also inject an element of overreaction. They intertwine with government bureaucratic inertia and tend to uphold projects which may have started from false or misguided assumptions. No government withdraws easily from projects previously strongly advocated. In fact, not all projects which come to fruition prove to be the best. But all of them contribute to the exacerbation of the arms race.

Third, as a corollary to the race in military technology and the long gestation in the development of new weapons and weapon systems, a compulsion emerges not only for the permanent maintenance of the military R&D establishment but also for its steady expansion, the so-called "follow-on imperative". Large bureaucratic institutions, especially in key state sectors, have an inherent tendency to grow and expand. In the case of military R&D, given the climate of intense technological competition, this propensity turns into a stringent urge. Mobilised skill and expertise have to be preserved, and new skill and expertise sought. Existing scientific and technical personnel have to be kept in constant preparedness, and new personnel enrolled to improve performance. Expansion lies in the very nature of military R&D. The development of a new weapon system generates the urge for more advanced arms, to counter the effects of the former. Any cycle of moves in the arms race necessitates a cycle of countermoves. In a sense, the spirals of the arms race are a reflection of the follow-on imperative in military R&D.

All these structural features in the function of military R&D are interrelated and reinforce each other. They combine to forge the phenomenon of self-perpetuating armaments — an arms race dynamic evading human control.

In this context we should recall the powerful socio-political forces with vested interests — "the web of special interests" in President Eisenhower's words[12] — which sustain the military R&D establishment as well as all the power behind the arms race. Apart from the technological-scientific community involved in military R&D, these vested interests include the military, never fully satisfied with the resources and arms at their disposal; the armaments industry, which profits from arms race prosperity; and the state executive bureaucracy, which relies on armaments as an instrument of policy and diplomacy. These four pressure groups form the competitive alliance of the military-industrial-technological-bureaucratic complex. This alliance of vested interests, though in different forms adapted to systemic peculiarities, exists both in the East and West.

In the political literature, the military-industrial-technological-bureaucratic complex is usually discussed exclusively in terms of its relation to the arms race. But given the harmful effect of diverting huge human and material resources from productive use and causing a general malfunction of society, we should also be concerned with the internal socio-political impact of this "web of special interests". It is worth recalling that Eisenhower's warning against the growing influence of the "military-industrial complex" was primarily directed not against the Soviets but against disturbing phenomena in the US society itself. Eisenhower was concerned about the corrosive social, political, and economic effects these influences may have on the American people. Thus Russians and Americans would do well, instead of pointing an accusing finger at each other, to reflect on the position acquired by the "web of special interests" in their own country and the impact this has on their well-being, moral health, prosperity and power.

A strategy of gradual suffocation of military R&D

Although problems linked to military R&D relate mainly to the United States and the Soviet Union — which together are responsible for some 80-85 per cent of global military R&D — the overall security impact is much wider. The superpower arms race in many ways governs the military horizons and security climate the world over and has a determining impact on security in Europe. It is difficult to discuss the armaments race in Europe without considering the underlying factors of the race in military technology between the United States and the Soviet Union. Obviously, Europeans have a vital interest in the quest of the international community to bring military R&D under control.

This may seem a tall order. But unless the challenge is squarely faced, we may not succeed in halting the arms race, not to speak of initiating disarmament. There is no way to dismantle military R&D at a single stroke. Yet a strategy of gradual suffocation is possible. One approach would be systematically to curtail resources devoted to military R&D. There is also a possibility of directly interfering with the very process of R&D. One could start with intervention in those stages of the R&D process which are visible, which can be observed and are susceptible to control and verification. Concerning nuclear armaments, this could be done at the testing stages, both of nuclear war-heads and delivery vehicles.

Speaking in practical terms, the most urgent task at the present moment is to arrive at a comprehensive nuclear test ban (CTB) now under discussion between the United States, the Soviet Union and Great Britain, and on the agenda of the UN Committee on Disarmament in Geneva. Given the direct relationship of such a treaty to European security, the call for a CTB should be vigorously taken up by the movement as an essential and integral part of its programme.

A comprehensive ban on nuclear tests, aiming at halting or at sharply curtailing the augmentation and improvement of nuclear arsenals of the great powers, has remained on the arms control agenda for almost three decades, since the conclusion of the Partial Test Ban Treaty in 1963 which prohibited nuclear tests in the atmosphere only. In the meantime, nuclear testing, mainly underground, has continued unabated. The number of tests in the period 1963-1980 almost doubled in comparison to the previous period of 1945-1963.[13] Instead of decreasing, the pace of development of nuclear weapons increased.

For a long time, one of the arguments against the conclusion of a comprehensive nuclear test ban was that it would be difficult to control and verify. But today, as stated by the UN expert *Report on a Comprehensive Nuclear Test Ban,*[14] "verification of compliance no longer seems to be an obstacle to reaching agreement", given a global seismic network, national and international, supplemented by satellite observation, electronic and other means of information gathering and, in specific cases, on-site inspection on "challenge".

The importance of a comprehensive test ban is summarised by the UN experts as follows:

> A comprehensive test ban is regarded as the first and most urgent step towards a cessation of the nuclear arms race, in particular, as regards the qualitative aspects . . . A comprehensive test ban could serve as an

important measure of non-proliferation of nuclear weapons, both vertical and horizontal.

A comprehensive test ban would have a major arms limitation impact in that it would make it difficult, if not impossible, for the nuclear-weapon States parties to the treaty to develop new designs of nuclear weapons and would also place constraints on the modification of existing weapon designs.[15]

The conclusion of a comprehensive test ban treaty is long overdue and deserves the highest priority in arms limitation efforts. It could, especially, have a beneficial effect on the situation in Europe and further arms control negotiations. In particular, in view of the freeze of SALT II, it could serve to ease the crisis and help to renew efforts to limit the nuclear arms race.[16] One could then move to negotiations on a ban on testing of new missile delivery systems, which would strengthen the limitations for increasing and improving the nuclear arms capabilities of the nuclear powers. As stated by the UN experts:

The arms limitation benefits of a comprehensive test ban could be enhanced, and the channels of arms competition among the great powers further narrowed, if the comprehensive test ban were followed by restrictions on the qualitative improvement of nuclear delivery vehicles.[17]

Thus, at the present juncture, the conclusion of a CTB is becoming the most crucial issue in arms control. It can be taken as a test of the real political will of the nuclear powers to limit the arms race.

Between deterrence and waging nuclear war

Military R&D has its correlate in strategic theory, and the ideological-cultural superstructure in the doctrine of nuclear deterrence. This relationship is mutual. On the one hand, the development of new weapon systems serves to inspire more extended and aggressive concepts of deterrence. On the other hand, the underlying assumption of nuclear deterrence — the pursuit of more destructive and efficient retaliatory power — has prompted greater efforts of military R&D to produce better and more sophisticated weapons. Deterrence has become the spiritual animator of military R&D.

Born in the West in the period of the Cold War, the doctrine of nuclear deterrence became mirrored in the East in the "war prevention" strategy. Nuclear deterrence policies grew to dominate behaviour in East and West and were institutionalised as a common guideline in the SALT process.

The main proposition of the doctrine of nuclear deterrence is that peace shall be maintained through the threat of retaliatory "assured destruction" and the infliction of "unacceptable damage" to those who would start war or would endanger key interests of the other nuclear power. This is *par excellence* a doctrine based on a system of threat and intimidation. By constantly aiming to improve and increase retaliatory power, it actually leads to continued war preparation. At the same time, existing nuclear arsenals are brought into the power play, even in times of relative peace, as instruments of policy and diplomacy.[18] One outcome is that threat and use of force have become widespread in international relations. Our very culture has become corrupted by the *de facto* acceptance of violence and use of force as a normal part and *ultima ratio* of the contemporary international socio-political reality.

It follows that though the doctrine of nuclear deterrence pretends to represent a defensive posture — and the threat of nuclear devastation indeed may have, to a certain extent, contributed to prevent war — in the long run, deterrence tends to fuel the arms race. Evidently, manipulation of threat, intimidation and fear is not the best way for political education and the promotion of real peace. The higher we move on the ladder of the "balance of terror", the greater the chance that deterrence may fail. Military build-ups and stable peace are inherently antithetic. A parallel can be drawn to the old Roman tenet *si vis pacem, para bellum*. Eventually, preparation for war led to war. The contemporary arms race should be no exception. As indicated by the late Lord Mountbatten: "There are powerful voices around the world who still give credence to the old Roman precept — if you desire peace, prepare for war. This is absolute nuclear nonsense and I repeat — it is a disastrous misconception to believe that by increasing the total uncertainty one increases one's own certainty.[19]

Deterrence has a pervasive evil impact on both external and internal relations. Externally, it feeds and sustains the threat system as well as the action-reaction-overreaction momentum of the arms race. Internally, it serves to legitimise armaments, and by nurturing and cultivating perceptions of hostility it tends to lock opposing camps into structured enmity. Threats directed against the enemy turn inward and actuate internal stimulants for armaments. Autistic, self-sustained dynamics of the arms race, inherent in the mode of operation of military R&D, are reinforced by autistic phenomena in the socio-political superstructure generated by the deterrence scare.

But, as indicated earlier, nuclear deterrence is not a static concept. Its strategic parameters have evolved hand in hand with advances in the technological instrumentation in nuclear warfare — both quantitatively as far as the increase in the numbers of nuclear war-heads is concerned, and qualitatively as far as the perfection of delivery vehicles are concerned. "Modernisation" of nuclear weapons has led to the "modernisation" of the strategic doctrine. War-dissuasion has turned into a war-waging doctrine.

The crude concept of "massive retaliation", aimed mainly at cities (the countervalue strategy), was stipulated by the United States in the 1950s at a time of US superiority in nuclear weapons. This gave way in the 1960s, as the Soviet Union acquired intercontinental missiles, to the strategy of "flexible response" linked to the concept of "mutual assured destruction" (MAD). The targeting policy as inscribed in the Single Integrated Operation Plan (SIOP) became in this period more "flexible", comprising not only cities but also military and economic objects, that could be covered by the increased numbers of nuclear missiles. Retaliation options were seen in a continuum from conventional to tactical and strategic nuclear weapons, with priority accorded to military rather than civilian objects. In 1974, Secretary of Defence James Schlesinger, after discussions which lasted for years, announced the adoption of a "counterforce" strategy which provided for still larger options in targeting policy. These included, in particular, "surgical strikes" against hardened missile sites made possible by the increased accuracy, speed and reliability of the new nuclear delivery systems — the MIRVs, the "smart" bombs, MARVs, etc.[20]

Finally, in July 1980 President Carter issued the Presidential Directive 59 providing for yet larger selective options in nuclear targeting known as the "countervailing strategy". The new emphasis is on a "broad scale deterrence", envisaging a wide range of military, industrial and political targets, including command, control and communication (C^3) centres, missile bases, sensitive industrial plants etc.[21] The adoption of this countervailing strategy was generally interpreted as a step beyond deterrence, towards actually waging nuclear war.[22] Under the mantle of nuclear deterrence, a nuclear warfighting strategy had emerged.

The disclosure of the PD59 caused an international uproar. But, as stressed by the Secretary of Defence Harold Brown, the countervailing strategy was in fact "not a radical departure from US strategic policy,"[23] It was only "a refinement, a codification" of actual developments "in the light of current conditions and current capabilities."[24] It was "a natural evolution of the conceptual foundation built over the course of a generation" with inputs of both Republican and Democratic administrations.[25] It meant "to improve the effectiveness of our strategic nuclear forces across the full range of threats."[26] New nuclear capabilities translated into war-waging strategies.

The real importance of the above evolution lies in the fact that the US countervailing strategy — mirrored in parallel capabilities of the Soviet Union — dangerously reflects an orientation towards the acquisition of a first strike capability. By this is meant such power of a surprise attack which would paralyse and destroy the retaliatory capability of the adversary, forcing him to surrender. Waging and winning a nuclear war is becoming thinkable in the military mind. In fact, a number of new weapon systems now in the R&D line point to this orientation — e.g., new Anti-Ballistic Missile (ABM) weapons, new techniques in Anti-Submarine Warfare (ASW), the so-called "stealth" bomber that makes the aircraft invisible to radar, the intensified arms race in space aimed to annihilate communication and intelligence satellites, the development of laser and particle beams arms, and the development and deployment of new first strike nuclear weapon systems in Europe.

True, at the present juncture the issues are more political and psychological than purely military. None of the superpowers is near to a real first strike capability. However, the very fear that the adversary may try to gain advantages by striking first — reinforced by the syndromes of Pearl Harbour and the Nazi June 1941 surprise attack against the

Soviet Union — may in a crisis situation lead to catastrophe. While the arms race is fuelled by "worst case" assumptions, history has shown that first strike scenarios are too often enhanced by "best case" assumptions. The speculative nature of deterrence theories opens vistas for unpredictability. Nuclear deterrence critically heightens the perils of nuclear war.

Nuclear deterrence and peace in Europe

There is special relevance to the problematic of nuclear deterrence and its impact on peace and war in Europe. Misconceptions are widespread. Available evidence clearly points to the fact that the doctrine of nuclear deterrence has contributed to the military build-up in Europe, especially in nuclear weapons, putting peace in jeopardy. However, a myth from official quarters to the contrary, that nuclear deterrence has helped to preserve peace, has gained wide credence.

Essentially, the myth of peace-sustaining nuclear deterrence, as presented in the West, builds on the Roman precept of defending peace by preparing for war. This has been revived in the two-pillar doctrine: peace through armaments, and détente. Yet the recent setback of détente while armaments tend to escalate points to the illusory nature of the two-pillar doctrine. Evidently, armaments are counter-productive in relation to détente and are detrimental to peace. In the nuclear age, and given the huge concentrations of nuclear weapons in Europe, the consequences can be disastrous, as stressed by Lord Mountbatten.

The dissuasion effect of nuclear deterrence, as claimed by the establishments, was devoid of credibility, although this was not perceived for a long time by many Europeans. As mentioned earlier, no credible military scenario was ever produced for the use of nuclear weapons in Europe, in an environment where the distance between towns does not exceed a few kilotons of nuclear explosives, without almost total annihilation.[27] Governmental leaders who still talk about waging nuclear war in Europe simply "disregard the generally accepted technical facts on nuclear weapons".[28] Moreover, from the moment any nuclear exchange in Europe threatened to escalate and endanger the homelands of the superpowers, the entire US security guarantee for Western Europe lost credibility. As bluntly admitted by H. Kissinger: "Our European allies should not keep asking us to multiply strategic assurances that we cannot possibly mean or if we do mean, we should not want to execute because if we execute, we risk the destruction of civilisation."[29]

Indeed, the whole strategy of "flexible response", envisaging "limited" warfare in Europe, reflected a trend to decouple US security from European affairs. The following SALT process focused on strategic weapons and the security of the superpowers' homelands, while opening wide the gates for an invigorated race in tactical "grey area" weapons adapted to the European scene, only emphasising this trend. Instead of protecting Europe, current nuclear deterrence strategies tend to transform the continent into a battlefield arena for "limited" nuclear war. In a crisis situation, Europe may indeed fall victim to nuclear dissuasion strategies.[30]

Nuclear deterrence has contributed little to preserve peace in Europe. The real reasons for the relative peace in Europe in the 35-year period after World War II must be sought elsewhere, above all, in specific historical circumstances.

The main underlying factor for the relative stability of the armed peace in Europe lies in the decisive outcome of World War II. This sealed the fate of Europe and the borders of great power influences in a lasting way, reflecting long-term basic great-power interests. Though controversies of a socio-political nature have persisted, the East-West meeting of minds and interests concerning the preservation of the division of Europe remains. Moreover, in the process of US and Soviet empire building in the wake of World War II, and the global redistribution of power in the wake of the anti-colonial revolution, the centre of gravity of world conflict has moved away from Europe. The new focus is the Third World, engaging the great powers in intricate political, economic and military contests. Overextension of superpower involvement around the globe and the preoccupation with many global issues has helped to give Europe a relative respite. Lastly, the shift in the arms race from quantity to quality, with the emergence in quick succession of new weapon systems not yet fully integrated in military theory and praxis, has contributed to some restraint.

The above determinants are clearly time-conditioned, part of evolving and transient historical processes. Winds of change are strong today. New constellations are emerging which tend to transform the parameters of concord and conflict in Europe in a challenging way. Some of these elements of change were mentioned in the introductory part of this paper. They are disturbing. There are signs of strain and of a legitimate crisis in both East and West. It is reasonable to expect that the 1980s will be difficult years for European security. Given the inert resistance of the established order to change, growing tension seems inevitable. This intertwines with the military build-up. Current trends in the arms race are not passing phenomena. Seen in the context of escalating military budgets planned for years ahead, the feverish pursuit of military R&D and the evolving strategic doctrines, we may anticipate progressive military destabilisation. Europe is full of explosives, in both the material and political sense. Unless they can be brought under control — détente revived and the military build-up halted — how can conflict be avoided? The greatest danger for Europe lies in the accumulation of nuclear weapons. That is why the containment of this process and final elimination of nuclear stocks is a matter of highest priority; yes, it is actually a matter of survival.

Crisis and impasse in arms control

It is a truism that arms control has failed to halt the arms race or even to limit its momentum. This failure can be measured in all fields of armaments; in the sharp rise of military expenditures; in the growth of arsenals, nuclear and conventional, strategic and tactical; in the global proliferation of weapons; and in the deadlock in arms control negotiations. The failure is the more distinct as historically arms control has come to replace "idealistic and impractical" disarmament efforts with "realistic" step-by-step measures within the framework of regulated and concerted armaments. Ambitious plans of General and Complete Disarmament have been abandoned; instead arms control has set as its declared goal to make the arms race more predictable so as to reduce the probability of war, to reduce the costs of armaments, and reduce destruction in case of war.

Yet today — after 20 years of arms control negotiations

and the signing of a number of arms control agreements — the arms race is out of international control. Rather than becoming predictable, it has become unpredictable. Rather than reducing costs, the arms race is absorbing ever greater human and material resources. Rather than limiting destruction in case of war, the destructive potential of the modern war machine has increased.

In fact, the protracted bargaining process of arms control negotiations contributed to the escalatory trend in armaments. Externally, the introduction of so-called "bargaining-chips" stimulated "speed-ups in strategic programs"[31] (e,g, MIRVs in SALT I and cruise missiles in SALT II). Internally, "SALT has been used as a lever to increase defence appropriations."[32]

The current crisis in arms control is both political and structural. Politically it reflects growing contradictions between the great powers, a setback of mutual confidence, and a deliberate effort to win military supremacy. The arms race has been transformed into an economic, political, and military contest. In a climate of suspicion and threat, each military move by one side is interpreted by the other side as political and military intent, to be matched by a higher spiral of the arms race. Thus, the arms race has turned into an open-ended armaments marathon. Disturbingly, there is little evidence of any remaining political will in the high quarters of the contending parties to gain control over this momentum.

At least as disturbing is the structural aspect of the crisis. The race in military technology has reached a point where arms control is becoming nearly non-negotiable. On the one hand, the introduction of mobile, interchangeable and easily hidden new weapon systems such as cruise missiles and mobile ballistic missiles makes it increasingly difficult to control and verify any accord on the modern weapons. On the other hand, there is tension between the quantitative approach in arms control negotiations and the qualitative arms race. In the course of the technological armaments race, the two superpowers have built up two force structures with different profiles adapted to specific strategic needs, geopolitical requirements, historically shaped strategic concepts and technological capabilities. So, for instance, the proportion in the strategic triad of the land and sea-based intercontinental ballistic missiles as well as bombers differs substantially in the US and Soviet forces. Their technological quality is also scarcely the same. To try to establish symmetry in asymmetrical situations is a Sisyphean undertaking. Each new weapon system tends anew to de-stabilise the situation, making agreements on older weapons meaningless and preempting new arms control accords. Unless both sides can agree to drop the simplistic number game and admit that the existing stockpiles of strategic weapons are more than sufficient for claimed deterrence purposes, there seems no real prospect for significant arms control.

There is an obvious connection between the emergence of new weapons systems, the appearance of more aggressive war-fighting, strategic concepts and the failure of arms control. Both the armaments process and the new strategic doctrines are adverse to control, however limited. The transformation of military horizons, technologically and strategic, has been so substantial in recent years that the very underlying theory of arms control has come under attack.

A basic tenet of arms control theories was mutual vulnerability, reflecting the doctrine of mutual assured destruction. An organic linkage was perceived between deterrence, mutual vulnerability and strategic stability. The attainment of invulnerability by one side would tend to eliminate the retaliatory threat of the other and thus undermine stability as assumed in deterrence theory. This line of thought formed the basis for the SALT I Anti-Ballistic Missile (ABM) Treaty, which limits the deployment of ABM systems. All those theoretical assumptions of arms control are now being questioned.

For one thing, the Mutual Assured Destruction doctrine, which aimed to make the population of big cities hostage to deterrence strategies, is termed obsolete. In Kissinger's words: "It is absurd in the 1980s to base the strategy of the West on the credibility of the threat of mutual suicide."[33] Such a strategy has to be replaced by "a plausible war-fighting capability".[34]

Moreover, acceptance of the principle of mutual vulnerability is now called nonsensical. As again emphasised by Kissinger, one of the original architects of arms control:

"It cannot have occurred often in history that it was considered an advantageous military doctrine to make your country deliberately vulnerable."[35] Thus, the problem of the termination of the ABM Treaty is being put on the political agenda.

Such questioning of the basic tenets of the arms control theory is indeed indicative of the depth of its crisis. In circumstances where nuclear war-waging, war-winning, and first strike capabilities are becoming the dominant concern of the great powers, the theory of seeking stability through mutual vulnerability has lost its validity indeed.

Conclusions

Obviously, arms control and arms control negotiations today are in disarray. Given the rapid advances in military technology and the hardening of the structural and political barriers to arms control, there seems no return to the old frameworks, even with far more limited ambitions.[36] If any conclusions can be drawn from the above analysis, they are these:

(a) There must be a radical change of direction in the security debate and efforts, away from arms control measures that seek to balance armaments by joint superpower steering of the arms race, and towards genuine and comprehensive disarmament; i.e. visible reduction of armaments and elimination of military potentials. It is imperative to return to the idea of General and Complete Disarmament, to be implemented gradually under effective international control. After all, this is an idea which once was agreed by the United States and the Soviet Union as a workable proposition which got the unanimous support of the United Nations, and which is still inscribed as the "ultimate objective" in UN resolutions.[37]

(b) Given the fact that the establishments of the great powers have largely fallen hostage to the political and structural barriers to disarmament, a correct action-oriented strategy would seek change through broad mobilisation of global public opinion. If the political will to disarm is not sufficiently available at government level, it would need to be animated and impelled by the political will, made vocal, of peoples and nations.

(c) Concerning Europe, there is a need to develop alternative strategies. These should aim not at perpetuating military build-ups by balanced arms control measures, but at considerable reduction of military forces and arsenals. Such strategies may start from broadly understood confidence-building measures,[38] encompass risk-free unilateral disarmament initiatives focusing on a shift from offensive to defensive postures,[39] and take up plans for gradual military disengagement and denuclearisation of Central Europe, as a preliminary step towards freeing all Europe from nuclear weapons. A matter of immediate urgency is to halt the deployment of new nuclear weapon systems, in both East and West.

In one of its cardinal statements, the Declaration on Disarmament adopted by the 1978 Special Session of the UN General Assembly stressed: "Mankind today is confronted with an unprecedented threat of self-extinction arising from the massive and competitive accumulation of the most destructive weapons ever produced."[40] For no continent is this statement so true as for Europe, the continent with the highest accumulation of such destructive weapons in the world. Disarmament, and especially nuclear disarmament, is for Europe a question of practical security, of stable peace and of life itself.

Footnotes

1. Text in *U.S. News & World Report,* January 26, 1981.
2. George B. Kistiakowsky, *A Scientist at the White House,* Cambridge, Mass.; Harvard University Press, 1977, p.425.
3. Cf. W.K.H. Panofsky, *Science, Technology and the Arms Build-up,* paper presented at the Colloquium on Science and Disarmament, Institut Francais des Relations Internationales, Paris, January 1981.
4. *Comprehensive Study on Nuclear Weapons,* United Nations, Doc. A035/392, September 12, 1980, para 297.
   Cf. also "The False Nuclear Alarms", editorial, *The New York Times,* July 1, 1980.
   According to an October 1980 US Congressional Report, there were, in an 18-month period, 147 false alarms serious enough to require an evaluation of whether they represented a potential nuclear weapon attack. Four other alarms were considered even more serious and resulted in orders that increased the state of alert of B-52 bomber crews and intercontinental ballistic missile units. Finally, there were also 3,073 lesser alarms, primarily caused by atmospheric disruptions. Another report quoted in the US press revealed that at least 27 accidents, so-called Broken Arrows, have occurred involving US nuclear weapons. One of them is reported to have left only one out of six control mechanisms intact to prevent the explosion of a 24-megaton nuclear weapon. It has further been alleged, in the same context, that 10 more accidents occurred in the territories of

other states. Though there is no similar information from the Soviet Union, there seems little reason to believe that the same false alarms, accidents and exposures are not occurring there too, as well as in a more limited way in the other nuclear weapon states. (From the statement by the Swedish Under Secretary of State for Disarmament, Inga Thorsson at the Geneva Committee on Disarmament on February 3, 1981).

5. Henry A. Kissinger admitted this in "The Future of NATO", *Washington Quarterly*, Vol. 2, No. 4, Autumn 1979, pp.5 and 7; "we never had a comprehensive theory for using theatre nuclear forces . . . we had no precise idea what to do with them . . .".

6. *Ibid.*, para 298.

7. Cf. Marek Thee, "The Doctrine of Nuclear Deterrence. Impact on Contemporary International Relations", *Strategic Doctrines and Their Alternatives.* Paris: UNESCO, forthcoming.

8. Cf. Klaus Jurgen Gantzel, "Armaments Dynamics in the East-West Conflict; An Arms Race", *The Papers of the Peace Science Society (International),* Vol. XX, 1973.

9. Cf. Colin Norman, *Knowledge and Power; The Global Research and Development Budget,* Worldwatch Paper; 31, July 1979.

10. Cf. Marek Thee: "The Impact of the Arms Race on Society — Significance of Military R&D", *Impact of Science on Society,* Vol. 31, No. 1, 1981.

11. Cf. US budgetary data. Thus, e.g. the budget for FY 1981 provided for a real increase in military R&D seven times higher than the real increase in general defence outlays.

12. Dwight D. Eisenhower: *Waging Peace, 1956-1961,* New York: Doubleday & Co., 1965, p.615.

13. See table in the UN *Report on a Comprehensive Nuclear Test Ban,* Doc. CD/86, 16 April 1980, p.57. There were 488 nuclear tests during 1945-1963, and 733 during 1963-1979. In addition came 49 tests conducted in 1980 *(International Herald Tribune,* January 30, 1981).

14. *Report on a Comprehensive Nuclear Test Ban,* op.cit., paras 152, 155 and 156.

15. *Ibid.*, para 154.

16. Cf. Dan Caldwell: "CTB; An Effective SALT Substitute", *Bulletin of the Atomic Scientists,* December 1980.

17. *Report on a Comprehensive Nuclear Test Ban,* op.cit., para 159.

18. Cf. Barry M. Blechman and Stephen S. Kaplan (eds.): *Force Without War, U.S. Armed Forces as a Political Instrument.* Washington D.C.: The Brookings Institution, 1978.

19. From the speech by Lord Mountbatten on 1 May 1979, *Pugwash Newsletter,* Vol. 17, No. 4, April 1980.

20. See *SIPRI Yearbook 1974.* Stockholm: Alquist & Wiksell International, pp.55-66, and *SIPRI Yearbook 1975,* pp.41-44.

21. Cf. Address by US Secretary of Defence Harold Brown, 20 August 1980, *Survival,* November/December 1980.

22. Cf. Richard Burt: "US Stresses Limited Nuclear War in Sharp Shift on Military Strategy", *International Herald Tribune,* 7 August 1980.

23. Address by US Secretary of Defence Harold Brown, op.cit.

24. *Ibid.*

25. *Ibid.*

26. *Ibid.*

27. Cf. the address by Lord Mountbatten, *Pugwash Newsletter,* op.cit.; and Lord Zuckerman: "The Deterrent Illusion: A Nuclear Fact World Leaders Must Accept", *The Times,* 21 January 1980. Both reproduced in *Apocalypse Now?,* Spokesman, 1980.

28. W.K.H. Panofsky: *Science, Technology and the Arms Build-up,* op.cit., p.15.
29. Henry A. Kissinger: "The Future of NATO", op.cit., p.7.
30. Cf. Alva Myrdal: "The Superpowers Game over Europe", in *The Game of Disarmament.* Ch. 2, New York: Pantheon, 1976 and Spokesman, 1980.
31. Gerard Smith: "There is No Other Way", *Arms Control Today,* Vol. 11, No. 1, January 1981, p.6.
32. *Ibid.*
33. Henry A. Kissinger, "The Future of NATO", op.cit., p.7.
34. *Ibid., p.14.*
35. *Ibid.,* p.6.
36. Cf. Leslie H. Gelb and Richard Burt: "The Future of Arms Control", *Foreign Policy,* No. 36, Fall 1979; and Barry M. Blechman: "Do Negotiated Arms Limitations have a Future?", *Foreign Affairs,* Vol. 59, No. 1, Fall 1980.
37. Cf. Declaration on Disarmament by the 1978 Special session of the UN General Assembly devoted to Disarmament, UN Doc. A/S—10/23.
38. Cf. "Building Confidence in Europe", statement by the IPRA Disarmament Study Group, *Bulletin of Peace Proposals,* Vol. 11, No. 2, 1981.
39. Cf. Marek Thee: "Arms Control and Security in Europe", *Co-operation and Conflict,* No. 4, 1979, pp.217-19.
40. Declaration on Disarmament, op.cit., part II, para 11.

The Committee on Foreign Affairs of the United States House of Representatives, chaired by Clement J. Zablocki, commissioned a study by the research service of the Library of Congress, which established the United States' official view of the background of the decision to install cruise and Pershing II missiles in Europe, and assessed international reactions to it. This informative document was published at the beginning of 1981, by the US Government Printing Office in Washington. Our excerpts below feature the second chapter of the study; further excerpts appear in a concluding chapter.

The Evolution of NATO's Decision to "Modernise" Theatre Nuclear Weapons

1. Alliance Concern

The formation of the Nuclear Planning Group (NPG) in 1967 facilitated the discussion and study within the alliance of various aspects of NATO's nuclear posture. The work of the NPG, and public attention generally, concentrated on the short range or battlefield nuclear systems which formed the preponderant part of NATO's nuclear arsenal. In 1977, however, attention began to focus on the long or medium range component. This change of emphasis was the result of several separate but related factors: first, the perception that strategic parity as codified by the SALT process accentuated existing imbalances at lower levels of forces; second, the development of cruise missiles which, many argued, had considerable potential for NATO defence, particularly as a counter to Soviet theatre capabilities; and third, suspicion on the part of many Europeans that the American administration, in order to secure a SALT II agreement, would accept constraints on cruise missiles that would prevent their utilisation in the European theatre. None of these factors was conclusive. But, in combination, they produced a powerful momentum that led to the process of LRTNF modernisation.

European concern over implications for the alliance of developments in the SALT negotiations was catalysed by West German Chancellor Helmut Schmidt. As previously noted, the Chancellor had long demonstrated an interest in, and understanding of, strategic issues. In his book *Defense and Retaliation,* his discussion of graduated deterrence anticipated the evolution of NATO's doctrine of flexible response, and he consistently stressed the need for NATO to maintain a balance of forces with the East. Writing in 1970, he emphasised the direct relationship between the theatre and strategic forces.

"Soviet superiority in the Central Sector is further reinforced by about 750 medium range ballistic missiles that have no NATO counterpart. This point more than any other drives home the lesson that, looked at in general and from the theoretical point of view of a conflict extended over a long period of time, there can only be an overall balance in Europe's central sector if strategic nuclear weapons are drawn into the equation.[1]

By the mid-1970s Schmidt had become convinced that this linkage and therefore the credibility of NATO's strategy was being undermined. In a speech to the North Atlantic Council on 10 May 1977, Chancellor Schmidt expressed his concern that:

". . . the SALT process may lead to a paralysation of the Soviet and American central strategic forces and that the strategic nuclear component will become increasingly regarded as an instrument of last resort, to serve the national interest and protect the survival of those who possess these weapons of last resort".[2]

During his speech to the International Institute for Strategic Studies (IISS) in October 1977, Schmidt extended his concern to the implication of SALT for other levels of forces, by noting that SALT neutralised the strategic capabilities of the two superpowers and therefore magnified the significance of the disparities between East and West in nuclear tactical and conventional weapons. He emphasised that strategic arms limitations confined to the United States and the Soviet Union would inevitably impair the security of the West European members of the alliance *vis-a-vis* Soviet military superiority in Europe unless the disparities of military power in Europe were removed in parallel with the SALT negotiations.

The main purpose of the Chancellor's speech was to make public his concern that under the bilateralism of the SALT process, certain aspects of European security were being ignored. Although he nowhere directly referred to theatre nuclear forces, his comments focused public attention on the concept that a gap was appearing in NATO's deterrent capability.

The analysis underlying the Chancellor's remarks had been in circulation for some time. Much of the criticism of the SALT process, and particularly the emerging SALT II treaty was directed at its implications for the alliance. Critics maintained that Europe was being neglected at two levels: First, they argued that strategic parity as codified by SALT must inevitably undermine the American strategic guarantee; and second, they pointed to the emergence of Soviet systems, notably the Backfire bomber and the SS-20 missile, that were outside the SALT process but were highly relevant to Europe, and of American cruise missiles which would assist Europe, and yet were under discussion in the SALT negotiations. While concern over this neglect was voiced predominantly by American analysts, it also found an echo among a number of European observers.

The Soviet "grey area" systems that attracted attention were the Backfire bomber, first deployed in 1974, and most significantly the SS-20 missile. Reference to the existence of the SS-20 emerged in official Western statements during 1975. The 1976 Department of Defence posture statement noted the SS-20 as a new and unique development, the 1977 statement saw its deployment as impending, and the 1978 statement assessed it to be operational.

Public attention was first drawn to the SS-20 in September 1976, when Fred Ikle, who was then the Director of the U.S.

Arms Control and Disarmament Agency, commented:

"The spectre of such weapons grows like a towering cloud over Europe and Asia. Why are they adding to this arsenal? What, must we ask with deep concern, is the possible political purpose?"[3]

The SS-20 represented a clear increase in capability over the SS-4's and SS-5's. However, differences existed within the alliance concerning the implication of these improvements for alliance strategy. Despite these differences, the SS-20 took on substantial political significance as it became the symbol of NATO's deficiencies in theatre nuclear forces and of the need for positive action on the part of the alliance.

At the same time that Soviet theatre force modernisation became a matter of Western concern, American technology was producing a system which many observers believed offered almost unlimited application to the alliance — the cruise missile. The characteristics of the cruise missile — accuracy, invulnerability and relative low cost — were said to permit its utilisation in a wide range of roles. In one of the first analyses to deal in detail with the implications of cruise missile development, Richard Burt, then Assistant to the Director of the IISS, described some of the potential roles:

"In the performance of tactical missions, cruise missiles may provide an attractive replacement for increasingly expensive strike aircraft in the performance of many missions. On land, where aircraft undertaking deep penetrative strikes are increasingly vulnerable to SAM defences, cruise missiles could become a more cost effective instrument for interdiction and counter air operations. At sea, they might possibly supplant the need for aircraft carriers with their large complements of attack aircraft. Perhaps even more intriguing than the cost advantages that might stem from the tactical use of cruise missiles was that they could carry out tasks now assigned to tactical nuclear weapons".[4]

The 1976 Strategic Survey noted that the U.S. Air Force had commenced studies on the possibility of replacing the F-111's stationed in England with GLCM's. In January 1977, the report by the Director of Defence Research and Engineering, Malcom C. Currie, commented:

"The advent of long range, highly accurate cruise missiles is, perhaps, the most significant weapon development of the decade . . . the cruise missile represents a high leverage investment which can be fielded at relatively low cost by utilising existing launch platforms while at the same time forcing the Soviets to divert resources to costly air defence systems."[5]

It was argued that cruise missiles would be of particular interest to France and the United Kingdom in their future planning for the renewals of their independent strategic deterrents. Much of this analysis was based on speculation. Cruise missile development was insufficiently advanced to establish whether performance was as good as claimed and little work had been done to evaluate the cost effectiveness and efficiency of potential application. Nevertheless, Soviet anxieties and American ambivalence concerning the U.S. negotiating position in SALT served to intensify European determination that their options should be safeguarded. In this sense, cruise missiles application in the theatre nuclear role provided the most politically visible and immediately justifiable rationale for their safeguarding the technology for future application.

Suspicion concerning American attitudes toward cruise missiles was not without foundation. Since the Vladivostock agreements which had excluded both the Backfire and cruise missile problems, the Soviet Union had been pressing hard for permanent constraints on cruise missiles, particularly a non-transfer clause.

A number of observers feared that in order to achieve a SALT II agreement, the Ford administration would make a deal including restrictions on cruise missiles.

This suspicion increased when the new Carter administration took over in 1977 with a commitment to proceed rapidly to a SALT II agreement. Some U.S. officials were in favour of restrictions on cruise missiles. Strobe Talbot, discussing the preparation of the Carter administration March 1977 SALT proposals in his book on the SALT II negotiations, comments that the chief SALT negotiator, Paul Warnke:

> Urged that the United States SALT position contain at least one provision that the Kremlin would welcome and some Pentagon planners would resist. This was to impose strict limits on the range of cruise missiles, particularly ground-launched cruise missiles . . . Warnke could not imagine the Kremlin accepting any new U.S. proposal that left long-range, ground-launched cruise missiles unconstrained.[6]

A number of observers were quick to point out the implications for the alliance of an agreement that included restrictions on cruise missiles. Richard Burt drew attention to the American predicament.

> "The most interesting military option available to the West for countering the expansion of Soviet Eurostrategic capabilities is already under discussion at SALT — the long-range precision-guided cruise

missile. In deciding whether to exploit cruise missile technology in this manner, the United States must therefore once again choose between placing priorities on strengthening the alliance ties and quickly obtaining a SALT agreement.''[7]

Burt developed this approach in a later article, concluding that:

"Over time, many Europeans may conclude that the United States — in order to reach an agreement — has mortgaged systems that are most likely to serve Western rather than American interests.''[8]

Concern that the United States should not negotiate away what appeared to be a substantial technological advantage was also expressed in official circles. The 1978 Department of Defense Report commented that:

"Cruise missiles may be tempting candidates for arms control, but because of their versatility and the verification issues they raise, considerable caution needs to be exercised in how they are treated within the framework of SALT.''[9]

The efforts of the Carter administration to solve the cruise missile problem through the mechanism of the protocol failed to satisfy the anxieties of either its domestic critics or those of its allies. Confirmation was continually sought that the duration of the protocol would be finite and under no circumstances would be extended. Similar assurances were sought for the ability of the United States to transfer technological "know-how" to its allies. As a U.S. Senate report noted:

"In the 19 formal North Atlantic Council consultations on the progress of the SALT negotiations before the Vienna summit — and in a number of bilateral discussions, especially with the British — the United States was repeatedly asked to clarify the noncircumvention position and regularly reminded of NATO's concern about it.''[10]

Allied concern over the American position was reinforced by the initial reluctance of American officials to admit that a theatre nuclear problem existed. The reaction of many American officials to European concern over the theatre imbalance was to attempt to persuade them that the problem was illusory. These officials argued that it was unrealistic to isolate the theatre balance from the overall strategic balance and they stressed that the United States had more than enough central strategic forces to cope with the Soviet medium-range threat. They also made efforts to strengthen existing theatre forces by deploying an extra wing of F-111's to the United Kingdom and doubling to 400 the number of submarine-launched re-entry vehicles assigned to SACEUR.

During hearings on the SALT II negotiations in October 1977, Secretary of State, Vance, confirmed that the alliance was taking a close look at its theatre nuclear posture, but said that with Polaris and existing forward-based systems no additional long-range ground- or sea-launched systems were required. But, such assurances on the sufficiency of American strategic capabilities were interpreted by several of the allies as self-serving and an attempt to divert European attention from the theatre nuclear problem and thus allow the SALT negotiations to proceed undisturbed. Chancellor Schmidt's speech was a warning signal that European interests could no longer be ignored in the strategic negotiations between the superpowers. In fact, his speech reflected a development that was already under way. As a result of European persistence, the United States agreed that the issue needed special examination and a "High Level Group" was established as the forum for this study.

2. The High-level Group: Origins and Mandates

The High Level Group (HLG) had its origins in the May 1977 summit of NATO leaders, a meeting at which President Carter called for increased allied efforts across a wide spectrum of defence areas including TNF modernisation. The action program which sprang from this initiative, the long-term defence program (LTDP), included a separate functional area, designated Task Force 10, dedicated to identifying needed remedial measures in the TNF field. NATO assigned the Nuclear Planning Group (NPG) responsibility for managing Task Force 10. At its October 1977 meeting at Bari, Italy, the NPG established the HLG as a subordinate body. The HLG's mandate was to examine the need for NATO TNF modernisation, and the technical, military and political implications of alternative NATO TNF postures.

The HLG's work concentrated on the implications of three factors for NATO's strategy of deterrence through flexible response: first, the condition of strategic parity; second, the ongoing modernisation of Soviet theatre forces; and third, the growing obsolescence of existing NATO theatre forces.

The HLG was made up of national officials from 11 member States of the alliance: the United States, United Kingdom, Italy, West Germany, the Netherlands, Norway,

Canada, Turkey, Belgium, Denmark and Greece. It was chaired by the U.S. Assistant Secretary of Defense for International Security Affairs and had no standing staff as such. Rather, it relied on existing NATO Defence Ministry staffs, with most staff work in advance of meetings done in Washington. Members of the HLG were drawn from the senior echelons of ministries of defence and were from diverse backgrounds in terms of functions.

In the course of HLG's examination, a number of important guidelines emerged:

—The LRTNF decision should reflect an "evolutionary" rather than radical change in NATO's defence posture. Thus it would not entail any increase in importance in the role of nuclear weapons in allied defence or any change in the strategy of flexible response; nor would it produce any change in the overall total of nuclear weapons in the European theatre.

—A direct matching capability to the SS-20 was not considered necessary, but merely an offsetting capability to provide a credible response; this requirement determined that the systems chosen should have range sufficient to strike targets in the Soviet Union from West Europe.

—To satisfy public perceptions concerning the credibility of response, it was considered that the systems should have as much visibility as possible. Hence a preference for land-based systems.

—Survivability — and thus mobility — penetrability, and high accuracy were also emphasised.

—Finally, it was assumed that a mix of systems would provide an optimal synergistic effect. While it was recognised that visibility inevitably compromises survivability, the need to enhance the credibility of response was considered sufficiently important for this aspect to be given priority.

Beginning in the late autumn of 1977, the HLG conducted an exhaustive examination of the various technical options, the cost effectiveness of the specific force mixes, and their associated penetration and survivability factors. The HLG examined the possibility of modernising and/or augmenting existing aircraft and SLBM types. By mid-1978 the HLG had reached a consensus that TNF modernisation should include the deployment on the continent of additional improved long-range nuclear weaponry specifically capable of reaching Soviet soil. Its attention then focused on force mixes drawing upon the following three LRTNF weapons systems:

A. PERSHING II EXTENDED RANGE (ER) MISSILE[11]

The Pershing II was originally planned as a replacement for the Pershing 1A (P-1A)[12] currently deployed with the United States and West German forces. 108 P-1A launchers are deployed with American Army Units in the Federal Republic and 72 launchers with the Air Force of the Federal Republic.

Initially the Pershing modernisation programme had as its objective improved accuracy and lower yield in order to reduce collateral damage and provide a more credible theatre nuclear interdiction capability. In 1977 following recommendation from the Secretary of Defence and SACEUR — then General Haig — the requirement for a substantial increase in range was generated. The range of the Pershing II ER will be close to 1,000 miles as opposed to 400 miles for the 1A.

The Pershing II ER will have a new two-stage missile and re-entry vehicle (RV) and will use a modified version of the present erector/launcher and other ground support equipment. Following SACEUR's recommendation, the Pershing II will resemble the 1A as closely as possible. The main physical difference will be weight, the new missile being approximately 15,500lb as opposed to approximately 10,000lb for the 1A.

Unlike the Pershing 1A, which follows a ballistic trajectory from RV separation to the target by an onboard radar, the all-weather radar will be activated during the terminal phase of flight to correlate radar returns from the area surrounding the target with a pre-stored reference map of the target area. Successive corrections during RV descent are expected to achieve accuracies of between 20 to 40 metres CEP compared with 400 metres CEP for the Pershing 1A.

The Pershing II will use either the W-85 or W-86 warheads either of which can employ selectable yields. The higher accuracy of the P-11 will allow the use of lower yields for a given mission.

During peacetime, Pershing II's will be deployed in casernes at quick reaction alert (QRA) sites, and will disperse during crisis conditions to their firing positions. While the Pershing II continues to be support and manpower intensive, its reaction time and deployment time on the move has been considerably speeded up.

The basic Pershing II firing unit is a platoon consisting of three erector launchers with one missile per launcher and associated ground equipment. The Pershing II is still in the development stage and thus expected improvements remain to be achieved. The earliest initial operational capability (IOC) for the system is August 1983.

The United States is preserving a short-range version of the P-11 to meet FRG or other NATO requirements. U.S. officals have indicated that while no formal demand has been made, they expect the FRG to buy the single-stage version of the P-II particularly as the FRG has bought all previous improvements to the Pershing and as the FRG has budgeted out year funds to upgrade its Pershing force.[13]

B. THE GROUND—LAUNCHED CRUISE MISSILE (GLCM)

Many observers believe that the evolution of cruise missile technology in terms of accuracy, penetration and survivability offers substantial potential for improving NATO's defence capabilities.[14] Having examined the air-, ground- and sea-launched options for cruise missiles, the HLG decided that the ground-launched version offered the optimum solution.

The GLCM will be a version of the Tomahawk cruise missile adapted for launch from air transportable, ground mobile platforms. It is powered by a turbofan engine. Guidance is by inertial navigation with terrain contour matching (Tercom) updates at periodic intervals. Flying at a speed of around .8 mach at an altitude of below 100 metres, the GLCM's operational range will be approximately 2,500kms with an anticipated terminal accuracy of less than 80 metres CEP.

GLCM's will be deployed with American Air Force units. The missiles will be transported four to a launch platform. Four transporter/erector/launchers (TEL) with 16 missiles controlled by two launch control centres will constitute a fire control unit or flight.

The GLCM will use the W-84 warhead which provides selectable yields.

Similar to the Pershing II, the prelaunch survivability of

the GLCM derives from the system's mobility. Unlike the Pershing, the GLCM will be deployed during peacetime at permament sites in hardened shelters capable of withstanding blast effects at up to 2,000 p.s.i. Given warning time, the GLCM could move from its main operating base to a field location.

As with Pershing, many of the performance objectives of the GLCM have still to be fulfilled in testing. Reports have suggested two particular problems regarding the Tercom guidance system: first, to date the cruise missile has not been tested over terrain representative of potential operational areas — much of the terrain which the missile would almost certainly traverse — western parts of the Soviet union — are very flat and lack the distinctive contours for which Tercom is best suited; second, the provision of the maps necessary for Tercom may be a more difficult problem than previously assumed.

The IOC for the GLCM in Europe has been given as December 1983. However, Department of Defense officials have recently indicated a 6-month delay in the testing of GLCM due to technical difficulties in the computer and communications equipment. This raises the question of a slippage in the IOC.

C. THE SEA—LAUNCHED CRUISE MISSILE (SLCM)

While it was acknowledged that the land attack sea-launched cruise missile (SLCM) had a number of advantageous characteristics, particularly in terms of survivability and deployment flexibility, it was thought to lack the political visibility considered essential for TNF modernisation. Furthermore, the cost of providing dedicated platforms seemed likely to make the SLCM option too expensive. However, substantial interest in the SLCM option continues to be demonstrated and further LRTNF deployments by the alliance could involve SLCM deployment. The United States has continued development of several versions of the Tomahawk SLCM (anti-ship and land attack nuclear and conventional) for deployment on both submarines and surface ships. The DOD has programmed the eventual procurement of 243 anti-ship SLCM's and 196 land attack SLCM's for deployment on 33 688-class attack submarines and 15 963-class destroyers. For fiscal year 1981 Congress authorised the procurement of 50 Tomahawk SLCM's. The DOD is also conducting a critical review of the possibility of converting eight Polaris submarines into cruise missile launch platforms.

D. A NEW MOBILE MEDIUM-RANGE BALLISTIC MISSILE (MRBM)

The Department of Defense developed a detailed plan for a mobile MRBM in the spring of 1979. However, after congressional criticism of unnecessary duplication in TNF programs, the MRBM was dropped from the Air Force budget.

3. The HLG's Proposals

During the meeting of the NPG in Florida in the spring of 1979, NATO Defence Ministers agreed in principle to the concept of a deployment in the early 1980s of some 200 to 600 warheads for long-range theatre delivery. It was agreed that a final decision would be taken in December 1979. In the intervening months, final details concerning numbers and types would be established, the program would be integrated with an arms control approach and acceptance of the plan by all allies achieved.

The final HLG recommendation was for the deployment of a total of 572 nuclear missiles in 5 European countries; 108 Pershing II launchers and 24 GLCM launchers (96 missiles) in the Federal Republic of Germany; 40 GLCM launchers (160 missiles) in the United Kingdom; 28 GLCM launchers (112 missiles) in Italy; 12 GLCM launchers (48 missiles) in Belgium; and 12 GLCM launchers (48 missiles) in the Netherlands.

There has been considerable speculation concerning the choice of the number 572. NATO officials have stressed that the figure was not "drawn from a hat" as some observers have suggested, but was an informed judgment based on a number of widely assorted factors such as system availability, in-flight reliability, penetration capability, risks on the ground, target coverage, cost, the need to make a major impact on Soviet perceptions, and arms control considerations.

NATO officials have also emphasised that the deployment of a mix of Pershing II's and GLCM's not only offered a force of high accuracy with great improvements in reliability and accuracy, but also that each system possessed distinctive characteristics that complemented those of the other. Pershing II offers a very high assurance of penetrating Soviet air defences, the capability of striking time-urgent targets, and particularly important, the opportunity to take advantage of the existing Pershing I-A infrastructure. GLCM will have lower life-cycle costs and longer range, providing the capability of attacking a wider range of targets from several different bases thereby increasing the opportunity for participation among member countries through deployment on their soil. In addition, it was pointed out that the deployment of a mixed ballistic/cruise missile force hedges against the failure of one type of system, provides the flexibility to select the best weapon for a given mission while complicating enemy planning.

While the cost of the development and production of these systems (estimated at $5 billion) will be paid for by the United States, the NATO allies will contribute to the infrastructure and support of the systems through their contributions to the NATO Infrastructure Fund.

The possibility of participating in the operational control of these systems through the "dual key" system, as with the Lance and Pershing missiles currently deployed, was offered by the United States. However, the Federal Republic said from the beginning that it was not interested in dual control, and none of the other prospective host countries finally indicated an interest in purchasing the launch vehicles and sharing in the control. The new systems will therefore be deployed with American forces only and under American command and control. It is possible that the United States will reach bilateral understandings with host governments concerning appropriate consultation in the event of a requirement to fire. But such consultation does not imply any actual inhibition on the capability of the United States to operate the systems.

4. The Political Dimension of Modernisation

It is essential to view NATO's decision to modernise its long-range theatre nuclear forces within its political context. The evolution of the proposal and the December 12 decision were heavily influenced by a number of political criteria, notably, the question of the nature of deterrence, the condition of East-West relations, European attitudes to nuclear weapons, and the mechanics of alliance cohesion.

The question of strengthening the linkage between the U.S. strategic guarantee and a conflict in Europe was one of the primary considerations behind the modernisation proposal. Inevitably, this revived the perennial question concerning deterrence. What level of forces, what degree of certainty, what degree of credibility are sufficient for the purposes of the alliance? Does the strategy of flexible response require a matching capability at every level or merely a capability sufficient to convince a potential aggressor that the risks are not worth the gains?

The conflicting interpretations of deterrence and particularly of the need to enhance the American guarantee to Europe through LRTNF modernisation were illustrated in speeches in the autumn of 1979 by Henry Kissinger and McGeorge Bundy.

Speaking to an international conference in Brussels on the future of NATO on September 1, Dr Kissinger declared that under current strategic conditions, the American strategy of mutual assured destruction no longer afforded a credible deterrent for Europe.

> "We must face the fact that it is absurd to base the strategy of the West on the credibility of the threat of mutual suicide . . . if there is no theatre nuclear establishment on the continent of Europe, we are writing the script for selective blackmail in which our allies will be threatened, and we will be forced into a decision where we can respond only with a strategy that has no military purpose but only a population destruction purpose.,,[15]

Kissinger argued, therefore, that in order to restore the credibility of the strategic guarantee, the United States must develop strategic counterforce capabilities and credible theatre nuclear forces.

McGeorge Bundy, in a keynote address to the IISS conference a week later, took a somewhat different approach, stressing that as nuclear weapons are very different from other weapons, their deterrent value rests on the unacceptable and unpredictable threat of their use, something that is not affected by marginal changes in overall numbers. Moreover, the credibility of the American deterrent rested chiefly on the presence of 300,000 American troops in Europe.

> "The strategic protection of Europe is as strong or as weak as the American strategic guarantee, no matter what American weapons are

deployed under NATO . . . The enduring effectiveness of the guarantee has not depended on strategic superiority. It has depended instead on two great facts: the visible deployment of major American military forces in Europe, and the very evident risk that any large scale engagement between Soviet and American forces would rapidly and uncontrollably become general, nuclear and disastrous . . . no one knows that a major engagement in Europe would escalate to the strategic nuclear level. But the essential point is the opposite; no one can possibly know it would not. Precisely because these weapons are different, and precisely because the existing balance in Europe is endurable to both sides, even a small risk of a large nuclear exchange is much too much.[16]

These speeches summarized the different perspectives that dominated the debate over the need for LRTNF modernisation. On the one hand, it was argued that extended deterrence could no longer rely on a strategy of mutual assured destruction and that credible war fighting options were now required, particularly at the theatre nuclear level. On the other, it was maintained that deterrence continued to rest on the awful and unpredictable nature of nuclear weapons which would insure that the risks entailed in their use would always outweigh the gains. Marginal adjustments, as in the addition of nuclear weapons to European territory, would not affect the bipolar nature of deterrence. Much of the argument for and against LRTNF modernisation centred around these different propositions — but as neither are provable, both depended on subjective interpretations of intentions and capabilities as well as the essential nature of deterrence.

The LRTNF proposal also focused attention on the problem for the alliance of striking a correct balance between the military demands of a credible deterrence strategy and the political requirements of assuring a stable and harmonious environment with which all aspects of the East-West relationship must operate.

The adoption by NATO of the twin tenets of defence and détente has meant a continual adjustment between the insurance and reassurance elements of its defence doctrine. The level of military preparations necessary to deter the Soviet Union to "insure" the alliance is continually influenced by the need to demonstrate and "reassure" the Soviets of the non-aggressive and reactive nature of these military actions. The defence and détente platform has meant that in the search for greater stability, considerable emphasis has been placed on dialogue and negotiation. NATO nations acknowledge the need to upgrade their armed forces in order to maintain a credible deterrent, and also to deny the Soviet Union a *droit de regard* over such actions. But at the same time, they are aware of the advantages of maintaining a balanced and harmonious relationship with the East, and of the adverse consequences a deterioration in East-West relations would bring. In this respect LRTNF modernisation has posed a classic dilemma between the conflicting demands of defence and détente.

NATO attempted to resolve this dilemma by stressing that in the December 12 decision, it was not provoking a further escalation in the nuclear arms relationship between East and West, but was "closing the gap" in theatre nuclear forces — a gap created by Soviet TNF modernisation. This emphasis on the reactive nature of the NATO modernisation proposal necessitated a parallel declaration by the alliance of the willingness to establish an acceptable balance in theatre nuclear forces through arms control negotiations.

The general aversion to nuclear weapons that existed among important sections of public opinion in several European countries was also an important factor in the evolution of an arms control approach. The arms control element was considered essential in order to gain parliamentary and public support for the NATO proposal in several countries, particularly those where the system would be based. A clear indication of the likely public reaction to the introduction of the new missiles had already been given by the widespread opposition to the proposed introduction of the enhanced radiation warhead (ERW). While the issue of LRTNF modernisation was of a different nature than that of the "neutron bomb", substantial opposition could be anticipated in the left-wing of the SPD, on a widespread basis in the Netherlands and to a lesser but unpredictable extent in Belgium. Moreover, it could be expected that the traditional "no nuclear" policies of Norway and Denmark would complicate their endorsement of the proposal. Three of these governments, Belgium, Denmark and the Netherlands, had relatively fragile coalition governments which could be vulnerable to an issue such as deployment of nuclear missiles.

The likelihood of strong public reaction against the deployment of additional land-based nuclear missiles indicated one of the paradoxes of the modernisation proposal — while the technical experts argued that visibility was necessary in order to enhance deterrence, it was precisely this visibility that would cause the adverse public reaction.

While concern over the situation in theatre nuclear forces was expressed in a number of alliance quarters, German officials, as previously discussed, were pre-eminent in voicing their anxieties. They adopted a positive and at times forceful attitude on the question of modernisation and on the duty of all members to act decisively and responsibly on this issue. However, the West German Government qualified its position regarding modernisation with a number of conditions aimed at minimising any adverse effect in the political sphere.

These conditions reflected Germany's sensitivity concerning its position in the alliance and its position vis-a-vis its Eastern neighbours. In other words, the desire to enhance Germany's security through modernisation was matched by an acute awareness of the need not to jeopardise the political gains Bonn had achieved in terms of improved relations with the East.

The terms of "political burden sharing" on which the Federal Republic of Germany made its participation conditional were:
— That NATO should decide on new systems on the basis of a unanimous decision — no negative votes and no abstentions.
— That the plan for LRTNF deployment plan must include, at a minimum, one continental non-nuclear State, in addition to the Federal Republic; this criterion was termed the non-singularity principle.
— That the Federal Republic had no intention of becoming a nuclear State or of playing any leadership role in questions of nuclear strategy. In this respect, German officials stressed that it was the responsibility of the United States to take the lead in nuclear decisions within the alliance.
— That any systems capable of striking Soviet territory and based in the Federal Republic would remain exclusively under American control with Germany providing only financial support and operating facilities. Unlike the arrangements for Pershing 1A, there would be no dual key

arrangement for Pershing II.

Bearing in mind the nuclear status of the United Kingdom and France, the no-nuclear-weapons policies of Norway and Denmark and current domestic problems in other member countries, the German participation criteria clearly focused attention on the Netherlands, Belgium and Italy.

German officials referred frequently to the collective responsibility inherent in membership of the alliance and of the duty of all members to share equitably the risks and burdens of collective defence. However, given the political conditions in Belgium and the Netherlands, the German criteria were bound to cause difficulties for both governments. In view of the German role in instigating the need for modernisation and then imposing its own conditions, a degree of resentment on the part of the smaller countries was inevitable — equality of risk, it was argued, should not necessitate equality of paranoia.

In the case of the United States, the LRTNF decision became a test of American leadership within the alliance. Given perceptions of American vacillation and uncertainty in other fields and the legacy of the ERW episode, LRTNF modernisation was viewed as an opportunity for the United States to demonstrate its ability to lead the alliance, particularly in the crucial area of nuclear weaponry, and for the alliance to show its ability to respond to this leadership. While initially reluctant to concede to European urgings on the need for modernisation, once the process had begun American officials were determined that it should succeed.

This determination was also reflected among NATO and national officials alike, partly the result of a similarly strong resolve that LRTNF modernisation should not follow the same course as the ERW. Agreement on the modernisation proposal was increasingly viewed in terms of NATO's ability to cope with the challenges of coalition decision-making, and to act responsibly and with unanimity on an issue of great significance and sensitivity. In this respect, the proposal eventually developed a momentum of its own as officials stressed that the process was so far advanced that failure to achieve a positive consensus would represent a serious set back for the alliance. As one observer has noted:

"In its extreme form, this view held that whatever military program was eventually decided on would, in the long run, be less important than the taking of the decision itself.[17]

Considerable pressure was exerted in the months immediately preceding the December 12 decision by American and NATO officials in order to sustain the official consensus. Consultations and meetings at a variety of levels were intensified to insure that a unanimous decision would be obtained.

The preparatory work done by the HLG on the strategic, military and technical considerations of LRTNF and the degree of consultation involved, was extremely thorough and reflected well on the ability of the alliance to develop a collective and coherent response on such a complex and sensitive issue. But, the irony of the LRTNF modernisation process was that this success was restricted to the level of government officials and did not extend to parliamentary and public opinion. The consultation and co-operation had been at the level of bureaucratic and technical experts, whose mandate had not extended to the political implications of a modernisation proposal. As a result, a gap existed between what military and civilian officials believed to be the most appropriate solution and what political circumstances were likely to permit. Only when a precise formula emerged from the HLG for Ministerial and Cabinet approval was serious attention given to public and parliamentary opinion. In several countries, the NATO proposal was introduced into the official governmental and parliamentary domain at a relatively short period before the NATO decision was due to be taken. When the modernisation proposal did become an issue of public debate, it was clear that domestic opposition existed in several countries, particularly the Netherlands, Belgium and Denmark, each of which had relatively fragile coalition governments.

Thus, the consensus that had been carefully developed at the official level was seriously threatened by domestic political reaction in several countries. This situation illustrates one of the problems that NATO must face in dealing with nuclear issues — the appropriate point at which questions of nuclear strategy and capabilities should become issues of public discussion.

Finally, the Soviet reaction was an important element in the political context within which the modernisation decision was taken. The issue of American nuclear systems based on the periphery of the Soviet Union — the so-called forward based systems (FBS) had long been a major source of concern to the Soviet Union, and predictably, Soviet officials reacted forcefully to the suggestion that new and more accurate systems capable of striking Soviet territory would be deployed in Europe.

While Soviet officials provided a variety of arguments against the NATO proposal, their statements consistently stressed three points: that a balance of forces existed in the European theatre, which the NATO proposal would disturb; that ongoing Soviet TNF modernisation did not represent any change in the current equilibrium, and further that the number of Soviet medium-range carriers in the European sphere had decreased overall; that the Soviet Union was prepared to make further reductions in its medium-range carriers and negotiate limitations but only if NATO did not approve the modernisation proposal.

Soviet officials focused considerable attention on the European members, particularly the Federal Republic of Germany, stressing that a modernisation decision would inevitably have an adverse impact on East-West relations. They also asserted that the modernisation proposal was being forced on the Europeans by the United States and was part of an American design to achieve strategic superiority and create another spiral in the arms race.

The Soviet campaign both helped and hindered the course of the LRTNF proposal. In one sense, the Soviet campaign had the reverse effect of what Soviet officials intended and strengthened the position of those in the alliance in favour of a modernisation decision. Soviet pressure enabled alliance officials to argue that NATO must not allow its decision making process to be influenced by Soviet tactics and propaganda.

In another sense, however, the Soviet campaign indirectly hindered the NATO decision, as it tended to obscure the deep-seated opposition that existed in several European countries, not only toward nuclear weapons in general, but also toward what was seen by many as an unnecessary escalation in the arms race. Domestic opposition in several European countries was frequently dismissed as purely Soviet-inspired with the result that the genuine problems that several governments faced were underestimated.

Despite the persistence and the intensity of the Soviet campaign against modernisation, Soviet officials do not appear to have realised until very late that NATO was likely to reach agreement on the modernisation proposal. The major speech by Brezhnev on 6 October 1979, which not only summarised the Soviet position but also contained several arms control initiatives, was a case of too little too late. It lacked the one proposal that might have successfully diverted NATO from the December LRTNF decision — an offer to freeze deployment of the SS-20. Had the Soviets made that offer, the December consensus would have been extremely unlikely.

As it was, alliance reaction to the Brezhnev proposals varied from highly sceptical in the United States to mildly positive in several European capitals. The Soviet move nonetheless strengthened the hand of those who argued that the evident extent of Soviet concern would enable the alliance to win substantial concessions in the forthcoming negotiations. The Brezhnev initiative therefore had little or no impact on the course of alliance policy. In the words of a senior British official:

"Mr Brezhnev may perhaps reflect that the ERW success was, in the end, dearly won, in that it perhaps taught the NATO Allies sharp lessons which they applied successfully to a much larger issue".

5. The Work of the Special Group (SG)

While the HLG was conducting its examination and alliance members were formulating their political criteria for participation in an eventual LRTNF decision, a growing body of opinion within the alliance came to recognise that NATO should not embark upon a major nuclear weapons programme in isolation of arms control considerations. Public and parliamentary support for modernisation could only be assured if the alliance demonstrated a willingness to close the gap through arms control negotiations. It was important to underline the continued commitment of the alliance to the twin objectives of defence and détente. In addition, alliance officials perceived that it would not be in NATO's interest to engage in an unrestrained arms race with the Soviet Union in theatre systems.

German officials in particular stressed that achieving

limitations on Soviet theatre forces should be a primary objective for the alliance.

In April 1979, NATO established a special group (SG) to examine the arms control implications of a LRTNF decision in parallel with the work at the HLG. The SG consisted of arms control specialists from alliance countries except France, and was chaired by the Director of Political/Military Affairs of the U.S. State Department.

The task of the SG was to develop an approach parallel to the work of the HLG so that the defence decisions of the HLG were not held hostage to expectations on arms control agreements, but also so that arms control itself had a reasonable chance of success. It was accepted that the work of the HLG constituted the basic point of reference for the SG.

The SG developed the following principles as basic guidelines for the United States in arms control negotiations involving TNF:

1. LRTNF arms control negotiations should be complementary to, and not a substitute for, LRTNF modernisation. The HLG had identified the need for an evolutionary upward adjustment in LRTNF and this modernisation requirement existed independently from arms control. Arms control negotiations would be neither realistic nor possible without an agreed modernisation plan and a decision to implement it.

—A decision in principle on modernisation, but suspending implementation temporarily, pending progress in arms control, would not be in NATO's interest. Postponement of the decision was proposed in a number of the small countries, particularly by certain sections of the social democratic parties. It was countered, however, by the argument that a postponement on these terms would mean that NATO defence planning was dependent on Soviet willingness to negotiate — an unacceptable position.

—Arms control negotiations could lead to a downward adjustment in NATO's LRTNF requirements, but, as negotiations were unlikely to eliminate the Soviet LRTNF threat, NATO LRTNF modernisation would be necessary. If and when arms control results were achieved, the alliance could decide whether to modify the scale of its

LRTNF deployments. This guideline acknowledged the position of those who sought the so-called zero option, or at least wished to minimise the deployments. However, it made it clear that such an outcome was not likely.

2. LRTNF arms control negotiations should be conducted within a SALT III framework.

3. Negotiations in SALT III on LRTNF should involve close and regular consultation within the alliance in an appropriate manner.

4. LRTNF negotiations and MBFR should be consistent and mutually supportive.

5. LRTNF negotiations should insure *de jure* equality in ceilings and in rights. It was particularly important for the alliance to maintain the principle of equality with the East, even if it chose not to exercise this right.

6. LRTNF reductions or limitations should be verifiable.

The special group also reached a number of tentative conclusions concerning the immediate objective for LRTNF negotiations:

1. The negotiations should be a step-by-step process focusing on narrow and selective areas, rather than attempting a comprehensive approach which would multiply the difficulties and complexities involved and minimise the chance of progress.

2. The first step of this approach would be to focus on limiting and reducing the most serious and immediate threat to NATO, the Soviet land-based missile force, particularly the SS-20.

3. The aim should be to achieve a reduction in the overall threat of the land-based missile force by limiting SS-20 deployment, and insuring the retirement of the SS-4's and SS-5's.

4. The effective unit of limitation should be the numbers of warheads on launchers; thus an SS-20 launcher would count as three because its missile carries three warheads, and a GLCM launcher would count as four because each launcher has four missiles each with one warhead.

5. Limitations should apply to worldwide land-based LRTNF deployments, but with regional subceilings on systems located within striking range of NATO.

6. To avoid complex and prolonged negotiations, long-

range aircraft would not initially be included, but serious consideration should be given to addressing this problem in future negotiations. Backfire, however, did pose a particularly serious problem and careful consideration should be given to ways in which Backfire could be constrained in the SALT III context, without jeopardising the possibility of obtaining limits on the long-range missile threat.

The SG's work contained a number of significant ambiguities which would clearly require further study and clarification:

1. The adoption of a very restrictive step-by-step approach which concentrates on land-based missiles is the most practical formula and the one most likely to achieve visible progress. But it is argued that such an approach distracts attention from the wider and more serious question of the across-the-board Soviet TNF modernisation; criticism of a different nature suggests that isolating a specific category of systems will effectively formalise the existence of a separate regional balance, a development which Europeans, particularly the Germans, are anxious to avoid.

While negotiations which dealt comprehensively with all nuclear systems in Europe and aimed for a collective parity in overall totals of all nuclear warheads, including strategic, would be politically desirable, it would be the most difficult to achieve.

2. The precise level of SS-20's that the alliance could tolerate or "live with" has not been established, nor the corresponding numbers of NATO LRTNF then required.

3. Establishing a *de jure* right to equal ceilings may create pressure on NATO to build up to those ceilings rather than accept permanent *de facto* asymmetry.

4. It is not clear whether the ceilings on land-based LRTNF would be SS-20 only or whether it would also include SS-4's and SS-5's.

6. Rationale for the NATO Proposal

Before examining the December 12 decision and its immediate consequences, it is worthwhile to review in detail the various rationales underlying the HLG's proposals — many of which have already been alluded to — as well as the criticisms directed at the NATO position.

During the course of the LRTNF debate, a number of separate but related rationales were advanced to justify deploying additional long-range systems in Europe. These included: to compensate for the consequences of strategic parity on the theatre balance; to close the gap in theatre nuclear forces caused by the substantial ongoing modernisation of Soviet theatre nuclear forces, particularly deployment of the SS-20 missile and the Backfire bombers; to replace existing obsolescent alliance systems; to reinforce the alliance strategy of deterrence through flexible response thereby provide additional political reassurance concerning the credibility of NATO's capabilities; and finally to demonstrate the ability and willingness of the alliance to act effectively and cohesively in the face of Soviet force expansion, and of the United States to exert its leadership role within the alliance.

The central argument for LRTNF has been based on the changing strategic relationship between the two superpowers, the perceived consequences of strategic parity as codified by the SALT process. Under conditions of strategic parity it is suggested that the functions of central strategic systems are confined to deterring either side from their use. In the current strategic environment, the U.S. guarantee to employ strategic systems in response to aggression against Europe is inevitably weakened. Accordingly, it is argued that under strategic parity existing asymmetries at the theatre and conventional levels become more significant and should be ratified.

In this respect, the theatre balance is now regarded by many as being adversely asymmetrical due largely to recent Soviet modernisation of its theatre forces with the SS-20 mobile missiles, the Backfire bomber, and a new generation of Soviet tactical aircraft capable of carrying larger payloads over greater ranges. While it is obvious that these Soviet medium- and long-range nuclear systems represent a clear improvement in capability over existing systems, what is in dispute is precisely the question of whether they represent such a quantum jump in capability as to necessitate a response from the West.

Proponents of LRTNF modernisation argue that the SS-20 gives the Soviet Union an in-theatre "selective" targeting capability that it previously lacked. The improved accuracy and reduced yield of the SS-20's warheads would permit the missile to be used against selective military (counterforce) targets in Western Europe, whereas the SS-4's and SS-5's could only be used against cities (countervalue). Furthermore, the mobility of the SS-20 makes it invulnerable to a counterstrike and gives the Soviet Union added flexibility in usage. Last, the reload capability of the SS-20 suggests to some observers that this weapon system, unlike the SS-4's and SS-5's, is designed for a sustained military campaign.

A more pragmatic case for LRTNF modernisation arguably lies in the deficiencies of NATO existing LRTNF systems — SLBM's and long-range aircraft. The limitations of SLBM's have been said to include those of accuracy, flexibility of yield, and targeting; the firing of a single missile would reveal the position of the submarine; and they would not facilitate a "single short" selective response because of the number of RV's on each missile. More significantly, SLBM's are considered too closely associated with the central strategic systems, a factor which might inhibit an American President from using them.

The long-range aircraft which currently complement the SLBM force apparently also have serious deficiencies. They are ageing, vulnerable to pre-emptive attack, and would have difficulty penetrating Soviet air defences. Under current circumstances, it is argued that NATO's LRTNF lack flexibility and thus do not provide a credible response to the threat posed by the new Soviet systems.

The combination of these factors, it is believed, creates a gap in the deterrence spectrum which the Soviet Union could exploit during a crisis. With its new capability to strike selectively at Europe, the Soviet Union has the potential in a conflict situation to escalate to a level at which NATO, deprived of the American strategic guarantee, would have no credible response. Accordingly, some observers argue that the Soviet Union might be tempted to engage in a pre-emptive strike disabling NATO's current theatre systems trusting that the United States would be self-deterred from retaliating with central strategic systems or with NATO-dedicated Poseidons, thus maintaining a sanctuary status for Soviet territory. For example, Secretary of Defence Brown cautioned that:

"In the face of improving Warsaw Pact forces, we must be alert to the possibility that the Soviets might seek a first strike capability with LRTFS's. [18]

The advantages accruing from this situation are more frequently presented in political/psychological terms than in direct military action. Few observers believe that the Soviet Union would actually use its SS-20's in a first strike role, but they argue that the possession of the capability and the perception of superiority it affords would permit the Soviet Union to extract political concessions from Europe in a crisis.

Finally, while the military rationale, and particularly the threat of the SS-20, was used consistently to gain public support for LRTNF modernisation, political and psychological factors provided the predominant criteria for the final proposal. Most officials conceded that the strict military rationales — other than the renewal of old systems — were not convincing. It is argued that little military advantage, in terms of the total numbers of weapons available and the additional targets that could be covered, would be gained by the deployment of an additional 572 warheads. This aspect was confirmed during a dialogue between Senator John Culver and Walter Slocombe, Principal Deputy Assistant Secretary of Defense for Internal Security Affairs. Asked by Senator Culver what military targets that are not now covered would be covered by the longer range capability, Slocomb replied:

"It is not a question of reaching additional targets . . . I want to be quite clear. The requirement for TNF modernisation is not principally an issue of hitting new targets.[19]

He went on to emphasize that the main emphasis for LRTNF modernisation lay in the psychological aspect of deterrence.

7. Criticisms of the NATO Proposal

Attitudes toward the proposal to modernise NATO's LRTNF can be divided into four broad categories: those who believe there is an urgent requirement for a serious NATO LRTNF capability and view the 572 warheads as a totally inadequate response; those who believe that NATO needs a credible LRTNF capability but more for political than military reasons; those who are generally sceptical of the rationales for LRTNF but believe the modernisation decision was necessary in order to achieve results in arms control negotiations; and those who reject the rationales underlying LRTNF modernisation and argue that the costs of modernisation will outweigh any marginal gains. Criticism of the NATO proposal has emanated largely from the first and the last groups.

The first group has criticised that NATO proposal as a totally inadequate response to a serious deficiency and further as hindering serious progress in bringing about the changes necessary to rectify the current imbalance. These critics argue that the NATO LRTNF modernisation proposal has focused on a single element of the theatre nuclear spectrum, and has thus distracted attention from the real problem facing the alliance in this respect — the across-the-board modernisation of all Soviet theatre nuclear forces.

"Moscow's nuclear modernisation program is not centred around a single system, but consists of several new weapons, including the SS-21, SS-22 and the SS-23 battlefield nuclear support missiles, the Backfire mediuim-range bomber, and the SU-19 Fencer attack aircraft . . . a comprehensive approach to theatre nuclear modernisation must be taken in replacing the alliances increasingly obsolete nuclear posture rather than taking the piecemeal and *ad hoc* steps now under way."[20]

Accordingly, these critics contend that the alliance can no longer choose between defence and deterrence. Because of the seriousness of the Soviet military threat and the wide range of military options the Soviet Union now has available, NATO, it is argued, must possess credible capabilities at all levels. This involves strong conventional forces but it also means usable theatre and tactical nuclear forces capable of carrying out a wide range of military options. In this sense, the 572 warheads should be seen as only the beginning of a thorough re-shaping of NATO's theatre nuclear forces.

Criticism of the NATO proposal has been directed at three levels:

1. In the terms of numbers, the introduction of 572 warheads is totally inadequate, representing in General Haig's words, "only political expediency and tokenism."[21]

2. It is argued that the NATO proposal has distracted attention from the real problem of making the alliance undertake a thorough reappraisal of its theatre nuclear strategy in order to evolve a coherent and credible doctrine based on usable nuclear capabilities at all levels.

3. The offer of arms control negotiations is considered a serious error because: first, NATO has no bargaining leverage and, therefore, the current imbalance can hardly be improved through negotiation; and second, negotiations could produce a number of constraints that could prevent the

alliance from carrying out the modernisation measures necessary to rectify the current imbalance.

The following comments by William Van Cleave and Charles Marshall illustrate this school of thought:

"Those Pershing II's are going to be distributed among 15 airfields. They have got to be an easy target. They have no reach. This isn't adequate, it seems to me, to compete with what is being proliferated against them. Hoping to make use of them in a trade-off seems to me the equivalent of an high school football coach hoping to make a player deal with the Dallas Cowboys." (Charles Marshall)[22]

"It just doesn't equate with the type of theatre nuclear modernisation the Soviet Union has engaged in . . . Cruise missiles are worthless unless they are deployed in large enough numbers and a large enough variety of purposes to saturate defences because they are easily defended against. And less than 200 Cruise missiles between now and the end of 1985 is no threat whatsoever.

"Pershing II's merely replace a very old system in small numbers with a new system with very old technology and the same small numbers . . . Pershing II isn't mobile enough to be survivable . . . I don't regard these moves as modernisation in any way whatsoever." (William Van Cleave).[23]

At the other extreme, there are a number of critics who believe that 572 new warheads are unnecessary. These critics do not accept the thesis that strategic parity neutralises the deterrent effect of central strategic systems for all situations except a direct attack on the homeland. They believe that the current and projected capabilities of the United States, plus its pronounced willingness to defend Western Europe, are sufficient to deter any Soviet leader from a move that could result in the destruction of Soviet society. For those Europeans who doubt the American commitment, it is difficult to see why a small increment of weapons should make any difference or why they should have more confidence that an American President would release a missile from Europe than from the United States. If, indeed, this is the case, they argue that rather than strengthening the escalation ladder, such deployments would weaken it by making possible the containment or limitation of a nuclear exchange to European territory.

Concerning Soviet views of the present balance, these critics argue, because the Soviet Union is faced by four major nuclear powers (the United States, the United Kingdom, France and China) it has specific regional concerns for which it has designed regional forces. However, there is nothing to suggest that the Soviet Union would perceive anything but a continuum of options ranged against itself, from the presence of U.S. nuclear forces in Europe to U.S. central strategic systems. It is therefore difficult, from this perspective, to see why Soviet leaders should perceive an exploitable gap in Western capabilities unless Western critics manage to persuade them.

With regard to the more precise question of the increase in military potential represented by the SS-20, these critics point out that the West has lived under the shadow of 600 MRBM's and IRBM's and the hundreds of medium-range bombers for 20 years. They question whether the military characteristics of these systems represent a quantum jump in capability sufficient to justify NATO's LRTNF proposal. Concerning the "selective capability" afforded the Soviet Union by the increased accuracy and reduced yield of the SS-20, they argue that the term "selective" is difficult to appreciate when used to describe the use of 150Kt warheads (each 10 times the yield of the bomb used against Hiroshima) on a heavily urbanised and densely populated Europe. Any attempt by the Soviet Union to preempt NATO's nuclear's assets would comprise, to all intents and purposes, a strategic strike of the most devastating nature.

Under these circumstances, they ask what political advantage could possibly be achieved that would make such an action, with the attendant risk of American strategic retaliation, worthwhile. Thus, if such an action is politically and militarily incredible, why erect a hypothesis of escalation dominance which, in reality, does not exist. These critics therefore believe that, as with "the window of vulnerability", the "escalation gap" in theatre forces is visible only to those preoccupied with the narrow and selective world of targeting criteria.

These critics also argue that, as with other areas of technology, the Western advantage in cruise missiles will be short lived and NATO will then face new problems when the Soviet union also develops cruise missiles. Furthermore, the introduction of cruise missiles into Europe will severely complicate efforts to obtain limitations on theatre nuclear weapons.

In summary, then, critics of the LRTNF proposal do not

accept that Western perceptions of, and confidence in, the nuclear capabilities of the alliance are being weakened by recent developments at the strategic and theatre levels, or that the Soviet Union perceives a theatre imbalance which it could manipulate for political advantage. They argue that it is unlikely that any amount of juggling with the geographic location of American nuclear capabilities could ever satisfy the permanent doubters of the American guarantee. This doubt is inherent in the geostrategic structure of the alliance and the physical detachment of the chief guarantor from its allies.

Two final comments should be made concerning criticism of the NATO proposal. First, a number of observers who were sympathetic to the need for LRTNF modernisation disagreed with the choice of land-based systems. They have argued that land-based systems were a bad choice because public opinion frequently reacts negatively to the appearance of new nuclear bases and thus sitings could prove difficult in several countries. Furthermore, despite the emphasis on survivability through mobility, the realities of peacetime deployment mean that they remain vulnerable to pre-emption. Many observers doubt whether, during times of tension, the necessary permission to deploy would be given because of the escalating consequences implicit in such a move.

Secondly, while sceptical of many of the arguments put forward to justify LRTNF modernisation, few of these critics believe that Soviet actions should go unnoticed or unchecked. They would prefer, however, to introduce control and stability through negotiation and would have preferred that these negotiations be tried before the NATO decision. Given Soviet concern and apprehension over the new American systems, they argue that the existence of the programs would have provided a sufficient basis for negotiations.

Footnotes

1. Helmut Schmidt, *The Balance of Power*.
2. *Survival,* July/August 1977, p.178.
3. Quoted in *The Security of the Alliance* by Patrick Wall, M.P., a report to the military Committee of the North Atlantic Assembly, Brussels, November 1976. Ikle's speech had not been authorised and the State Department did not circulate the text.
4. 'The Cruise Missile and Arms Control', Richard Burt, *Survival,* January/February 1976.

5. *Program of Research Development Test and Evaluation. Fiscal Year 1978,* statement by the Honorable M.R. Currie, Director. DRE to the 95th Congress.
6. Strobe Talbot *Endgame, the Inside Story of SALT* (Harper and Row) 1979, p.57.
7. Richard Burt, 'The SS-20 and the Strategic Balance' *The World Today,* January/February 1977.
8. Richard Burt, 'The Scope and limit of SALT', *Foreign Affairs,* July 1978.
9. Annual Defense Department Report Fiscal Year 1978, p.56.
10. 'SALT and the NATO allies', a staff report to the Subcommittee on European Affairs of the Committee on Foreign Relations, US Senate, October 1979.
11. This study provides a general description of the technological characteristics of the LRTNF systems. A more detailed technical study is currently being prepared by the General Accounting Office for the Subcommittee on Europe and the Middle East.
12. The Pershing missile was first deployed in Europe in 1962 to provide medium-range nuclear suport to NATO forces. The original Pershing was a mobile system with a large 60-400Kt warhead and a range of about 100-499nm. Deployment of an improved system — the P-1A — was carried out from 1969 to 1971.
13. See the statement by Dr. Percy A. Pierre, Assistant Secretary of the Army, to the Subcommittee of the Committee on Appropriations, U.S. House of Representatives, 15 April 1980.
14. For discussion of the potential application of cruise missiles within Nato, see the forthcoming Brookings Institutions study on cruise missiles.
15. Dr Kissinger's remarks as quoted in *Survival,* November/December 1979, the International Institute for Strategic Studies.
16. Ibid.
17. 'The Role of Nuclear Weapons in Alliance Strategy', Klass de Vries, report to the Military Committee of the North Atlantic Assembly, November 1979.
18. Department of Defense Annual Report, Fiscal Year 1980, p.85.
19. Hearing before the Subcommittee of Research and Development of the Committee on Armed Services, 10 April 1979.
20. Richard Burt, 'Washington and the Atlantic Alliance', *Strength to Weakness, National Security in the 1980's* (The Institute for Contemporary Studies, 1980).
21. *Atlantic News,* 12 September 1979.
22. *From Strength to Weakness, National Security in the 1980's,* op.cit.
23. Ibid.

Part II
Europe Under Threat

Robert Havemann is currently held under house arrest in East Berlin, where he has been an outspoken critic of his government. When asked by Western sympathisers whether he wished the Russell Foundation to organise a Tribunal on his, and other, cases in the German Democratic Republic, he replied "organise a peace conference instead".

After the Thirty Minutes War

Robert Havemann

350 years ago, between 1618 and 1648, the 30 Years War raged across all Germany. When the Treaty of Westphalia ended this war, barely three million people had survived.

Since the coming into force of nuclear stalemate, there has been peace in Europe: a foreboding peace of fear and terror which persists only because it is enforced by atomic parity. The nuclear stalemate means that any future attack will not only destroy those against whom it is directed, but also bring upon the aggressor an inevitable catastrophe. If this peace, which has already lasted for 30 years, comes to an end, the war which results (yes, it will be a very brief war) will leave behind it fewer living persons than did the 30 years war 300 years ago.

The few survivors of such a war will themselves waste away, destined to die, unhappy victims of a cataclysm in which all hopes for a future more human world will have disappeared for ever.

But we still have the possibility of avoiding such a catastrophe, and for this reason it is necessary for everyone to understand, in all its uncertainty, the danger which is menacing us, and to learn to take this danger seriously.

The Hiroshima bomb had an explosive force of 20 thousand tons of TNT. A medium sized hydrogen bomb has an explosive force of 20 million tons of TNT, or 1,000 times that of Hiroshima. This explosive force corresponds roughly to that of all the bombs and explosives used by all the belligerent nations taken together during the Second World War. The number of bombs of this kind which exist at the moment can be calculated to amount to something between 50 thousand and 100 thousand.

An intercontinental missile can set down on its target, with considerable accuracy, ten or more similar bombs, having travelled half way round the world to do so. For its ballistic flight it takes 45 minutes to traverse 20,000 kilometres and therefore 22½ minutes to cover 10,000 kilometres. The time needed to fuel the missile is approximately half-an-hour, maybe longer. But since it is very likely that the loading of several intercontinental missiles can be observed by satellites, and because there is an interval of an hour between the issue or orders to attack and arrival on target, the adversary too can launch the majority of his missiles. The result of such an attack with intercontinental missiles would thus be mutual destruction. An attack of this kind is therefore a race to suicide. Upon these facts rests the thirty-year peace of nuclear stalemate.

Now, the American plan to arm all the European NATO States with new medium-range missiles constitutes an attempt to overcome the stalemate, and to control the choice of war or peace without needing to fear an annihiliating Soviet counter-blow. The American plan has a very simple logic. Previous NATO middle-range missiles had a range of roundabout 1,000km. With such missiles it was impossible to launch an attack on the USSR from Western European bases.

Now, "middle-range" Pershing II and Cruise missiles are to have a range of 5,000km. Such weapons, after NATO's decision of December 1979, will be sited in bases in the territories of America's European allies. Pershing II has the same speed in flight as an intercontinental missile. Due to their enormous range and speed, they can hit all the important military targets in the Soviet Union in a maximum of ten minutes. Because they rely on solid fuel, they are ready to fire at any time. Since they are not sited on fixed bases it is impossible to pinpoint their temporary locations and pre-empt their firing.

At the same time, a new American strategy, only recently unveiled, targets these missiles not on cities and industrial centres, but on "important military objectives and operational centres". Everything is transparent. With the aid of such missiles Russian missile silos can be destroyed in a pre-emptive blow. In less than 5 minutes, which is the necessary time for a Pershing II to arrive on target, it would be impossible, even in the most favourable conditions, to fuel even the odd Soviet intercontinental missile.

Those Soviet ICBMs which are placed in the East, too far away to be reached by European medium-range weaponry, would be attacked at the same instant from Alaska. After such a surprise attack by medium-range missiles, the Soviet Union would then be rendered defenceless to American ICBMs. The only response open to the Russians would be the launching of their own medium-range missiles against the NATO European allies. Europe would then become a heap of rubble impregnated with lethal radioactivity. The danger which would still threaten the USA would be that of poisoning by fall-out from the innumerable nuclear explosions which would have taken place all round the globe. One may suppose that some American "whose job it is" would have brought into being an adequate system of filtration of water and air supplies.

NATOs justification for arming itself with new medium-range weaponry derives from the fact that the USSR for its part has brought into being a corresponding medium-range missile with multiple war-heads, which can attack the West

European NATO States at any time.

For this reason the December 1979 NATO decision, taken under heavy pressure from the United States, has been described as a move to "recover equilibrium of forces", as if NATO were simply matching what had already been done by the forces of the Warsaw Pact, levelling up to the mark already established by the USSR and removing its consequent advantage.

But evidently such a misrepresentation only serves to deceive world opinion. What possible purpose could be served by an unprovoked Soviet attack on Europe, as long as Russia is not seriously menaced by NATO? Russia would not derive the least benefit from turning Europe into an atomic desert: with a folly of that kind it could only bring its own existence into extreme jeopardy. The only power that can possibly envisage any political or economic advantages deriving from a preventative medium-range missile attack is the USA. Europe, in this case, would be seen as a protective shield behind which, from a safe distance across the ocean, Americans could wait for the tragedy to end.

Let us suppose that talks between the USA and the USSR, respectively between NATO and the Warsaw Treaty Organisation, continue, but without achieving results. The United States will begin to plant their missiles in Italy, in West Germany, in England, in Norway and in Benelux. How long can the USSR simply observe this process of preparation for a sudden attack which threatens its very existence? Can they afford, in general, and not just in their own interest, simply to watch passively?

To remain completely impartial, is it thinkable that the United States is aiming at a powerful military position (who doesn't, after all?) but nevertheless only for its own security, purely defensively, without any intention of risking a nuclear war? There are political leaders in Federal Germany who seek to justify to their own consciences verbal consent to NATO's decision by appealing for "trust in the pacific spirit of the United States". By such appeals they would like to smother the doubts which torment the rational sides of their minds. Maybe they might manage the task. But such political men ought to remind themselves that trust in American pacific intentions cannot be taken for granted among *Soviet* leaders.

Neither can one expect such trust, even after nice speeches and assurances: it would be a light-minded response. The USSR paid with 20 million dead for the fact that Stalin believed Hitler's declarations about non-aggression. How many million dead people may have to be paid in *this* case, for any rupture of America's pacific spirit? Meanwhile, the Americans are building, right under their gaze, an offensive nuclear force which could destroy the USSR with practically no risk to themselves.

Thinking deeply, thinking enough to the consequences of this confrontation, one is compelled to the conclusion that, in talks about medium-range weapons which are now being discussed, the lives of millions of Europeans are in jeopardy.

I am convinced that the USSR is willing to take any possible step, even a step of great significance, which might lead to the end of tension in Europe, to the end of the arms race and to actual disarmament. Within this ambit they are not aiming at unilateral military advantage, but are guided only by their search for security from nuclear attack. Further, détente and peaceful co-operation, even from an economic viewpoint, are today more than ever in the interest of the USSR.

I think that, more than people suspect nowadays, the key to the solution of European problems may be found here in Germany.

Translated by Tamara Coates

Rudolf Bahro was given an eight-year sentence as a "spy" because he allowed the West German Trade Unions to publish his book The Alternative. *After widespread protests, the German Democratic Republic released him under an amnesty declared for its 30th Anniversary, and deported him. He became a leading voice in the ecological "green" movement, and the representative of the Russell Foundation in Germany.*

The Russians Aren't Coming

Rudolf Bahro

The crisis of Western military strategy happens to coincide in time with an increasing crisis of general political stability in the Eastern bloc, ultimately tending to affect the Soviet Union itself. Given a total product that is less than half that of the USA, a productivity that is still further behind, and the very much less favourable integration of the military sector into the economy as a whole, the Soviet Union with its poorer population has to spend at least twice as high a proportion of its national product to keep step in the arms race.

It is common knowledge that, with the exception of a leap

forward in missile propulsion from the mid-1950s to the early 1960s, the Soviet Union has always lagged behind in military technology. Nothing of this has changed. It has no equivalent to the Cruise missiles that adapt to the contours of the terrain and can fly beneath the enemy's radar defences. Comparisons of troop numbers, which are so fondly bandied around and purport to show a superiority on the part of the Warsaw Pact forces, in actuality prove just the opposite.

The Eastern bloc finds itself forced to make up by quantity what it lacks in technological quality. In the key field of nuclear war-heads, NATO has numerical superiority, as a result of its typical lead in MIRV technology, even though the Soviet Union has a greater number of missiles as such. The gigantic Soviet tank armies are designed above all for invading its allies and for use in less developed countries, being of little use against NATO's armoury of anti-tank weapons.

A Clear Imperative

The dynamism and efficiency of the Soviet economy, moreover, are significantly on the decline. Even if it will not be so easy to stifle the Soviet economy purely through the arms burden, the logic of mutual deterrence contains a real danger of technological defeat for the Soviet Union in terms of the advance of electronics and computerisation, which the Western arms industry already plays on, a danger which will surface in the current decade. The only indubitable strength that the Soviet Union possesses, today more than ever, is its gigantic territory. The peoples of the Warsaw Pact countries, with only a twelfth of the earth's population, occupy more than a sixth of its surface, with a more or less complete spectrum of natural resources, even if access to these is sometimes difficult. The Soviet Union's geostrategic situation, in the context of the present bloc confrontation, thus indicates in the long run a clear imperative of stability. It seeks to gain time, and expansion into more industrialised regions, rich in population but poor in raw materials, would be a senseless goal.

There is no doubt that the SS-20 missiles enable a Soviet missile attack on Western Europe, though the Soviet Union has no motive for a pre-emptive strike so long as the space between Poland and the Urals is not threatened from

Western Europe, or the Warsaw Pact attacked in any way. I hope that the Soviet Union will be ready to withdraw these weapons in exchange for the Americans abandoning Pershing II and Cruise.

WTO Weaknesses

One thing however is obvious, in view of the Polish situation (and quite apart from the fate of Soviet intervention in Afghanistan, which it is to be hoped will be a salutary failure) — the greater number of soldiers in the Warsaw Pact forces can only be introduced into the debate today to impress the uninitiated. The situation in Eastern Europe is clearly showing that, except in the event of blatant Western aggression, an emergency would mean not only that the troops of almost all the East European countries would have to be subtracted from the Warsaw Pact forces, but so would considerable Soviet contingents.

Adelbert Weinstein offered the following noteworthy assessment in the *Frankfurter Allgemeine Zeitung* of 12 February 1981:

"The Warsaw Pact, too, has its weaknesses, for example the strategic situation in Poland. For months now, 26 Russian divisions have been waiting at the Polish borders. How monstrous this situation is can be seen from a comparison. What would it mean for NATO if the Americans had to invade West Germany on this scale in order to hold the strategic zone of central Europe for the West as a field of operations? For on top of the ideological danger, the unrest in Poland is a warning to Russian strategy. The 20 Soviet divisions in the East German glacis can be used neither for attack nor for defence unless their supply lines through Poland are firmly in Moscow's hand.

Then there are the psychological burdens afflicting the Warsaw Pact. Already, both Polish and Russian troops have been put to a severe psychological test on account of the unusual situation . . .

A violent solution . . . would release forces which in normal times remain concealed, though they are not politically inactive: those historically conditioned elements of tension that have contributed for centuries to determining the lives of the East European peoples. These emotional forces would also have their effect on the fighting power of the satellite armies, if it came to a military showdown with the West. The Poles could only be mobilised to fight against NATO if they believed that the Bundeswehr was threatening their country. In that case, their dislike of the Germans would be greater than their antipathy towards the Russians. But the Polish soldiers have scarcely any hostile feelings towards the Americans, French or British. The Czechs, for their part, see the East German forces as their enemy rather than the West Ger-

mans; it was the East Germans, after all, who invaded Prague. The
other Western allies, especially France, the Czechs view as potential
friends. No Hungarian or Romanian can be convincingly motivated for
war against the West. The Warsaw Pact countries are mostly made up of
conscripts, and conscripts are not readily influenced by ideology.''

Because of its internal constitution, the Soviet Union is
quite incapable of effectively securing the political system it
has dictated even in its immediate sphere of influence in
Eastern Europe. The positive significance of the Polish example for Western Europe consists above all in that it has
decisively removed from the realm of what is rationally conceivable the prevailing fear of the post-war era that the Soviet
leaders have it in mind to incorporate the population of
Western Europe into their empire.

The 'Bolshevik Danger'

The Soviet system has totally exhausted its original revolutionary impulse. As far back as 1945, its *counter-attack* to the
Elbe (and it is only in the form of counter-attack that the
Russians have ever advanced massively to the West, drawn in
by the armies of Bonaparte, Wilhelm II and Hitler) was in no
way inspired by the socialist ideals of the October Revolution, themselves borrowed from the West, but rather by the
idea of the Great Patriotic War. The 'Bolshevik danger',
whatever positions people took towards it when the Russian
revolution still exerted an influence beyond its geographical
limits, simply no longer exists.

We have proof of this in domestic politics in the decline of
Third-International communism in most of Western Europe,
and its hopeless political isolation in those countries, such as
France, where it still has a certain numerical strength — for
reasons that are only indirectly to do with the Soviet Union. I
don't know of any party less dangerous to the *status quo* than
the PCF. Compare the situation today with the importance of
Comintern communism for Western Europe in the 1920s!

Just as in the 19th century, Russia today is once again
under pressure from the West to adapt its political system to
the requirements of its self-preservation as a continental empire, now however in conditions where its shadow is cast not
only over Europe, as before, but over the whole world, in its
role as the second superpower. In this connection, the Soviet

Union is fundamentally on the defensive, additionally troubled at its rear by a newly industrialising China. The Soviet Union is overburdened by its great-power status, quite irrespective of whether the Moscow general staff may not still think more in terms of preventative attack rather than a more indirect strategy, as might become appropriate depending on the conjuncture of the arms race and international military balance.

A 'New Ostpolitik'

This situation has led to a relaxation in West European political debate that is already becoming apparent. Even in West Germany, the anti-Bolshevik neurosis is losing its virulence. There is an increasing space for rational discussion of the Soviet Union and East Germany, with the increasing generational distance from 1945 also making its contribution here. This might gradually open the way for a 'new Ostpolitik' of a quite different kind to that of twelve years ago.

Naturally, if we were to continue identifying the prospects for peace with the balance of terror, the decline in Soviet power would be a matter for concern not just to those who still identify with Soviet interests. On the left, residues of traditional illusions as to the supposed socialist character of the Soviet Union and the Eastern bloc combine with reverence for the ideology of deterrence in the tendency to tolerate the efforts of the materially weaker of the two super-powers to achieve military parity. This leads to an untenable and indeed unrealistic position. We should be well aware that such a balance has never existed, and that given the internal situation of the Soviet Union and the Eastern bloc it is less attainable today that ever before.

The inability of the Soviet Union to control 'its' East European perimeter is in no way the result of any intervention by the Western left in favour of the forces of reform. The most optimistic perspective, from the standpoint of peace too, is that of a profound renovation of the entire social system in these countries. A certain advance by the ecology and peace movement in the West would be expedient, as this would secure the room for manoeuvre that the Eastern bloc countries need for this development, and prevent reactionary forces in the West from taking advantage of the transformation of institutional structures in the East; but this advance of the West over the East is in any case an accomplished fact.

The European Fracture

Since the East has irrevocably crossed the threshold of advanced industrialisation, and the military form of conflict cannot be repeated between industrialised societies, there is only one reasonable perspective for the long run. This is the integration of Eastern Europe and the Soviet Union into a European community of nations of a new kind. In the last analysis, the underlying cultural basis of Russia is no more distant from the West than is that of Turkey. (I note here in passing that the contrast in economic organisation between *so-called* market economics and *so-called* centrally planned economics is customarily exaggerated; both in fact combine elements of market and of planning, if with different emphasis).

This idea naturally presupposes what I have already said, i.e. that the European fracture, as expressed in the frontier between the blocs, is no longer historically productive, and we must recognise on the contrary that the two systems, both in their different ways non-socialist, mutually obstruct each other's chances of internal development. Because they both have the same industrial foundations, and ultimately both face the same — i.e. ecological — challenge, they should both aim to evolve towards an identical goal. Ecological humanism and democratic socialism provides its governing co-ordinates.

This article forms parts of A New Approach for the Peace Movement in Germany, *to be published by* New Left Review *later in the year. (Translated by Dave Fernbach).*

The Dutch Inter-Denominational Peace Council (IKV = Interkerkelijk Vredesberaad) is a peace organisation in which, since 1967, the following churches participate: the Mennonite Brethren, the Evangelical Lutheran Church, the Moravian Brethren, the Society of Friends (Quakers), the Reformed Church in the Netherlands, the Netherlands Reformed Church, the Old Catholic Church, the Remonstrant Brethren and the Roman Catholic Church. In 1977 the IKV launched a campaign against nuclear armament under the motto: "Help remove nuclear weapons from the world, to begin with, from the Netherlands".

Aktion Sühnezeichen (Action for Reconciliation) was founded on a synod of the Evangelical Church of Germany, when this church was torn by political differences over a military chaplaincy treaty and the question of nuclear armament.

Common Resistance to the Common Threat

A Statement by
Action of Reconciliation (West Germany) and the
Inter-Church Peace Council (Holland)*

Action of Reconciliation (ASF) in the Federal Republic of Germany and the Inter-Denominational Peace Council (IKV) in the Netherlands, who came together in a Peace Week Initiative have decided to intensify their co-operation in the future in order to resist the so-called LRTNF modernisation (Long Range Theatre Nuclear Forces). The ASF and the IKV have worked together for some time already, primarily in the churches and among church members in regard to consciousness raising and the stimulation of a willingness to act.

*Issued for the Conference on Nuclear War, Groningen, The Netherlands April 1981.

Because of the seriousness of the situation, they are now focusing their co-operation on the question of the LRTNF modernisation, primarily because of the great risk that Europe will suffer irrevocable ruin in a hopeless nuclear arms race, the end of which can only be disastrous.

The ASF and IKV are working for a Europe free of nuclear weapons, in which the relations between peoples and nations will be determined by a politics of détente and in which armaments will be reduced to the lowest possible level. In such a Europe there will no longer be a place for rigid block formation in military alliances. Instead, collective agreements must form a guarantee for "peace and security". We — the ASF and the IKV — will do all we can to influence the politically responsible bodies to develop policies directed toward the realisation of this goal.

It is necessary to take account of the dissimilar positions of both countries, the Federal Republic of Germany and the Netherlands. The geographical situations are as different as the positions of political power. But the political developments of the last years have also shown that both countries can and must, each in its own way, make an optimum contribution to the creation of a more peaceful Europe.

Since the end of the sixties West Germany has apparently seen that it is in a unique position in regard to formulating and carrying out policies of détente between East and West. West Germany seems to have understood its historical task in regard to "Ostpolitik", even if it has always coupled détente to a policy of security in which the formula of the "balance of power" has prevailed, regardless of the extent of armament involved. As long as the arms race continues, these two political components will be in conflict with each other, which, in all likelihood, will usually occur at the expense of détente.

The LRTNF modernisation is a typical example of this. It is being imposed upon us for the sake of the balance of power. But in the age of insane nuclear overkill such reasoning loses all meaning. The whole matter becomes even more shameful inasmuch as there are substantial reasons for viewing the LRTNF modernisation of NATO not so much as a response to arms developments on the part of the Soviet

Union, but instead as a military response to internal political tensions between the United States and Western Europe regarding interpretation of the so-called American nuclear guarantee.

For the ASF and the IKV both rationalisations are unacceptable because they in effect lead to the same result. The nuclear arms race in Europe would continue unimpeded, and a new policy of détente, which would include measures for disarmament, would be frustrated before it began. Therefore we will do all we can to prevent the stationing of Pershing II and Tomahawk (cruise) missiles in West Germany.

After centuries of neutralist politics the Netherlands has, since World War II, integrated its security policies in the Atlantic alliance. Since then the Netherlands has been known as a docile ally. It has subordinated itself as a matter of course to the wishes of larger and more powerful countries in the alliance. That attitude is beginning to change, and rightly so. Significant sectors of the Dutch society are realising that for a small country there is a middle position between neutrality and docility. The IKV describes this middle position as follows: a critical membership in the NATO and an independent policy for peace. An independent policy for peace would be directed in the first place towards forming new alliances and coalitions with other (small) countries in order to create a new power base against the arms race and against a policy of "domination and oppression" of which the superpowers in practice still avail themselves.

If the Netherlands want to be able to give form to such an independent policy for peace, then it will need to lend support to disarmament initiatives of other countries (e.g. nonproliferation agreements and nuclear free zones) and to resistance to the arms race by groups in other countries, by removing all nuclear weapons from Dutch territory and from the Dutch armed forces.

There can be no question of allowing a new generation of nuclear missiles to be placed in the Netherlands. And the refusal to do so must be clearly tied into the demands of a West German policy for peace such as described above.

The ASF and the IKV will have to do all they can to assure that the Dutch government this year rescinds its assent to the NATO decision of December 12, 1979. That means more than just not placing the Tomahawks on Dutch Territory. We are seeking nothing less than a break with the principle of unanimity in the NATO. Underlying the modernisation decision of December 12, 1979 was an "obligatory" consensus. The Netherlands must now demonstrate that there was only an apparent unity. In this way a turnabout can be effected in the modernisation discussion, and an independent Dutch policy take shape.

The ASF and the IKV advocate a new policy for peace that truly does justice to the pursuit of détente and that therefore makes use of the specific possibilities which the various countries have. We ascertain that up until now the arms limitations talks have too often, even exclusively, fulfilled the function of an alibi for the armaments process. The "double decision" of December 12, 1979 is just another example of that. The proposals for arms limitations which have come from the NATO do not signify any deceleration in the arms race, and at best can only be interpreted as an attempt to establish a "balance" at a higher level of armament.

More than ever we are convinced of the present necessity of working out serious disarmament proposals. To begin with a favourable climate must be created, particularly by means of calculated unilateral steps. We must demonstrate the political will to truly pursue the path of détente and disarmament. The nullification of the LRTNF decision is such a calculated unilateral step.

In the near future the ASF and the IKV will be developing many various activities directed against the LRTNF modernisation.

We will seek an understanding with the churches in whose commission we work and with whom we feel related.

Together with other peace movements we will organise demonstrations.

The Peace Weeks will be marked by resistance to the modernisation. We will confront our governments and political parties in various ways with our request that the modernisation decision be reversed. The arms race must finally be stopped and turned around; with the LRTNF modernisation as a start, for the sake of a livable future, here and around the world.

Pax Christi began a nationwide discussion throughout Holland in 1981, on the basis of an advisory report which was submitted to the Roman Catholic Bishops' Conference. This document is summarised in this official resumé, which has relevance far outside Dutch frontiers.

The Netherlands Against Nuclear Weapons

Pax Christi, Netherlands

Introduction

In February of 1980 the InterChurch Peace Council (IKV) submitted a number of questions to the Dutch Bishops' Conference.

These questions are, among other things, concerned with the position of the Church with regard to the proposal of the InterChurch Peace Council "Help rid the world of nuclear arms, let it begin in the Netherlands", and with all sorts of activities of the Church in which it could co-operate with the Council.

From the Episcopal Commission for Administration of the Bishops' conference, Pax Christi received the request to advise the bishops in answering these questions of the Inter-Church Peace Council. The National Board of Pax Christi has now drawn up a report, in which it gives a detailed justification for its support of the InterChurch Peace Council proposal. In addition the Board points out in this report, why the bishops should comply with the request of the Inter-Church Peace Council to strengthen the ties with the Christian Peace Movement and to support the concrete proposal of the InterChurch Peace Council.

Analysis of the situation

In an introduction the report gives a short summary of the present situation in the field of nuclear armament. There is also a reference to the developments which, in the past 15 to 20 years, have led to a considerable worsening of the situation. For a more detailed analysis of the situation the "Guide to Nuclear Armament" of the Dutch Reformed Church of 1979, is referred to.

Ethical Considerations

In the first chapter the National Board gives a survey of the pattern of thinking in the Catholic Church about the ethical view of nuclear weapons. The report then describes and analyses successively the developments that, from the beginning of the sixties, have occurred in that pattern of thinking, on the level of the World Church, the pronouncements of the Popes and of the Holy See, on the level of two national Bishops' Conferences, the American and the Dutch Conference, and the developments in Pax Christi Netherlands.

The conclusion is that gradually the Church is abandoning its tolerance with regard to the possession of nuclear weapons, as part of a deterrence strategy, after it has more and more explicitly come to reject the use of any nuclear weapon.

In the light of worsening developments, the Church more and more tends to reject the possession of nuclear weapons as unlawful.

Closely associated with this is a development in the pronouncements of the Church about disarmament. It is no longer a question of the Church, in its statements, confining itself to the summing up of the traditional criteria that should be fulfilled for the disarmament process. The criteria in question were then mutual balance, multilateral, via treaties etc., in broad outline exactly what the various states always and everywhere bring forward.

In view of the poor results of this approach, the statements of the Church show an increasingly strong feeling for other approaches, among which is a disarmament policy, based on unilateral initiatives towards a bilateral disarmament.

Pax Christi advises the bishops:

1. To reject use and possession of nuclear weapons on ethical grounds, in order therewith to confirm the development in the World Church in this direction, and to help accomplish it.
2. To emphasise, in the World Church, as a consequence of the condemnation of the possession of nuclear weapons, the moral necessity of striking out on to a new road towards disarmament.
3. With regard to other states to plead for a policy of unilateral steps in the direction of bilateral disarmament, and to help a further development of the moral standards to be fulfilled for responsible steps on the above-mentioned road.
4. Before the Dutch Catholic religious community and Dutch society as a whole, once more to bring to the fore the "NO" of the Dutch Council of Churches against any progressive development and extension of nuclear armament.
5. Before Dutch society to support proposals for unilateral steps on the part of the Netherlands, in particular the proposal of the InterChurch Peace Council for denuclearisation of the Netherlands as a first step.
6. Once more to give their moral support to the work of the Christian Peace Movement in the Netherlands, as it is given shape in Pax Christi and the InterChurch Peace Council. That means that the Bishops, if necessary, should take that work under their protection when it has to suffer from unjustified attacks.

Scientific Considerations

The National Board distinguishes three ways in which to strive for disarmament.

—The way used up until now by the states, consisting of a combination of two methods, namely negotiations about mutual arms control and arms reduction and at the same time continuation of the armaments process.

—Next there is the way of completely unilateral disarmament.

—And there is the approach in which the states, by means of unilateral disarmament steps, try to set in motion a process towards bilateral disarmament.

Pax Christi notes with regard to the first way, which has been applied now for 35 years, that it has produced completely negligible results, and that the risks we run through armament have only increased. The second way is also rejected by Pax Christi because (a) this way does not take sufficient account of the needs for security that exists among people, and (b) because insufficient social and political support is to be found in our society for this way.

Pax Christi pleads that states, in international politics, should try, in the third way, to bring nearer arms reduction and disarmament. We have indicated elsewhere the criteria to be fulfilled for unilateral steps according to behavioural scientists who developed this method.

The most important criterion is that the step(s) one commits oneself to, and which one thereupon takes independently, are not made dependent on a reaction from the opponent, a reaction the latter would have to bind himself to beforehand. That is the procedure in negotiations and they do not lead to any positive results in the field of disarmament.

However we do not mean to imply that after the setting in motion of a mutual process, negotiations could be dispensed with. But it is certainly necessary that in taking unilateral steps to consider whether the opponent reacted to the preceding step with a move on his part, and what the importance of that response was. If the judgment passed on it is positive, a following more important step can be taken. If no significant response comes forth, the process will not be mutual. In that case continuing with unilateral steps would mean passing on to unilateral disarmament, and that is not the intention; it is also contrary to the starting point of this approach. The unilateral initiatives will than have to cease.

The following advantages of the method of unilateral steps are:

—real steps towards disarmament are taken;
—the other need not bind himself to anything in advance, and can answer without loss of face;
—parties can regain the initiative;
—a party can carefully assess the risk it takes;
—parties can clearly show that they renounce armament as an instrument of superior power policy.

Political Considerations

In the past ten to fifteen years ever more sophisticated and accurate nuclear arms were developed, and gradually a change has taken place from the conception that nuclear wars cannot be waged, to the strategy of the limited nuclear war, which can not only be fought but also be won. All negotiations about arms control and disarmament have been quite unable to prevent this development.

The politicians in East and West have not stabilised the type of deterrence of the sixties. They have not, from that situation, proceeded to mutual arms reduction. But that was exactly what was hoped for and expected at the beginning of the sixties. Why did not East and West seize the opportunity and why have they allowed us to drift into a much more perilous situation?

In international politics there is a suction, the Board of Pax Christi says, in the direction of a superior power policy The military way of thinking about balance and deterrence is inextricably linked with the aim of dominating the opponent. It is that policy of superior power that is deeply rooted in our society. Domination, not service, is the standard guiding us in our relations with our fellow men.

In the rejection of this principle of domination, in our own behaviour and in society, the plea of Pax Christi for a policy of unilateral steps finds its deepest roots. A policy like this is at right angles to the deterrence way of thinking and the policy of superior power. Such a policy can also mobilise

137

people of goodwill to form a force at the service of those politicians and military people who cannot cope with it merely by their own efforts, but who are fully prepared to avail themselves of that force.

Pax Christi is clearly in favour of an integration of the denuclearisation of the Netherlands into a policy of unilateral initiatives of NATO. It pleads however that the Netherlands should take that step alone if NATO is not willing to co-operate. For Pax Christi does not rule out the possibility that the Warsaw Pact, via one of the East European States, would respond to the denuclearisation of the Netherlands, to show NATO that it is interested in a continuation of that course.

Pastoral Considerations

When the Church pronounces itself on the problem of nuclear armament, it should do so in a way that is politically relevant. In practice this means that it must make its pronouncements as concrete as possible. If the Church does not do this, and confines itself to making very noble statements that everyone can easily accept, it acts in a politically irrelevant way, and consequently — what is worse — pastorally irrelevant. With regard to the problems of survival, the Church will have to try to point to a way out, drawing on the deepest inspiration from which it lives. The way it shows will have to be of real help to men. Therefore the Church must express itself concretely about the courses to be taken. Thus the feeling of impotence can be broken through. Both the impotence of those who feel caught and oppressed in the security dilemma, and the impotence of those who, it is true, reject a continuation of the present armament policy, but who feel absolutely powerless to influence developments in this direction.

Pax Christi stresses the fact that the proposal of the Inter-Church Peace Council has, quite clearly, been brought forward in order to give people a concrete means for affecting a change. The proposal was also made from pastoral considerations. For in all Church statements, while it is pointed out that the influence of public opinion is of the greatest importance, nearly always these statements fail to offer people concrete means by which they can effectively give shape to the responsibility laid upon them.

Pax Christi then shows in its report what objections are made against concrete political pronouncements of the Church:

—Does the Church sufficiently consider the security dilemma, when it chooses a policy of unilateral initiatives?

—When the Church pronounces itself on concrete political questions, are not its views just as fallible as those of others? What then is the authority of these statements really based on, and in what way may Church statements be used and in what way may they not be used?

—Does not the Church run the risk of being identified with certain political and ideological systems, and can it avoid this risk by keeping silent, or does it then rather run the risk of being identified with the established system?

—Is there not a danger of the armament problem painfully dividing not only the individual consciences of people, but also Church communities and parishes?

—Will not the Church lose much of its privileged position in our society when it has been recognised as a concrete opponent of the deterrence system and of the superior power policy? Will it not be reproached for playing into the enemy's hands, or even worse: of being in league with him?

—Or is it rather that the Church shrinks from the reproach of encouraging the faithful to believe that war and armament can be conquered, and in so doing fostering human pride?

Pax Christi summarises its answers to these questions as follows: "Let the Church preach Jesus and not be worried about itself. Let the Church develop man's conscience and stimulate the belief of Christians, and thus foster a reluctance to follow the road we are stuck on: nuclear armament to maintain our security". The Church may rely on the unity among the faithful to grow, when, in Christ's spirit we talk with one another about what is to be done by we Christians in these "problems of survival". Are not we greatly failing in confidence in His spirit, when we fear, in spite of His guidance, to embrace totally different approaches?

This piece is extracted from The Roman Catholic Church, Nuclear Weapons and Disarmament, *published by Pax Christi, Netherlands.*

The Communist Party of Italy, when NATO took its December 1979 decision on "modernisation" of Theatre Nuclear Forces, appealed for a new effort to agree accurate estimates of the nuclear balance between the blocs in order to negotiate disarmament down towards agreed thresholds, rather than to accelerate armament up to alleged levels. These documents explain the Party's reasoning on this matter.

Eurocommunism and the Bomb

Documents from the Communist Party of Italy

1: The Path of Negotiations against Rearmament*

The Executive Committee of the PCI has discussed the problems of security and defence in Europe in the light of the more recent developments of the international situation and in relation to the polemics and controversies on the strategic-military balance in Europe and the United States proposal to NATO to install 572 Pershing II and Cruise missiles in various Western European countries, including Italy. These developments have aroused deep concern and alarm.

*Executive Committee Resolution — L'Unita, 18 October 1979.

We are witnessing an overall worsening in international relations: local conflicts and clashes of various origin in points and areas of the greatest importance, interventions and acts of interference in the affairs of other countries, dramatic tensions. The atmosphere of détente has deteriorated.

The SALT 2 agreements — and the possibility of embarking on SALT 3 — have raised new hopes and expectations, but also strong resistance. The controversy over the balance of forces has arisen, and today we are faced with the threat of a turn in the opposite direction from détente: in the direction of a new surge in the arms race. And we are dealing with increasingly destructive and less controllable weapons. This is an awesome prospect in a world where existing nuclear arsenals are already far more than sufficient to destroy life on earth.

Unless this tragic logic is broken, all talk about hunger and underdevelopments, the security, independence and freedom of peoples, and civil progress and renewal of society would be in vain and deceitful.

The gravity and complexity of these issues require that they be studied and discussed with the utmost seriousness and objectivity in relation to the vital interests of peace, international co-operation and European and national security. All attempts to exploit these questions for domestic political purposes (or, even worse, to use them as a means of provocation and blackmail) must therefore be rigorously avoided.

The Communist Party reaffirms its line of consistent struggle in defence of peace, for the consolidation of détente and for new forms of international co-operation based on the principles of national sovereignty and non-interference in the domestic affairs of other countries and aimed at promoting the autonomous development of the emerging peoples. All tendencies to find solutions to problems and contentions in a more rigid bloc policy and in building up hostile groupings against other countries must be overcome. It is these principles that must guide us in making all the efforts necessary to solve existing conflicts and tensions, halt the deterioration of international détente and give it new impetus.

The problem of the now existing military balances and alliances must be tackled in this context. While setting as its goal the overcoming of the bloc logic and the progressive dissolution of the blocs themselves, the PCI does not question Italy's international alliances and realistically does not ignore the existence of the blocs and the related balance of forces as facts from which we must start in order to make the process of détente more vigorous and operative.

But the dilemma facing us today is either a balanced control of armaments, aiming at gradual measures for disarmament, or a new spiral of rearmament. Reopening the arms race, particularly in the present international situation, would have incalculably grave effects as it concerns not only the security, but also the economic development of the various countries. The whole problem of the Eurostrategic nuclear weapons and conventional armaments deployed in Europe must therefore be dealt with through negotiations.

The time has come for the difficult question of military balances to be tackled and solved at the negotiation table, launching proposals and measures that lower, rather than raise the level of armaments, guaranteeing conditions of security for everyone. Europe needs less rather than more weapons. This is a vital necessity for Italy and for the world as a whole.

Obviously, to this end, the immediate approval and ratification of SALT 2 is necessary. In this way, it should be possible to begin negotiations for SALT 3 immediately.

More generally in the face of the present polemics on the balance of forces in Europe and the opposing analyses and judgements set forth in this connection, the PCI proposes that negotiations be rapidly undertaken in the proper forums — which might be a conference between the Atlantic Alliance and the Warsaw Pact — to establish the real state of nuclear armaments in Europe and, if situations are found where the balance turns out to have been altered, to correct them, restoring the balance at the lower level.

Proposals advanced or needs affirmed by various political forces and governments in Western Europe reveal ample possibilities to undertake a political and diplomatic initiative in this sense, also grasping and verifying the possibilities offered by the recent statements and proposals of the government of the USSR.

In addition, concrete possibilities exist to make headway in the Vienna talks for the reduction of conventional forces and to arrive at the next session of the Conference on Security and Co-operation in Europe, to be held in Madrid, with proposals and measures designed to restore an atmosphere of trust between the sides. The PCI Executive Committee holds that the Italian government can and must make a positive contribution in this direction.

The PCI invites the political forces, the popular masses, the democratic, peace loving, cultural, religious and moral forces and all men and women who aspire to peace, to discuss these assessments and proposals. We are at a crossroads for the future of mankind. Everyone must do his part to create a vast movement for negotiations, for agreements with the goals of disarmament, détente and peace. We hold that the road to disarmament passes through the search for and establishment of balances at decreasing levels of armaments. We are therefore also convinced that every decision to increase armaments, by whichever side, tends to produce a new leap in the disastrous spiral of the arms race.

To contribute in fact and not only in word to defeating hunger in the world, to avert the mortal threats hanging over Italy, Europe and the whole world, to relieve each country from the crushing burden of military spending and facilitate efforts everywhere for economic and democratic progress, the Communist Party invites all the democratic and peace loving forces to join in a common search and effort to make an effective contribution to peace and détente. In particular, it is our job to work for security in Europe, the continent that has benefited the most from détente and today is in danger of becoming the theatre of a new, serious confrontation, in order to free Italy from the threat of a possible nuclear catastrophe and help to create a situation in which the resources of all countries can be devoted to the pursuit of civil progress, freedom and peace.

The PCI Executive Committee appeals to all Communist organisation and militants to discuss these problems and mobilise for broad-based initiatives.

2. Negotiate First, Suspend Deployment*

Q. On the "Euro-missile" issue, certain political circles and

*Paolo Bufalini, Interview on the Missile Question (Rinascita, November 9th, 1979).

press organs are attempting to distort the PCI's position, interpreting it as a backslide with respect to Euro-Communism and committing, in the effort, some awkward blunders of the sort that forced Mr Piccoli to make a retraction. What is the purpose of this campaign?

A. First of all, this campaign is part of an anti-Communist offensive designed to counteract the greater interest and objectivity our proposals, positions and initiatives begin to encounter today, with the deep crisis in the DC and the travail within the Socialist Party. It is sufficient to recall the tales published over the past few days concerning fights within the Party leadership and, if I may say so, the recent distortions and fabrications with regard to my own positions: fabrications that anyone who has a collection of *l'Unità* and *Rinascita* and re-reads my polemics against the DC in 1978 and 1979 can easily confute. But let's turn to the specific question of the nuclear weapons in the European "theatre".

I believe, and the more honest commentators have recognised, that the position we have taken on the SS-20's and the Pershing missiles is an important one for two reasons. First of all, it is important to the ends of the cause of peace and the defence of our national interests. Secondly, it is important as a concrete test of the validity of the principles of that new internationalism, that new conception of international relations, which underlies Euro-Communism.

The position set forth in the Executive Committee Resolution of October 17th is very clear. We did not say that the military balance is intact or that the United States is wrong out of hand. We said that as far as we know, neither Italy nor other governments have sufficient, decisive elements to reach a conclusion in one sense or the other. And we called for a rigorous ascertainment of the real state of armaments, to be carried out in the forums considered most opportune and with the involvement of the Atlantic Alliance system and the Warsaw Pact system. If it turns out that this balance has been broken, we hold — and this is what characterises our position — that it must be restored, re-establishing parity at lower, not higher, levels; removing the factors (missiles, in the concrete) responsible for having upset the balance. It is the strength of our proposal, its autonomy from all preconceived stands, that certain circles would like to hide, twisting it or pretending that our position with regard to the SS-20's is still ambiguous.

Q. Attempts have also been made to exploit the parliamentary debate on the Italian stand, accentuating the differences between us and the other parties. In your opinion, what really came out in that debate? Did it widen or shorten the distance between the various positions on the issues of the military balance, whether or not to deploy Pershing and Cruise missiles in our country and negotiations for disarmament?

The parliamentary debate unquestionably showed that there are political forces in Italy who are totally subservient to US demands, forces which have no hesitations when it comes to embarking on a qualitatively new arms race that could directly involve Europe in a nuclear conflict. But it also showed that there are more responsible, concerned forces whose positions leave room for an approach aimed at the preservation of peace and addressed to both the United States and the Soviet Union. We have serious reservations on the specific proposals advanced by these forces (namely, a policy decision to go ahead with the missile programme, linked — more or less firmly — to future disarmament negotiations), and we said so. But our proposal for *beforehand ascertainment* allows a certain leeway for discussion with regard to the forums for negotiations, which we nevertheless feel must begin immediately, *before* any steps are taken in the direction of a new rearmament. There could thus be points of contact between our position and other positions that emerged in the debate, motivated by serious concern over the US request. In any event, the important thing, I think, is the breadth of the grouping that called for rapid ratification of SALT 2, still blocked by the US Senate, and for negotiations between NATO and the Warsaw Pact. Pointing this out does not mean "swallowing the bitter pill of the missiles" as stupidly claimed by *Il Manifesto,* whose editors initially seemed to have understood and approved our position.

Q. In your opinion, how can we arrive concretely at negotiations between the Atlantic Alliance and the Warsaw Pact with the aim of lowering the level of the present strategic balance between the forces of the two blocs?

I have already said that the forums and modes for negotiations can differ widely. The most simple would be a direct approach, involving all the members of the Atlantic Alliance (and therefore also France) and all the members of the Warsaw Pact. But I would not be too rigid, because what interests us is the end result, not the ways and modes or this or that forum.

What I would like to stress is that the worst way, a way involving really serious risk, is to agree beforehand to install the Pershing and Cruise missiles in the hopes that subsequent negotiations will make their deployment unnecessary. We hold that negotiations must come *first,* and, as concerns us, we have no reluctance in saying that if it is ascertained that the missiles to be removed or not to be installed are the SS-20's of the Warsaw Pact, we shall take the suitable initiatives together with the others. But are the others, those who criticise and question our position, equally independent as concerns the American Pershings? I would say more. As Comrade Natta has already stated in his address to the Chamber, we have suggested that the Italian government propose to the USSR, the US and the NATO countries, together with immediate negotiations, the suspension of the construction and deployment of both the SS-20's on the one side, and the Pershing and Cruise missiles on the other. If the Italian government moves in this direction, we shall support it.

The dilemma facing us today — I repeat what the Executive Committee has already said — is either a balanced control over armaments, with the aim of gradual measures for disarmament, or a new arms race.

We must avoid every act, every attitude, pushing in this second direction.

The seriousness of the crisis gripping us today, the appeal of those countries where millions of men, women and children are still dying of hunger, makes this imperative.

I would like to add one further thought. Is the imbalance the United States fears really only a military imbalance, or isn't it something with far deeper causes? Doesn't the real imbalance (above and beyond what may be found to be the case with regard to the specific imbalance said to exist in the European strategic theatre) stem from increasingly deep and acute contradictions emerging within the Western countries and in relations between these countries and the Third World nations? Does the solution to this imbalance lie in rearmament, in the waste and squander of rearmament, or in the pursuit of détente, co-operation and a new economic order (involving the East as well, if possible), policies that prior consent to a new arms race would make impossible or in any event much more difficult? Is it easier to ask Moscow to suspend the production of its SS-20's on the basis of negotiations — and we are ready to support such a cause — or on the basis of a decision to deploy Pershing missiles in Italy and other NATO countries? I don't think there can be any doubt about the answer.

3. Lower that ceiling*

On the eve of the parliamentary debate on the US proposal to install the new Pershing 2 and Cruise missiles in Europe, the Italian Communist Party presented a motion in the Chamber of Deputies signed by Enrico Berlinguer, Pajetta, Di Giulio, Alinovi, Spagnoli, Cecchi, Chiovine, Rubbi and Bottarelli. Following is the text of this motion.

The Chamber, in reaffirming the foreign policy line sanctioned in Parliament with a significantly broad vote — in the Senate on October 19th, 1977, and in the Chamber of Deputies on December 1st, 1977 — emphasising Italy's commitment to undertake an effective initiative for international détente and co-operation, while honouring its existing alliances and in particular within the framework of the Atlantic Alliance and the European Community of which Italy is a member;

Sensitive to the concern and alarm expressed by broad strata of public opinion, not only in Italy but in all the countries of Europe and other parts of the world, for the deterioration of the international situation, the eruption of new crises, the sharpening of already existing tensions and finally, the concrete threat of a new nuclear and missile arms race in Europe;

Considering that today such an arms race would entail a qualitative leap towards increasingly sophisticated, terrifying and uncontrollable types of weapons and involve heavy and economic costs such as to destroy all possibilities to root ou

*Motion presented in the Chamber of Deputies *l'Unita,* December 2nd, 1979.

hunger, underdevelopment and other scourges afflicting the world;

Considering at the same time that the decision to proceed with the construction and stockpiling of such weapons would start a process which would be extremely difficult to stop and reverse and would inevitably create an atmosphere of distrust, division and sharper tensions in international relations, seriously obstructing the indispensable search for negotiated agreements;

Observing that various governments and large numbers of political forces and organisations and associations of various political, cultural and religious inspirations in Europe have called for the immediate opening of negotiations;

Invited the government of the Republic to advance the following set of proposals to the Atlantic Council:

a. the suspension or postponement for a period of at least six months of all decisions for the construction and deployment of the Pershing 2 and Cruise missiles;
b. the invitation to the USSR to suspend the construction and deployment of the SS-20 missiles;
c. the immediate opening of negotiations between the two sides with the aim of setting a ceiling on the military balance in Europe at a lower level and such as to guarantee mutual security.

*The Socialist International set up a
study group on disarmament, following
Olof Palme's initiative at its 1978
(Helsinki) Congress. Kalevi Sorsa, of
Finland and Walter Hacker, of Austria,
were chairman and secretary,
respectively, of this body. In Madrid,
during November 1980, the International
adopted a comprehensive report, from
which these pages are excerpted.*

Ridding Europe of Nuclear Weapons

A Statement by the Socialist International*

Disarmament and development

Disarmament should not be divorced from development.
Disarmament will relieve human and material resources to
combat poverty, hunger, ignorance and other social in-
justices.

International and national plans must be urgently prepared
for diverting resources such as capital, human and natural

*From the Final Report of the Socialist International Study Group on Disarma-
ment, adopted by Socialist International Congress, Madrid, 13-16 November 1980.

resources and technology from the armaments sector to development co-operation.

A minimum of 5 per cent of the capital formerly invested in military procurements and the maintenance of armed forces and armaments should be used for additional development aid. An agreement must be reached on a standardised evaluation of defence budgets and military expenditure.

The research potential released from the armaments sector should primarily be diverted into efforts to solve development problems.

A special international fund should be established to finance various projects of converting resources from military purposes into social and economic development, especially in the least developed countries. The main contributions to this fund should come from the principal arms producers and those maintaining major armed forces.

Nuclear disarmament

The disarmament negotiations should be extended to deal at appropriate fora, with the limitation of all nuclear weapons in the world. Every effort must be made to strengthen the non-proliferation regime in order to make it universal. The ultimate goal must be the total elimination of all nuclear weapons.

The USSR and the United States should continue their bilateral talks on the limitation of strategic nuclear arms. The further SALT agreements should lead to a reduction of the total number of nuclear weapons. Parallel to this, the qualitative development of nuclear arms and their delivery systems should be effectively halted.

Development, production and location of new nuclear weapons should be limited by agreement. New weapons systems must be prohibited before they reach the stage of deployment.

During the negotiations, all parties should refrain from developing and testing new arms and delivery systems.

The Comprehensive Test Ban Treaty should be concluded as soon as possible *inter alia* in order to resist the qualitative development of nuclear weapons and to limit the growth of nuclear weapons arsenals. Such a test ban would also reduce the reliability of existing nuclear stocks that are subject to erosion and thus further reduce the probability of their use and to make the use of existing arsenals less reliable and thus less probable. The Treaty should be permanent and cover all nuclear test and detonations, military as well as peaceful. The CTB must be respected by all States.

The negotiations on the control and reduction of nuclear weapons in Europe should be started without delay. The immediate objective is to prevent a new round of the nuclear arms race in Europe. Hence, before the concrete limitations are agreed on, all governments concerned should agree to avoid in the meantime any measures which could aggravate tension and render the forthcoming negotiations more difficult. The negotiations should bring about significant reductions of medium and short range nuclear arms systems in a balanced way. In Europe, the continent with the heaviest concentration of nuclear weapons, the objective must be a gradual and in long range total elimination of the stationing of all nuclear weapons. Appropriate fora should negotiate on the reduction of all offensive weapons in Europe.

China should be encouraged to join the disarmament process, including the negotiations for the limitation of nuclear weapons, at the earliest possible time.

Agreements, global and regional, on the reduction of tactical nuclear weapons should be concluded by the nuclear powers, with due participation of the states on whose territories such weapons are stationed.

The nuclear powers should agree on refraining from developing and deploying new types of so-called battlefield nuclear weapons. Any developments tending to blur the distinction between nuclear and conventional arms should be blocked.

Strengthening the security of non-nuclear powers against nuclear weapons is also of special importance for non-proliferation. All nuclear powers should give internationally binding guarantees not to use or threaten to use nuclear weapons against non-nuclear powers.

The establishment of nuclear-weapon-free zones aiming at enhancing the security of the states concerned should be furthered on the basis of the common purpose and co-operation. In Latin America, the provisions of the Tlatelolco Treaty, establishing the nuclear-weapon-free zone in the region, must be signed by all states of the region and universally respected. The interests of the states in Africa, Asia, the Middle East and the Southern Pacific should be translated into corresponding effective non-nuclearisation arrangements.

Regional Control

The modernisation and deployment of medium-range nuclear weapons have recently been intensified and the problem of their regional control has also been brought to the forefront by the limitations imposed on intercontinental systems in the SALT treaties. Even on the medium-range level, new procurement tendencies are accompanied by the emergence of dangerous doctrines concerning nuclear wars with a limited geographical scope and lowered threshold of escalation into the nuclear sphere. The bulk of medium-range systems are stationed or are to be deployed in Europe and hence they are mainly a European problem.

Medium- and short-range nuclear weapons have largely remained outside disarmament negotiations so far. After recent deployments and decisions on the production and deployment of medium-range systems in Europe, both the Soviet Union and NATO made offers for negotiations on the control of medium-range weapons and have started preliminary consultations. No common ground for starting such talks is in sight however.

It is evident that the Soviet Union and the United States are in a key position in any negotiations on medium-range systems. It is however obvious that such bilateral talks are but a first step. France and the United Kingdom have nuclear weapons of their own deployed in Europe. Other states in the region are also involved.

A nuclear war in Europe and even a new round of the nuclear arms race on the continent would greatly affect the security and position of all countries there, including neutral and non-aligned.

The states where such nuclear weapons are stationed have a particular interest in the negotiations. But also all states that remain within the range of such weapons have their national security interest affected. Proposals for European disarmament fora have been made. The subject matter of these proposals differ but they all bring to the fore the necessity for a broader approach to arms control in Europe. The Vienna talks also provide a forum for discussion on certain problems of nuclear arms control.

The British Labour Party has decided on "a pledge to close down all nuclear bases, British or American, on British soil or in British waters".

The idea of establishing nuclear-weapon-free zones has gained wide support among nations. It has been regarded as a feasible method of decreasing regional tension and preventing the proliferation of nuclear weapons, as well as of diminishing the risk of a nuclear attack against the countries in the region. A number of concrete plans pertaining to certain regions or sub-regions in Africa, Asia, Europe, Latin America, Middle East and the Southern Pacific have been presented. The plans have not however, led to arrangements in practice, except in the case of Latin America. The concept of nuclear-weapon-free zones remains on the agenda for international deliberations especially within the UN.

Johan Galtung is at the Geneva University Institute for the Study of Development. He was a member of the Third Russell Tribunal in the Federal German Republic.

What kind of
Defence should we have?*

by Johan Galtung

Today is April 9, 41 years after Nazi Germany invaded and occupied Norway, and I shall only make the point that our image of April 9 is moving. From the image of a Norway made defenceless by a Labour Party hostile to the military, invaded and occupied by Germany, we are now on the way towards an image of Norway as an area of deflection in order to tie German forces, by diminishing the pressure on our pro-

*This paper was given at Politisk Forum, Oslo, 9 April 1981; and at the GPID/SAREC meeting on Militarisation, Development and Alternative Security Strategies, Oslo, 25-27 May 1981.

tector, England and to some extent France; a Norway with an officer corps more worried that Norwegian soldiers should turn the gun the other way round than that they should have something to turn against the enemy. Each generation will produce its own image of April 9. With a more mature view of the situation we will perhaps one day permit outselves to have all of these images in our mind at the same time: there is something to learn from all of them. But what can be learnt is never unambiguous, for that the situations are too different. A militarily well-reasoned extermination of perhaps 50% of Norway's population in order to eliminate strategically important goals, such as the NATO Headquarters, the Norwegian Defence Headquarters, our airports, all places that could serve American strategic interests — for instance in a prepositioning connection — warning and communication installations such as NADGE (and perhaps also AWACS elements) did not belong to the strategic picture in 1940. Norway was perhaps worthy of a fight, but not worthy of being eliminated out of anxiety for what could come from Norway in terms of quickly remodelled bombers with enormous destructive capacity. We are in a qualitatively different situation today. But nevertheless we note that those days, 41 years ago, it was perhaps also from our own, from the object of our anglophilia, England — *perfide Albion* as it sometimes is referred to — that an important threat was forthcoming; and that our inner class struggle played an enormous role in the formation of "our" defence policy. Both classes were afraid that much of the military power should fall in the hands of the other class!

What kind of defence should we have? The first pillar that a defence should rest on would have to be the concept that it should be a *purely defensive* type of defence, a defence that cannot go abroad, or reach abroad, except as troops for the United Nations, a defence nobody could possibly feel threatened by. This will have to be valid, both in times of peace and in times of war — if it is only true in times of peace then it is by and large uninteresting, except as a political tranquilliser domestically. Our two self-imposed constraints directed against atomic weapons and bases for foreign powers (should have been foreign troops) on Norwegian soil in times of peace are insufficient: they do not define our defence as purely defensive. The stronger the integration into NATO joint defence and the more markedly United States stands as a leader capable of pushing through its will, the more justified the other party's suspicion that there is an American finger around the Norwegian finger around the triggers on Norwegian soil. Our peaceful intentions become uninteresting, the American intentions are what counts. As the Soviet Union is at least as convinced as the United States that the other party wishes world domination if they could only manage, and are convinced that the United States in a situation of crisis would brush Norwegian objections aside, possibly also dominate a crisis-government, it is only through a defence that is not automatically integrated into a United States led NATO that our own defence can become purely defensive.

This is not the same as a 'No' to NATO. It is not even the same as a 'No' to a United States dominated NATO or a 'Yes' to something that perhaps once could become a reality: a NATO without United States. What is implied is only to go one step further along the line that Norway and Denmark already have been walking: a looser attachment, more independence in military and political decisions, less integration into systems that, with justification, can be seen as aggressive, even as aggressive in a nuclear sense, meaning as first strike systems — the prepositioning and warning/communication installations. The Soviet Union does not have to be paranoid in order to characterise the prestocking agreement as "a new step in the intensification of NATO's military preparation". The 24 155mm guns can even — as far as one can understand — take ERW weapons, meaning neutron grenades (TIME, 21 July 1980, p.10). Of course, the Soviet Union, with its SS-20 (now substituting for the SS-5 on the Kola peninsula), SS-22 and SS-23 now substituting for Scaleboard and the Scud rockets has not much to say to the Americans when it comes to "modernisation", except that it can be maintained that the US all the time has been ahead in the qualitative arms race. The superpowers have their own logic: *The Observer* for 29 March had two examples, the new Soviet ammunition, some kind of dum-dum with enormous damage effects for the new gun AK-74, and the United States with a Pentagon entangled in a court case from once in

September 1950 when they were exercising in biological warfare against their own population in the bay of San Fran-
cisco, with many who became ill and one who died. The point
is that *we* do not have to be suspected of being a party to this
system.

The proposal about nuclear weapons free zones is in this
direction: in return for not becoming a more or less conscious
subject of a strategy involving nuclear weapons, nor shall we
become an *object* of such a strategy. I am of course an
adherent of this, and will only add three further comments.
First of all: this should concern not only procurement and
production, testing, deployment and stocking, training and
use, nuclear ships calling on Norwegian ports, passage and
use of Norwegian airspace, but also communication installations — these should be mentioned explicitly. And secondly:
we can very easily risk that the best becomes the enemy of the
good if we insist on the solution that includes parts of the
Soviet Union or all of middle Europe from North to South. A
Nordic zone is better than no zone at all, and if one cannot
manage this the Norwegian zone would be better than no
zone at all. If we had a popular vote about membership in the
European Community because it concerned Norwegian
sovereignty there should be even more reason to have a vote
on this question! And thirdly: let those who claim that
through a nuclear weapon-free zone we renege on our best
negotiation card come forward with examples that such
negotiations ever succeed!

The second main pillar in a development of our defence
concept would be to do what we have already done: look
around in the world and discover that we are not alone. We
are surrounded by like-minded countries, from Canada to
Finland, (and in increasing degree, Netherlands, Belgium and
Luxembourg). The eight Nordic countries (when we also take
into account Greenland, the Faroes and Aland islands)
together with Canada, the Netherlands, Belgium and Luxembourg constitute a tremendous territory, and very much more
homogenous than the NATO territory as such. Six of them
are NATO countries, others are integrated communication-
wise. The cultural community is considerable. Politically it is
absolutely clear that these are parliamentary, not presidential
democracies; they are mixed economies that have been and

still constitute an important part of the north-western corner of the world and have benefited from the economic relations to earlier colonial countries.

Militarily and politically one can find in all these countries an increasing anxiety about the United States without this in any sense leading to weakness, servility or attitudes supporting the Soviet Union. The Nordic countries are in a process of becoming a third block of opinion and in Great Britain Labour has already reflected this anxiety in their resolution to make Britain a nuclear-free zone. In Netherlands not only public opinion and the Labour Party in opposition pronounced themselves in this direction; it also seems clear that the American Congress Committee that concluded that the fact that there is little chance that the Netherlands will accept the theatre nuclear force (TNF) implies a serious foreign policy dilemma for the United States will be proven right. One should also note that the Netherlands, and perhaps also Belgium, is moving in a Norwegian-Danish direction, but not beyond our self-imposed restrictions. The German condition that it should not be the sole recipient of cruise and Pershing II missiles will not be satisfied by the American client country Italy and a Great Britain which it is very difficult to make any clear prediction about. In other words, *we are not alone,* and the steps the Social Democratic parties have been taking in order to build up some kind of community feeling are to be welcomed. Things are moving already, something that Reagan's foreign policy adviser, Allan, is aware of, and with a certain nervousness.

In the history of the two systems since 1945 France and Rumania have played relatively parallel roles. They are interesting because they are still members of the alliances, but with strong restrictions on the freedom of action of their superpowers relative to them. The way in which de Gaulle protested against the leadership role of the United States in the alliance and argued in favour of a directorate of three powers (USA, England, France), and finally took France out militarily except at the top level at the same time as the political membership in NATO continued, abrogated the agreement about a headquarters for NATO in Paris and US bases in France in the middle of the 1960s, is well known. Less known is the corresponding development in Rumania.

At the beginning of the 1950s the Rumanian leader, Gheorghiu Dej, was a very servile Stalinist. But in 1956, after the revolution in Budapest, he was sent there by the Soviet Union in order to help install Kadar. He saw reality very clearly, driving in a car through empty streets because people stayed at home in protest. As early as 1958 he made Khruschev withdraw Soviet troops from Rumania. But Dej did not argue about the danger of intervention. His arguments were the classical arguments against foreign troops: that they eat too much of the food originally destined for the civilian population, that they steal watches, rape women — that they harm good relationships and friendship. Khruschev understood the signals. At the beginning of the 1960s the Rumanians went even further and a law was passed to the effect that Rumanian troops should not be used abroad to participate in manoeuvres — except at the top level. Also Rumanian and only Rumanian troops in Rumania in peace time; Rumanian troops not abroad in peace time! In other words, important and explicit restrictions on the alliance membership. When Nicolae Ceausescu came to power in 1965 he was able to get some political leverage out of this and also out of the forceful 'No' to the so-called socialist division of labour within Comecon. Since then he has been a centre of unrest in the Warsaw Treaty Organisation. Just like the Gaullists he has outdistanced the opposition when it comes to having an independent attitude relative to the superpowers. On the other hand, he is not against the intervention in Poland "if socialism is threatened" — meaning if the leadership of the party is threatened. Dubcek was a party man, Walesa is not . . .

There is something to learn from this. Dej experienced the Soviet Union as a repressive power, as an imperialist in the streets of Budapest and drew the correct conclusion: if the Soviet Union can do this in Hungary they can do it in our country, too. The Warsaw Treaty Organisation and the Comecon system are there above all to protect the political *status quo* in Eastern Europe, meaning partocracy, the rule of the party — against external and internal enemies. NATO and the European Community have a corresponding role: to protect democracy and capitalism — perhaps sometimes in the opposite order — against external and internal enemies. Chile and El Salvador are not located in Europe, Poland is — but the logic is the same and there is considerable pressure on Norway to join in the USA's struggle against liberation movements in non-European countries, and including the limits for the area of NATO activities. At this point it looks as if Norway and Denmark have given a clear answer even if the Danish 'No' made more impact in the international press than the Norwegian. More and more explicit indications of that type is what is needed, of the countries singly and in combination — assisting each other politically in the open.

The third main pillar is the actual content of the defence. It has to be clearly defensive, it should be beyond suspicion of being at the disposal of one of the allies, or all of the allies, or of forces inside Norway for offensive purposes, not even in the sense of using attack as defence — and this would already be implicit in a clear 'No' to nuclear weapons. How should one build this kind of strong defence? In my view by adhering to some very simple principles that today are quite neglected.

The first principle one sees rather clearly by asking the question why Switzerland has such a strong defence and gives an impression of being so unconquerable. *Answer:* (1) because it is not part of an alliance with a strong superpower that has a demobilising impact on the country because people start thinking that, when the chips are down, the superpower will take care of their defence; (2) because Swiss defence is not so centralised that the rest of the country becomes demobilised because all initiatives come from the capital headquarters; (3) because not all of the military technology is so complicated that it has a demobilising impact on the creativity of people themselves. I will stand by the assertion that the more a country is "integrated" under a superpower, the more centralised its defence precisely because defence efforts are concentrated very heavily at very few points and in few persons who are absolutely dependent materially and non-materially on the superpower. If in addition there is a suspicion that one is actually fighting the superpower's war rather than one's own, the defence motivation will be minimal. Those who are building a defence capacity of this kind are, for that reason, truly enemies of defence. A self-respecting country needs something better than that.

The second principle is the main principle in ecological

thinking: If you want to be strong, or "mature" as the ecologists say, then base this on diversity, variety, complexity. Not only one defence system, but several. More concretely: a defence consisting of both conventional military defence, guerilla and non-military defence would be much, much stronger because there is always something to fall back upon if one of them should fail. I am not going into any kind of detail, only mention two rather obvious points:

—these forms of defence draw on the capacity in different parts of the population. The violent forms will, above all, be used by men, young and middle aged — even if here some kind of equalisation between the two sexes has taken place recently. The non-violent form can be used by the whole population.

—a division of labour between these is in no sense impossible. The conventional defence would be a *first line* defence, a marking of borders, a defence against transgression — but it would not be able to stand up against a very powerful enemy. The other two will come into the picture in occupied areas — their task would be to make the country so indigestible for an antagonist that he will think twice before he starts attacking. In other words, the two constitute a defence *in depth*.

Of the non-military forms of defence one should mention such things as sabotage against one's own property in order to make factories etc., useless for an antagonist — not the same as scorched earth tactics — non co-operation and civil disobedience; every part of the country, every municipality, every organisation that produces something, every voluntary association would have its own non-military defence plan with clear ideas as to what one could do.

Personally, I would, for a number of reasons, prefer to work in this third sector — I believe most in that one. But I know that we who have a more pacifist inclination constitute a minority, although not that small. The majority of the Norwegian people want military defence: in a democracy they are then entitled to have it. But this majority does not have the right to prevent a minority which also wants to contribute to defending its country in its own way from being participants should an attack come and an occupation ensue from it. They have a right not to be regarded as potential traitors, herded into concentration camps, or whatever plans there might be for conscientious objectors. In the same way I could also have argued above: the majority of the Norwegian people support NATO; but the majority does not seem to adhere to a policy which to such a large extent will make Norway a bomb target during the first days of the war — the first hours — even minutes — and for nuclear bombs, not ordinary bombs.

In this diversity we should learn to see a source of strength, not a source of weakness. If our entire population had had only one view and only one inclination in this important question we would have been in a weaker position that we are today — we would have less to draw upon. Precisely this complexity should permit an elaboration of possibilities for non-conventional military defence and for non-military defence. There cannot be anything to lose from this except, perhaps, for people who will have two worries in mind:

—would this not threaten the military monopoly of the defence function and thereby threaten the status of the military sector in our society in general?
—will a population trained in guerilla and also in non-military defence not be a population totally ungovernable by its own legitimate government?

No doubt there is something to these two trains of thought, and for that reason they should be taken seriously.

To the first, one might argue that this has already happened to a large extent. It is generally recognised today that our security perhaps depends more on skilful foreign policy than on military policy in a more narrow sense. In addition to that we have a concept of total defence in which economic and psychological defence, and civil defence, form a part. The military sector in a conventional sense is already a part of a more comprehensive whole, and has in our democratic society accepted this position. A defence concept where both military and conscientious objectors find a place side by side would be problematic to start with, but if we have a country where Christians and non-Christians can live side by side in most contexts this should also be possible. There are strong national currents in both groups that should have a unifying power, and there is a common fear of the nuclear insanity and of the limitless arrogance of the superpowers that also will have a unifying effect. Finally, one should not underestimate the role of bureaucracy as a unifying factor. An office, later a section in (the extended) department of defence would organisationally place the two parties more in the same setting. Such thoughts have already been entertained at so-called high levels — they should be revived again, they should be put into action.

The second argument is an argument about class struggle. There is no doubt that there is something in this: a population trained in non-violence will be able to carry out non-violent resistance, with the Samic minority and Norwegians side by side, against hydro-electric dams in the northern part of the country, frequently and more effectively. They would be able to, yes, that is not the same as saying that they would do it — just as little as the Swiss soldiers have made use of the guns they have at home in their wardrobes — every single one of them — against their own people. Perhaps it creates confidence when authority gives the population a source of power so that it does not have to build it up itself, clandestinely and amateurishly? Perhaps one could also think of a new social contract at this point, something in the direction of agreeing that non-violence should only be used when fundamental values, and special fundamental rights are threatened, such as the freedom of an ethnic group, its identity — and not on all kinds of occasions? A foreign occupation is clearly such an occasion, a dictatorship of the majority against the cultural minority is another one. We have the strength and the power to live with such problems — they can only develop and strengthen our democracy even further. These are the problems of a mature society.

My conclusion is therefore clear: not only *is* there an alternative defence based on a looser coupling to a superpower dominated NATO, on co-operation with like-minded countries as a third block which also could establish contacts in the Third World, and on a defence which is composed in a diverse manner of conventional and non-conventional, military and non-military components. *We are actually already on the way on all these points,* and have been so for a long time — because it seems to be appropriate for us. Norway is small and has some tendencies towards becoming a client State — we have been dependent on others for such a long period in our history. But the sense of national identity is strong, the ability to improvise likewise. A Norway which went further along such lines would be a path breaker in the desperately dangerous situation today — so dangerous that I do not even want to describe it in detail because I am not convinced that doomsday visions work constructively. They seem rather to be paralysing, people become apathetic, saying, 'OK, it is probably unavoidable'.

In Norway today there are clear initiatives in all these directions. Among the more conservative we find people who wish for a stronger national defence. From the extreme left, to well beyond the centre of Norwegian politics we find a scepticism about the United States — the former white angel who saved us from Nazism. In the Labour Party we find new trends of thinking in the direction of nuclear weapon free zones and co-operation with like-minded parties and like-minded countries; an effort to find a new foothold in an ever more complex world with the image of the United States undergoing changes every day. Even Reagan, poor man, in hospital, would probably today, perhaps, be willing to admit that the Soviet Union is not behind every enemy action to which an American President can be exposed? And in the Liberal Party we find considerable new thinking about the whole concept of defence as such, and not so different from what has been indicated here. Another point should also be mentioned in this connection: whereas in 1948 closer defence co-operation among the Nordic countries would have been a psychological impossibility due to the negative attitudes towards Sweden arising from the Second World War, today such feelings have yielded to a genuine feeling of brotherhood, shared visions and positions in a problematic world. In Norway something of this may have to do with the changing economic roles: an oil-strong Norway relative to an economically weaker Sweden which it is more easy to love than the tremendously successful and technically competent Sweden of yesteryear.

But why this division of labour in attitudes to defence among the various parts of the Norwegian political life? All of these thoughts and currents constitute a whole — why not try to make them pull together! To the advantage of a Norway with a real defence, not a Norway thrown into the cynical play of the superpowers, superpowers who always will be more than willing to sacrifice a small pawn in the total game if that can serve their own interests.

RAIMO VÄYRYNEN

Raimo Väyrynen is Professor of Political Science at the University of Helsinki.

The Nordic Region and the World Military Order

by Raimo Väyrynen

The idea of a nuclear weapon free zone in the Nordic area cannot be comprehended unless we begin with an historical account of the evolution of the security policies of the Nordic countries. In addition to this historical perspective we have to pay attention to the development of nuclear weapon technologies, and the doctrines which relate to them, by the great powers. Present problems in Nordic security are characterised by the closer integration of the countries in the area, especially of those belonging to the military alliances, in the face of the global threat system. Their security is increasingly conditioned by the measures adopted by the great powers in their nuclear strategies; hence their autonomy in the security field is decreasing. As the confrontation between great powers is intensifying and increasingly assuming a military character the pressures on Nordic countries are simultaneously becoming greater than before.

The changing military reality and the growing probability that Nordic countries will be drawn into a nuclear war if such a conflict, against expectations, breaks out, has been a catalyst to the recent outburst of security proposals. These have injected new elements into a situation which had been largely stalemated for thirty years. At the same time disagreements about preferable security policies have increased in Nordic countries and have resulted in a certain polarisation of political opinion. Although no big changes are to be expected, the security policies and doctrines shaping them have become more dynamic; they are seeking new ways of expression but collide continuously with the existing framework which is rather resistant to any major changes. That is why any change in the security position of the Nordic area has to be gradual and to take place within the existing structure of the system.

Nordic security has to be analysed in fact, at three separate, but intermingled, levels; global, regional and national. Especially important are the interfaces between these levels, such as, how global strategic developments influence regional security in the Nordic area and how the regional and national aspects interact. The Nordic region is typically a subordinated system in the global military game and hence its ability to steer international development is minimal. The interface between the regional and national aspects of security is somewhat more complicated. The fact that the Nordic countries are following different types of security policies means that regional security is shaped by national considerations and their interaction. On the other hand the Nordic countries form a certain type of security system, which is to say that their security needs and policies are interconnected and affect each other. The nature of this security system cannot be comprehended without an historical review of its emergence.

Historical evolution

In the aftermath of World War II the Nordic countries were rather separate from each other and were preoccupied with their own specific problems. Norway and Denmark were recovering from the Nazi occupation and settling the wartime political issues. Both of these countries were neutralist in their foreign policies, favoured a strong United Nations and wanted to pursue a bridge-building policy between the two power blocs. Sweden emerged as the most prosperous nation in postwar Europe and also opted for neutrality. Finland had started to build workable political and economic relations with the Soviet Union as a semi-sovereign nation because of the presence of the Allied Control Commission in the country. Finnish politicians gradually realised that the only viable way in the foreign policy was to build Finnish-Soviet relations on trust and mutual co-operation.

The post-war wave of neutralism did not last long however. The Nordic area was drawn into the global logic of the military rivalry between the great powers. When the Cold War broke out in 1947 or so, the United States began to conclude military alliances in order to strengthen her global hegemony and to encircle the Soviet Union. It has been pointed out that Washington did not need her new allies to add their resources to her own economic and military capabilities — her hegemony was undisputed anyway — but she did seek to use their territories for strategic purposes. The strategic usefulness of the allies included the establishment of military bases and installations on their territories and their integration into the U.S. military command systems and weapon deployment plans.[1] From the very beginning the role of U.S. allies was to serve as forward bases in the global struggle with the adversary, the Soviet Union. Nordic countries had to face this fact and to respond to a combination of gentle invitations and political pressures.

After the abortive attempts to conclude a Nordic defence alliance between Denmark, Norway and Sweden in 1948-49 the two first countries soon joined the NATO in April 1949. They became integrated in the military and political plans of NATO, which were largely drawn by the United States. Denmark and Norway had, however, some reservations, and they wanted to apply restrictions to their alliance membership. In

Norway in particular these restrictions were motivated by the desire not to challenge openly the neighbouring great power. Thus Norway as well as Denmark gradually developed provisions concerning the foreign military bases and nuclear weapons on their territories.

The Norwegian policy on foreign bases simply states that she will not enter agreements allowing the armed forces of foreign powers to stay permanently in the country unless Norway is attacked or subject to the threat of attack. The nuclear weapons policy states, in turn, that Norway does not intend to stockpile nuclear weapons on her territory; it is somewhat unclear whether this provision concerns only peacetime or whether it is valid also during a period of crisis. The most recent statements indicate that the latter interpretation might be also valid.

These facts mean that Norway — and Denmark for that matter — is applying a restrictive alliance policy and is unwilling, largely because of her exposed geographical position, to adopt extreme forms of NATO allegiance, at least during peacetime. The Norwegian base policy is not, however, as restrictive as it may appear. It is not normally interpreted to exclude allied military manoeuvres or short visits by the allied air and naval forces; neither is the pre-stocking of heavy military material from the United States rejected, as the recent decision to establish that kind of storage in Central Norway indicates. Norway also participates in the surveillance, navigation and command systems of NATO as well as in the planning of its nuclear operations. Thus the Norwegian restrictions on her alliance membership are in many respects flexible and optional and can be rather easily removed, if it is so decided, during an international crisis.[2]

After having settled her political course on neutrality Sweden started to emphasise the strength of her armed forces as a precondition of her foreign policy. Military capability was considered, together with the policy of non-alignment during peacetime, a sufficient means to preserve the neutrality of the country during war. These premises required, in turn, the maintenance of an extensive and self-sufficient arms industry to develop and manufacture weapons for the army. Sweden's economic and military strength, as well as her active policy of neutrality, made her the most significant country in the Nordic area, which position she has so far preserved.

Sweden's economic crisis, together with the rapid rise in the development and production costs of advanced weapons systems has been shaking the foundations of this powerful position. The Swedish military has become more dependent on foreign technology and the viability of the domestic arms industry has been partly called in question. The net result of these developments is that the military economic foundations of Sweden's armed neutrality are not as credible as they used to be in the past. This conclusion cannot be extended, however, to the credibility of Sweden's policy of neutrality which has more or less maintained its previous strength.[3]

Finland's international position evolved gradually from a semi-sovereign status in the immediate post-war period to a policy of active neutrality which has been practiced during the last twenty years. Finland's neutrality has a special character because of the security arrangement concluded with the Soviet Union through the Treaty of Friendship, Co-operation and Mutual Assistance (FCMA). According to this treaty, from 1948 Finland may receive military aid from the Soviet Union if she is subjected to an armed attack by Germany or States allied with it. The FCMA Treaty recognised a certain military interest of the Soviet Union in Finland which has been rejected earlier as incompatible with sovereignty.[4] This was the price which Finland paid to the global logic of military rivalry in order to meet Soviet security concerns on her north eastern border.

This brief account of the post-war development of the Nordic security system shows that it has been considerably transformed by the global logic of the political and military competition of the Cold War. Denmark and Norway were drawn into a military alliance and Finland concluded a special security agreement with the Soviet Union. Sweden participated in the military rivalry by building up her own arms industry and armed forces and contemplating, until the second half of 1960, the acquisition of her own nuclear weapons. The Cold War logic drew the Nordic countries apart from each other in security policy, while economic and political collaboration continued, though not always without frictions. Thus one of the pertinent issues in the Nordic co-operation has been how these diverging tendencies have been matched to each other to allow further collaboration, but to take also into account the incompatibility of security interests. The problem is, in other words, how to make the Nordic security system sufficiently stable and how to restrict the unwarranted penetration of great power interests into the area.

Some of these problems are illustrated by the Nordic relationship to the nuclear arms race. Basically the situation is that Finland has been forbidden, in the Paris Peace Treaty of 1947, to acquire nuclear weapons or their delivery vehicles. Sweden gave up the nuclear option during the 1960s and Denmark, as well as Norway, have restricted the stationing of foreign nuclear weapons on their territories. The Non-Proliferation Treaty (NPT, which all the Nordic countries have endorsed, further stipulates that they will not develop nuclear weapons themselves and that nuclear weapon powers will not supply them with these weapons for their own deployment. In this sense the NPT strengthens the *non-nuclear status* of the Nordic countries.

The Nordic countries are not, however, entirely non-nuclear, because of a loophole in the NPT which does not forbid the transfer of nuclear weapons systems to other countries provided that the nuclear weapon power in question does not cede control to the recipient. If Sweden preserves her policy of non-alignment in peacetime and neutrality in war, she cannot receive atomic bombs. In theory the Soviet Union could transfer nuclear weapons to Finland as a part of the military aid to repel an attack specified in the FMCA Treaty. In the cases of Denmark and Norway their restrictive alliance policy has so far eliminated the possibility of stationing nuclear weapons on their territories. It is not excluded, however, that the outbreak of a serious crisis in the region would invite U.S. nuclear armaments to these countries.

This possibility may be, in fact, regarded as the most serious threat to the stability in the Nordic security system. The Finnish interest in foreclosing this channel of insecurity has been manifested in repeated efforts to establish a nuclear weapon free zone in the Nordic area. The Nordic members of NATO have, in turn, resisted this idea because it would have considerably affected the character of their alliance obliga tions. Only recently has more active discussion on this question surfaced in these countries, partly as a consequence of the changing position of the Nordic area in the global military competition between the great powers.

Nordic countries in the global military game

Until the 1960s the security of Nordic countries was mostly affected by the political and military developents in Central Europe and in the Baltic area. Confrontations between great powers over Berlin and the two Germanies were reflected in the north and the extension of NATO's activities to the Baltic region from the late 1950s onwards also transformed the situation. The Soviet Union became more worried about her own position in the area and started to criticise the Nordic countries for closer military collaboration with NATO. These types of tensions were first felt in Norway and Finland.

During the last dozen years the situation has, however, changed. The political atmosphere in Central Europe still has, of course, significance for the Nordic countries but the increase in the military weight of the northern flank has gradually bypassed it. Until the 1960s the Northern Atlantic was largely controlled by the NATO fleets. At that time the Soviet Union made strategic decisions to expand the strength and range of her fleet and, as a result of this, Soviet naval operations were gradually extended to the Northern Atlantic and beyond.

A concomitant tendency was the shift of emphasis in strategic weaponry from silo-based ICBMs to submarines carrying intercontinental nuclear missiles. The SALT I Treaty accelerated this development, which considerably enhanced the significance of the Murmansk base to the Soviet Union. The strategic forces in the Kola Peninsula became an essential ingredient in the so-called central balance between the United States and the Soviet Union, with which *Norden* must live.

In fact the northern flank may now be (alongside the Persian Gulf) the most sensitive point of confrontation between the great powers. This means that they have to make attempts to regulate this confrontation in order to avoid immeasurable consequences, including the nuclear holocaust. The Soviet interest in the area is to guarantee the free movement of her submarines from the Barents Sea to open waters to avoid the possibility that they might be blockaded in shallow sea areas in the vicinity of Murmansk. Although the increase in the range of the most modern SLBMs has been reduced, it still determines Soviet strategy to a large extent. The U.S. interest, in turn, is to monitor Soviet military movements from as close a distance as is feasible in order to obtain necessary information. In case of war the United States would apparently strive to contain Soviet submarines in their own waters and destroy them, if possible, there.[5]

From the Norwegian point of view it is difficult to avoid the conclusion that the strategic principle of U.S. alliance policy is also relevant to its prospects. In short, the alliance relationship with Norway is maintained primarily because of the strategic value of her territory *vis-à-vis* the Soviet union. It is easy to agree with Sverre Lodgaard that the decision to pre-stock heavy military material for a US marine brigade in Trondelag, Central Norway, is not critical as such because this military material can in reality hardly be used for offensive purposes. More important is what kind of military operations the brigade will carry out and h ow it will be supported in the air and sea. The crucial issue is whether these forces will be used in operations against the Soviet military bases and if so, when and under what conditions.

Norway is in many ways integrated in the global military strategy of the United States. The surveillance and navigation stations in Norway can be used for the purposes of U.S nuclear strategy, both in anti-submarine warfare (ASW) and in outright offensive operations. Nuclear-capable bombers such as F-111 and Vulcan, can use Norwegian airports, which are currently being improved for more extensive military uses. Furthermore, Norway is deploying AWACSs, the flying command stations, on her territory.[6] The crux of the matter is whether these military installations of various types would be used by the United States for offensive purposes against the Soviet Union, and whether, even if this did not happen, Moscow might regard these installations as so threatening or otherwise problematic that they had to be destroyed by nuclear or conventional strikes.

Behind this reasoning there is the basic question of whether the military integration of Norway into NATO lowers or heightens the threshold of its incorporation into military con

frontations between the great powers. Although the pre-
stocking of heavy material and other related military solutions have been defended, by arguments relying on the deterrence model, claiming that they decrease the probability of
Norway becoming a participant in military clashes, the opposite conclusion seems to be even more plausible. Any
minor military skirmishes in the northern flank are highly im-
probable because of the strategic weight of the area and
dangers affiliated with it. If war did break out the result
would be full scale military confrontation in which NATO's
military installations in Norway would immediately draw it
into the conflict and make any neutral option impossible. (It
may be out of the question anyway).

It has been predictable that the Soviet news media would
criticise Norway for her policy of closer military collaboration with NATO. In fact, the target of criticism has not
focused so much on the specific geographical location of U.S.
heavy military material. The pre-stocking issue is seen in
Moscow in the wider context of U.S. military strategy and
Norway's place in it. This was made plain by the Soviet
Foreign Minister Andrei Gromyko to his Norwegian counterpart Knut Fryderlund and repeated, for instance, in the
following newspaper commentary: 'US stores in Norway are
nothing else than a foreign network of bases which is a
material precondition for shaking the foundations of
Norwegian defence policy'.[7]

The position of the northern flank is becoming even more
exposed with the new military strategy of the Reagan administration. During the Kissinger era, the United States
avoided military escalation in Northern Europe so as not to
irritate the Soviet Union. Brzezinski started to change this
policy in his efforts to achieve military parity with the Soviet
Union in different parts of the world. Reagan is now starting
to complete these endeavours by increasing the strength of
the U.S. navy and by allocating a greater share of its ships,
supported by aircraft carriers, to the Northern Atlantic.[8] The
Soviet Union will, no doubt, respond to this move; probably
by increasing her own naval strength in the area. Consequently, the outcome will be an escalation of military tensions in
the northern sea areas.

Sweden's security policy is based on a combination of

peace policy, aimed at the promotion of peaceful and stable development in Europe and in the world in general, and conventional deterrence, which can be achieved by a strong military capability. Both the policy of peace and deterrence must be credible in order to convince the other countries that Sweden is serious in her political and military endeavours. The emphasis seems to be, however, on the comprehensive 'total defence' which forms the foundation of the country's security policy. Sweden's military strength and the policy of neutrality are, furthermore, considered an important factor of stability in the Nordic area: Denmark and Norway being members of NATO, and Finland having a security treaty with the Soviet Union; Sweden is seen to stand in the centre, and to balance the policies of the neighbouring countries which may be drawing in different directions.[9]

A key word to fit the Finnish attitude to the political and military constellation in Northern Europe, and in Europe in general, is also stability. This does not mean, however, that the present situation is considered an ideal one, or that it should not be changed at all. The escalating arms race in the European continent, together with political confrontation, breeds instability and threatens the existing patterns of security arrangements. The negative military and political impact of bringing Eurostrategic missile systems into Europe is a good example of developments which endanger the prevailing stability. That is why the present situation is preferred to these future alternatives.

In the Finnish case the problems connected with Eurostrategic systems has some special implications. These are due to the vicinity of those military and civilian targets in the Soviet Union which may be aimed at by the Euromissiles. In particular, cruise missiles would violate Finnish air space on their way to the Soviet territory. As a sovereign nation Finland should be able to defend herself against these missiles. This need is further enhanced by the provisions of the FCMA Treaty because an attack by cruise missiles against the Soviet Union would be defined as an aggression in the sense the Treaty stipulates it.[10] Although there are no reasons to dramatise too much the military impact of cruise missiles on Nordic security, they will at any rate considerably transform the military environment in the area.

All in all, one may agree with the following evaluation of the impact of the new weapon technologies on Nordic security:

> New weapons technology tends to increase the significance of the Nordic and Baltic region and its immediate milieu for regional and global military operations and planning of the great power alliances. Certain permanent factors are arising which may bring Northern Europe into the structures of the alliance defence systems in a new way . . . New types of middle range nuclear systems, especially cruise missiles, could draw the Nordic region into the sphere of nuclear politics . . . New features of NATO alliance politics form another new issue. The increased participation of Norway and Denmark in NATO nuclear planning activities and forthcoming new policies, and their growing importance due to the grey area controversy, draw the effects of nuclear competition into the region once again.[11]

In this light it is not excessive to conclude that the Nordic countries are, in one way or another, hostages of the global logic of the nuclear arms race and other manifestations of the military rivalry between the great powers. NATO is intensively extending her military strategy to the Nordic region, while the Soviet Union has mainly invested in the development of her naval capabilities in the northern sea areas. At the same time she has openly criticised the Norwegian policy for too close an integration with the US strategy. It remains to be seen whether the Soviet Union might at some future stage consider that U.S. military activities in her geographic neighbourhood have become so expansive that measures might be taken to limit Western influence in the Nordic region.

A Nordic balance?

Some Norwegian scholars, especially Arne Olav Brundtland, have coined the term 'Nordic balance' in which the Finnish-Soviet treaty one one hand, and the NATO membership of Denmark and Norway on the other hand, are seen to balance each other; while Sweden, with significant military capability, is the fulcrum around which the balance hovers. According to this view the Soviet pressure on Finland, for instance, would necessitate closer collaboration between NATO and its Nordic members.[12] In more general terms one may say that the Norwegian interpretation of the Nordic balance connects it with the balance of power in the central relationship between the great powers. If Soviet influence in the Nordic region is considered to have increased, the balance has to be restored by linking Norway more closely to the military capability of NATO.

I would like to suggest, however, that this model of the Nordic balance is incapable of explaining the actual developments in Nordic security systems. In fact, most of the recent developments in *Norden* cannot be captured by this model. To start from the south we may focus on the resistance of the Danish government to increasing military expenditure by the required annual rate of three per cent. The underlying reason for this is, no doubt, the economic crisis faced by the country. This tendency cannot be comprehended however, by the balance model. The question may be, in fact, more of a Danish-Norwegian balance; the Commander-in-Chief of the Norwegian armed forces, Sverre Hamre, has proposed that the Norwegians will have to shoulder that part of the military burden which has been given up by the Danes. This statement is related, of course, to the overall military balance between NATO and the Soviet Union in the northern flank, and is apparently inspired by official Norwegian thinking on the Nordic balance. The related model cannot be, however, used to account for this statement because of the negligible role of the Soviet Union or Finland in the problems of the Danish defence economy.

The hollow character of the model of Nordic balance is also illustrated by the pre-stocking debate. Although the decision to pre-stock heavy American military material in Norway can be argued by pointing to Soviet military strength in the area, and has led to some Soviet counter-reactions, the model fails in predicting some more nuanced developments. According to the model the pre-stocking decision should have been either a consequence of a tightening Soviet grip on Finland, or would have alternatively contributed to this outcome. Both of these claims are difficult to substantiate, because there are no new political developments in Finnish-Soviet relations.

The Finnish model of Nordic security is based on unlinking it from great power confrontations, and on efforts to promote co-operation and mutually acceptable security arrangements between the Nordic countries themselves. The primary interests of Finland in Nordic security are the maintenance of stability and of the relative autonomy of the region. If the pre-stocking of heavy military material on Norwegian territory would have endangered the Nordic stability the Finnish attitudes towards it would probably have been negative. So far, this has not turned out to be the case. If cruise missiles would prove to be a destabilising factor (as they most probably would), the official Finnish reaction would be critical, as it already has been. If the reduction of the Swedish military capacity would upset Nordic stability the Finns would probably oppose such cut downs. In fact this was the point made by the Swedish Under-Secretary of State, Leif Leifland, in his recent memorandum.

It was maintained in this memorandum that the decision of the Swedish Riksdag to cut the Swedish military budget by a basically nominal sum would upset the Nordic balance. Furthermore, it was pointed out that the Finnish authorities, among others, had expressed their reservations about the decrease in the credibility of Swedish defence. Yet, recently, the Foreign Minister of Finland stated that no such apprehensions had been transmitted to Sweden. In fact, it would have been difficult to comprehend any such intervention by the Finns.

The Leifland memorandum indicates a concrete weakness in the model of Nordic balance. It is too mechanistic and relies too heavily on balance-of-power thinking. As a consequence of this, even minor variations in the level of military preparedness are interpreted to have visible political implications. In my opinion the stabilising role of Sweden in the Nordic system is predominantly related to her neutral foreign policy and its credibility and only secondarily to her military capability. In this connection, one may also observe that in reality Sweden is less able than before to rely on the strategy and ideology of military deterrence, so that foreign policy is assuming a more central role in her efforts to guarantee the security of the country.

From the Finnish point of view stability is, thus, a keyword in the Nordic security system. In fact one could discern a common element in practically all the foreign policy initiatives made by Finland since the early 1960s, independently of whether they deal with the nuclear weapon free zone in the Nordic area, the Finnish-Norwegian border area, disarmament and arms control, European security or the relations with the German States. This common element has been to enhance by preventative diplomatic measure the stability of *Norden* and Europe in general and to remove in advance sources of political and military frictions. An underlying factor in this policy has been the lessons learnt from the Finnish-Soviet crises of 1958 and 1961 which have convinced the Finns that destabilising elements in their environments would elicit Soviet counter-reactions to Western moves.[13]

The relations between Finland and the Soviet Union are based on a security arrangement, satisfactory to both sides, as well as on the model of co-existence; which means economic and cultural co-operation and recurring political consultations between countries. In this framework Finland has been able to pursue a policy of neutrality and to contribute to all-European security and co-operation. The maintenance of stability in the Nordic region and in Europe in general is a precondition for the smooth functioning of co-existence and the security arrangement with the Soviet Union. International tensions, military threats and the formation of new political, military and economic coalitions would bring strains into these arrangements and would hence complicate Finland's foreign international position. This makes the central role of stability among Finland's foreign policy goals understandable.

A Nordic nuclear weapon free zone

In 1963 the President of Finland, Urho Kekkonen, proposed the establishment of a nuclear weapon free zone in *Norden*. This proposal was inspired by such international developments as the Undén plan on the club of non-nuclear countries and the preparation of the Tlatelolco Treaty in Latin America. Furthermore, the military instabilities brought about by a new surge in the arms race increased the relevance of Kekkonen's proposal. In the situation that prevailed in 1963 the Nordic countries had a common denominator in their nuclear policy: they did not allow the stationing of nuclear weapons on their territories during peace time. This did not foreclose, however, the possibility that Denmark and Norway would, during a crisis, accept the nuclear weapons of their allies on their territories. There has been some discussion whether President Kekkonen advocated an absolute or only a conditional ban on the stationing of nuclear weapons in Denmark and Norway, but he wanted, at any rate, to disconnect the Nordic region from the nuclear strategies of the great powers.

Since then Finland has, on different occasions, continued to support the idea of establishing a nuclear weapon free zone in the Nordic area, but Denmark and Norway, and to a lesser extent Sweden, have been critical of this idea. Since the late 1970s the Kekkonen plan has received more understanding among other Nordic countries than before. This 'third wave' has stemmed from concern about the instability created by the new weapons technology.[14] This aspect of Kekkonen's proposal was detailed in his speech in Stockholm in May 1978:

> As the disarmament talks draw out and developments in military technology enhance the risk of nuclear conflict in Northern Europe, the Nordic countries should in their own interest enter into negotiations among themselves and together with the great powers concerned about arms control. The object would be a separate treaty arrangement covering the Nordic countries which would isolate them as completely as possible from the effects of nuclear strategy in general and new nuclear weapons technology in particular.[15]

This proposal differed in certain respects from the earlier ideas put forward by Kekkonen on the Nordic zone:

> We observed that the third 'wave' of Kekkonen's proposal has grown out of its original framework in which an increase in stability obtained through a political treaty was the aim. A transition has now been made from adjustments to political regulation of weapon systems. It is no longer enough to have political guarantees concerning the potential use of weapons. Now there is a desire to discuss the weapons themselves and their location in the Nordic region and its vicinity.[16]

The objection most often heard from other Nordic countries was that Kekkonen's proposal was one-sided, favouring the Soviet Union, and that it had to be balanced by including some parts of the Soviet territory and the Baltic Sea in the zone. The Swedish government has reservations in this respect, but continues to support the zone proposal in general terms.

The original Finnish view was that the nuclear weapon free zone should include only the territories of the four Nordic countries. This view has remained by and large, unchanged. Some Soviet commentaries have also clearly indicated that she has no willingness whatsoever to include any part of the Soviet land or sea territory in the nuclear weapon free zone. For instance, the Soviet missiles in the Kola area are a part and parcel of the strategic balance with the United States and not targeted against the Nordic countries.[17] In these circumstances the discussion on the nuclear weapon free zone in *Norden* has become stalemated as the views held by the relevant actors are too far from each other in such central matters as the boundaries of the zone.

This disagreement still prevails and, in fact, recent exchanges of views have proved that it is rather deep. This has not prevented some new tendencies from appearing in the debate. Within the Norwegian Labour Party an influential minority has demanded discussion on the Nordic nuclear weapon free zone as a means of strengthening Norway's security.[18] The Norwegian government has partly turned down this idea by insisting that Norway could be included in a nuclear weapon free zone only as a part of a wider nuclear free arrangement. This apparently means that there should be a more extensive zone free of nuclear weapons in Europe, or that the inclusion of Kola Peninsula would be a precondition for Norway's decision to give up the stationing of nuclear weapons on her territory, even during wartime. In the present conditions this means that the Norwegian Labour government does not consider the Soviet offer on the extension of negative security guarantees a sufficient reason for entering Kekkonen's zone. Norway apparently prefers firm alliance commitments with the United States to any special arrangements with the Soviet Union.

At the political level, a nuclear weapon free zone in the Nordic area has thus been connected with a wider arrangement in Europe. As the inclusion of the Murmansk area in this kind of zone is hardly probable, it has to be extended to Central and Southern Europe. Ambassador Jens Evenson,

one of the influential figures behind the Norwegian campaign, has proposed in an interview that a kind of buffer zone
has to be created across Europe. He would include in that arrangement Poland, the German Democratic Republic, the
Federal Republic of Germany and Czechoslovakia, in addition to the Nordic countries. In Evensen's opinion there are
also other potential members of a nuclear weapon free zone
in Europe, viz Holland, Belgium, Luxemburg, Switzerland,
Austria and even Greece, Bulgaria and parts of Turkey.[19]

A related idea has been launched by Alva Myrdal who,
after having paid due attention to the problems involved, ex-
plores the opportunity of establishing a nuclear weapon free
zone in Europe consisting of the countries included in the
Kekkonen plan, the remaining neutral countries (viz.
Switzerland and Austria) as well as those mentioned in the
Rapacki plan in the 1950s. Myrdal proposes that the gradual
implementation of this zone could be started from Finland
and Sweden which could declare their own territories a
nuclear weapon free area, on top of the legal and political
commitments they have already made in this matter. These
two countries could provide a political example for others to
follow.[20]

A conclusion

The Nordic countries have been gradually drawn into the
global military competition between the United States and the
Soviet Union. This is especially true for Denmark and Norway, which have been integrated more and more closely into
the nuclear doctrines, strategies and operational plans of
NATO. Sweden and Finland have been able, as neutral countries, to stay partially outside the great-power competition,
although it is also constantly modifying their own security
position. In Sweden there are worries about the sufficiency of
her military defence and deterrence, sharpened by the
reliance on military means, compared with political ones, in
the security policy of the country. In Finland the provisions
of the security treaty with the Soviet Union, although designed for a crisis situation, also naturally have relevance for
peacetime security policies.

In these circumstances the Nordic area cannot be
autonomous in its security policy, while external pressures

make any balance unstable. Further military integration within NATO affects the Soviet policy in the region which, in turn, results in new decisions and measures in the Western capitals. In general the Nordic region is now more connected than ever before to developments in Europe as well as to the global nuclear arms race. There are no signs that there will be any appreciable changes in the future, other than that the strategic arms race will continue.[21]

Expectations on the achievement of a stable military balance in the Nordic region are unrealistic, because there is no such balance in the nuclear arms race, neither locally nor globally. That is why the only starting point for the disarmament process is the acceptance of the *status quo,* although it may contain imbalances as it does in the Nordic region. The prevailing situation provides a certain measure of political and military stability on which one could build initiatives to promote disarmament. In Northern Europe these initiatives should aim at enhancing the autonomy of the region and at disconnecting it from most dangerous consequences of strategic rivalry. This is possible only if the great powers can show restraint in their military policies.

The promotion of stability and autonomy in the Nordic security system is a long and difficult process. It is not, however, hopeless because, as a consequence of a dialectical process, people are again becoming conscious of the frightening consequences of the nuclear arms race. Disarmament initiatives are now enjoying wider support than ever they have during the last twenty years. This is partly due to the fact that these initiatives have been, and have had to be, more concrete than before to connect the political process and conceivable outcomes to each other; in a word to make action for disarmament meaningful.[22] The ideas concerning nuclear weapon free zones, which have special relevance in *Norden,* are instrumental in this respect. Though the zone proposals in Northern Europe cut across existing security policy commitments and hence create political problems, it is in the longer run a viable alternative which can be extended also to other parts of Europe.

Footnotes

1. See Harvey Starr, 'Alliances: Tradition and Change in American Views of Foreign Military Entanglements', in Ken Booth & Moorehead Wright (eds),

RAIMO VÄYRYNEN

American Thinking about Peace and War. New York 1977, pp.50-55.

2. On the Norwegian policy see, e.g. Johan Jorgan Holst, 'Norwegian Security Policy', in Johan Jorgan Holst (ed), *Five Roads to Nordic Security,* Oslo 1972 and Osmo Apunen, 'Nuclear Weapon Free Areas, Zones of Peace and Nordic Security', *Yearbook of Finnish Foreign Policy 1978.* Helsinki 1979, pp.4-8.

3. A representative collection of views on Sweden's security policy is *Elva asikter om svensk säkerhetspolitik.* Trosa 1979.

4. See, e.g. Osmo Apunen, Finland's Treaties on Security Policy. *Co-operation and Conflict,* 4, 1980. pp.249-61.

5. The official viewpoints of the Nordic countries on the increase in the northern strategic significance of the northern flank are put forward in the following publications: Forsvarskommisjonen av 1974. *Norges offentlige utredninger, NOU 1978:9.* Oslo 1978, Andra parlamentariska försvarskommitténs betänkande. *Kommittébetänkande 1976:37.* Helsinki 1976, pp.16-19, and Var säkerhetspolitik. *Statens offentliga utredningar 1979:42.* Stockholm 1979, pp.66-71.

6. Malvern Lumsden, 'Norge som anglo-amerikansk flybase' and Sverre Lodgaard, 'Förhandslagringen i strategisk perspektiv', both articles in Magne Barth (ed), *Förhandslagringen i Norge?* Oslo 1980, pp.41-68 and 119-47.

7. *Pravda,* 26 October 1980; see also *Pravda,* 22 November 1980.

8. Statement by Mr John Lehman, Secretary of Navy, published, for example, in *Helsingin Sanomat,* 4 March 1981.

9. Var säkerhetspolitik . . . *op.cit.* 1979, pp.101-14.

10. This is pointed out by a Soviet pseudonym Yuri Komissarov in *Suomen Kuvalehti* 47, 1979, pp.42-46. The Swedish concerns regarding the cruise missiles are analysed in Nils Andrén and Birger Gripstad, *Grazonsvapen.* Trosa 1980, pp.81-90.

11. Kari Möttölä, *On Factors of Détente and Tension in Northern Europe* (unpublished manuscript). Helsinki 1979, pp.3-4.

12. Theories of the Nordic balance is explored, for instance, by Nils Andrén, *Den nordiska balansens framtid.* Trosa 1976. See also Arne Olav Brundtland, Urho Kekkonen ja 'Pohjolan tasapaino', in Keijo Korhonen (ed), *Urho Kekkonen. Rauhanpoliitikko.* Keuruu 1975, pp.111-37.

13. Some of these recent developments are explored in Raimo Väyrynen, 'Finlands utrikespolitik inför generationskiftet'. *Internationalle studier* (Stockholm) 1, 1981, pp.6-10.

14. Kekkonen's proposals have been analysed in detail by Apunen *op.cit.* 1979, pp.2-19, and Unto Vesa, *Planen pa ett kärnvapenfritt Norden. Tampere 1979.*

15. The text of the speech has been published in *Yearbook of Finnish Foreign Policy 1978.* Helsinki 1979, pp.64-66.

16. Apunen *op.cit.* 1979, p.15.

17. Yuri Komissarov, Kohti ydinaseetonta Pohjolaa. *Kanava* 9, 1978.

18. A representative compilation of these views is Thorbjorn Jagland *et al* (ed), *Atomvapen och usikkerhetspolitikk.* Oslo 1980.

19. *Sydsvenska Dagbladet,* 18 November 1980. See also Jens Evenson, 'Norge i en farligere verden' in Thorbjorn Jagland *et al* (eds), *Atomvapen og usik- kerhetspolitikk.* Oslo 1980, pp.43-45.

20. *Dagens Nyheter,* 11 abd 12 December 1980. Myrdal has responded to her critics in *Dagens Nyheter,* 12 February 1981.

21. See Anders Sjaastad, SALT II: Consequences for Europe and the Nordic Region. *Co-operation and Conflict* 4, 1980, pp.237-48.

22. On this point see Raymond Williams, The Politics of Nuclear Disarmament. *New Left Review,* No. 124 (1980), pp.35-36.

Part III
Détente and European
Nuclear Disarmament

Fernando Moran is a member of the Senate in Spain, and foreign affairs spokesman of the Spanish Socialist Party, PSOE.

Restoring Détente

Fernando Morán

The decade of the 80s has begun with a backdrop of serious tension between the superpowers, economic crisis and the militarisation of political thought. Tension and the militarisation of political thought act reciprocally. The crisis has created a climate of insecurity which has coloured the assessment of the international situation. This insecurity is, nevertheless, relative; in other words, insecurity is being experienced on the understanding that the balance of power has not changed sufficiently for either block to gain advantage from an offensive action. The deterrent, the equilibrium of terror, still functions. As does the conviction that the superpowers still maintain between them an ultimate and solid relationship based on common interests; a relationship which is irreplaceable for both parties and which united them with their respective allies: the maintenance of balance in the one-to-one relation and, as a consequence of this need, the justification for each party to exercise discipline over their collaborators, allies or satellites. There is an over-riding need for the USSR (and a critical one for the United States) to re-establish the bipolarity of power on which doubt has been cast by certain very important events. If this does not mean a return to the vision into zones of influence, it does signify the re-establishment of bipolarity. This rested on the capacity of both to work together to globalise any more or less peripheral situation; that is to say, to reduce a given situation to a condition whereby it only or principally affects the relationship between the superpowers.

The essential features of the decade from which we have recently emerged is that bipolarity was questioned, criticised and even challenged. The seventies began, as we shall see, with a consciousness of the power of bipolarity and of the fact that its upkeep did not necessitate a physical presence in all, or even the main, areas of the world. An indirect presence is all that is required; whether it be by means of an intermediate power which combines its own interests unquestionably with the defence of the interests of the superpower (in other words, by means of the "zonal guardians"), or from control of the overall economic relations.

Combined with strategic control, the seventies advanced — up until the last years — in a world in which cultural pluralism had been granted respect, as a consequence of the major revolution resulting from de-colonisation, but when this pluralism had not yet produced a sufficiently strong strategic and political challenge to necessitate a *more direct action* to try and re-establish, as far as possible, the hegemony of the industrial world in its two versions, capitalist and socialist.

The seventies were the inheritors of the optimism of the happy sixties, in which the industrial world showed — or thought it had shown — that political pluralism could be conceded; that the emerging world could be developed and dominated not at this stage by physical means, but by their intellectual and psychological counterparts: the accuracy of Western Eurocentric industrial analyses in defending and predicting any peripheral eventuality. These concepts were to undergo a crisis — were, in fact, to be challenged — at the end of the decade. Each superpower was to be obliged to act to reduce the complexity and relocate security on the basis of a single proposition: that the most important thing is, and must be, the one-to-one relationship between the super-powers. However, this conclusion — which established a common interest in bipolarity — did not lead to an understanding between the superpowers; on the contrary, the breakdown of bipolarity was made manifest at this time by a breakdown of détente and an attempt by the United States to improve its strategic position and political control by means of strengthening its dominion over its allies, principally the NATO members.

This tendency towards military build-up came about during an economic climate and a crisis of the policies of the White House under Carter which led to the most crushing defeat ever of an incumbent President and the elimination of the liberal-leaning senators from the foreign affairs forum where they had, over the last fifteen years, done much to change the mentality of the Senate.

The failure of the methods of indirect control — zonal guardians, areas screened off from a foreseeable confrontation — in conjunction with facts on military parity has produced a strategy aimed at achieving local or regional balances through *direct* action by the superpowers themselves. The Soviet intervention in Afghanistan in December of 1979 is an example; a cause, and also a consequence, of this new attitude of direct confrontation; that is to say, the approach by one power, the USSR, to a zone of possible tension and direct confrontation.

The present situation is the result of the development of a number of factors during the seventies and, specifically, since Helsinki in 1975. As in all underlying processes, the data and factors which produce the new phase developed gradually over a period of time. During that period, those factors tended towards the new direction; in other words, in favour of détente in the one-to-one relation. This talk aims to briefly outline these opposing tendencies and to show how the factors working against détente gained the upper hand, without forgetting those factors which will operate in limiting the confrontation nor those which allow us to hope for a new phase of détente to succeed the current situation. For this to happen, it is necessary for the progressive forces of European nations, dedicated to the wellbeing, independence and possibility of creating a freer and more just society, to undertake a realistic analysis of the situation without becoming a prey to the simplifications which the militarisation of approach prevalent among the far right might induce them.

The Conditions which led to Helsinki — The Strategic Considerations

After an election campaign in which the Republican candidate adopted a "hawk" stance on questions concerning relations with the USSR, with an America in the throes of a moral crisis — especially among the university young — thanks to the Vietnam war and at the height of the apprehension that the slogan "America the Invincible" was not proving true in the rice fields of Indo-China, Nixon came to the Presidency in 1968. And in 1969 talks began between Dobrynin, the Soviet Ambassador in Washington, and the then advisor for national security affairs, Kissinger, who sought, if not neutrality, then Soviet military abstention in Vietnam and the summit meeting so longed for by Nixon, which would globalise relations between the superpowers. The American policy and the Soviet reply were possible, thanks to a concrete assessment of the strategic situation.

During the period which runs from the dropping of the atomic bombs on Nagasaki and Hiroshima, up to maybe 1952, the United States was the military hegemonic power. What the military experts call a "one unit veto system" was established. A single power, acting alone, could veto the action of any other power with the threat of a nuclear reply, to which the aggressor would be defenceless. Imbalances in conventional arms and forces were compensated for by the nuclear threat which acted as a sufficient deterrent. The nuclear superiority, the nuclear monopoly in fact, allowed for a graduated response. Only the required megatonnage would be used. It is important to remember that this was the basis on which the North Atlantic Treaty was signed and the whole NATO system and organisation established. As far as we Spaniards (officially semi-ostracised, but subject to American diplomatic and political support) are concerned, this was the basis of the treaty setting up American bases on Spanish soil, signed in 1953. The US Strategic Air Force, much more important to the American Strategic Command then, than later, when the other two feet of the tripod (nuclear submarines and missiles) were set up, was the guarantor of the deterrent and the principle element of defence. Within that framework the Spanish bases played an important role.

From the middle of the fifties onwards the "two unit veto system" comes into being. Each of the two superpowers can veto any imprudent action by its opposite number. An equilibrium of mutual threat is established. The bipolarity of power is so absolute that the central one-to-one relationship is sufficient; the rest of the zones are deadweight in terms of their influence on the overall situation.

The doctrine current in the West assumed compensation for conventional inferiority by means of the nuclear deterrent. As a considerable nuclear arsenal began to appear in the East, the prevailing doctrine came to be that of "massive retaliation". Any guarantee of the contact zone between the two blocks, Europe, against a calculated or limited threat, had necessarily to consist of a general or very extensive response. From the time of the sixties, however, Western Europeans began to ask themselves whether, in the case of a conflict limited initially to Europe, the massive American response would automatically come into effect; placing at risk, as such actions would, the huge conurbations on the other side of the Atlantic. This doubt was increased when Defence Secretary McNamara changed the "massive retaliation" doctrine for the "flexible response" without getting this change, so vital for Europe, agreed to by the Europeans. As we know, insecurity about the automatic triggering of the full American capability led General De Gaulle to develop his "force de frappe" and, in 1966, withdraw from NATO.

Europe then, as now, found itself between deterrent and détente. Countries like West Germany, in which any conflict would be decisive and catastrophic, wanted to increase the deterrent capacity and, at the same time, explore the possibilities of détente, gradual disarming and a balance of forces.

The seventies produced a parity which both sides considered acceptable. There also existed the idea that a conflict would be limited, something which gave the Americans greater confidence, but not the Europeans, the immediate targets of the initial phases of a nuclear conflict. Escalation, escalation control and what the experts call "escalation dominance" (that is to say the relative strategic superiority which allows one power to progressively mark out the levels or thresholds of a possible conflict) are terms which came to be accepted as functional by the Pentagon.

The important point to grasp is that from the middle of the sixties and during the seventies up until around about 1978 it was considered that an acceptable parity existed.

But if parity is acceptable for the superpowers, Europe needed détente to reduce the risk of error or the likelihood of a local or tactical conflict; this is why Europe or, to be precise, West Germany, pursued détente.

Détente, which is different from disarmament, was acceptable to the superpowers for obvious reasons: (a) in the first place, because détente does not imply the dismemberment of the two blocks (its logical conclusions might lead to this, but there is a big difference between logic and reality); (b) because détente would not affect the division into zones of influence.

In his memoirs, Kissinger relates how from an initial dubiousness and reluctance faced with Bahr and Brandt's ideas for a German "Ostpolitik", the White House (preceded by the State Department and followed by the Pentagon) began to appreciate, in very precise terms, how détente, up to a point, would not affect the central relation between the superpowers and how it might permit certain advantages for security and produce a relationship that was beneficial for both sides. Today we hear that "détente is indivisible"; in fact, when the White House proposed it at the end of the sixities and beginning of the seventies, détente was a favourable factor in achieving Soviet co-operation for American moves to withdraw from the hornets' nest of Vietnam.

In the heyday of Kissinger's *realpolitik,* the Under

Secretary of State, Sonnenfeldt, explained to a meeting of American ambassadors in Europe the doctrine of zonal division. He even went as far as to say that it would be better for Yugoslavia to maintain its independence without veering further towards the West and for the other nations of the Eastern block not to attain a more flexible situation in order to protect the *status quo*.

The certainty that both clusters of allies would keep to their own side of the fence gave security to both superpowers and allowed other factors of a political and cultural nature to come into play; all this on the basis of economic and social assumptions which appeared to be solid.

The Economic and Social Assumptions

The economic crisis we are now suffering may have begun around 1973-4, but it did not become manifest before 1977-8 in spite of the effects of oil price hikes in Kuwait and Teheran of 1973 following the Yom Kippur War.

Before the crisis the capitalist world had lived through the previous twenty years, despite the periods of alternating acceleration and deflation (stop-go), in the conviction that Keynesian techniques would avoid an event such as the 1929 crash and that the system would progressively adapt to the combined productive forces without any need for radical structural changes. The instruments used to achieve this were: Keynesian control of demand, indicative planning of supply and a model of welfare based on rising public expenditure. The foundations, however, were somewhat weaker: lack of control over multinational corporations which, as Stuart Holland has pointed out, had direct effects on industrial strategy and development; a system of world trade based on a progressively unfavourable trade balance for two thirds of the planet, the developing countries to which the industrialised nations — with an inevitably inflationary system — would transfer their inflation; a monetary system based on the convertibility of the dollar and on the dollar/gold parity which allowed the leading industrial capitalist country to incur trade deficits while at the same time maintaining the value of its currency. The political assumptions amounted to the possibility of integrating the industrial proletariat and the middle classes within the system, thus defusing and dispersing the class struggle so long as public spending could be increased. Keynesianism and monetarism avoided facing up to the problems of social structure. However, if the foundations were weak, the statistical fact of growth during this period at a rate of not less than 5 per cent and the well orchestrated relations of dependence on the Third World and peripheral capitalism created a climate of confidence in the techniques and the system which made profound structural changes appear unreasonable. Given this security and military parity, ideological and political confrontation with the other industrial system could be controlled within boundaries which permitted dialogue and encouraged co-operation. The European Economic Community, once the so-called "Common Market Crisis" of the sixties caused by De Gaulle's attack on the supranational elements contained within the Rome Treaties had been overcome, turned towards a possible, and to some extent ambitious, integration, as is shown in the Harmel report on economic union in 1970. The first expansion converts the community scheme unquestionably into one more piece in the structure of the industrial world.

In the East, to be more precise, in the Soviet Union, the technocratic policies of the Kosygin-Brezhnev team manage to unblock a number of bottlenecks in the productive system at the same time as consumption is improved and the relation between heavy- and light-industry planning is made a little more harmonious. The lack of a concrete reaction to the intervention in Czechoslovakia gives Moscow (at this time paying progressively more attention to its own Eastern flank, China) greater confidence.

The two rival systems do not, therefore, feel threatened at the beginning of the decade of the seventies.

The Intellectual and Cultural Assumptions

In spite of the Vietnam war, that period was not a time when attitudes were militarised. In the United States liberal intellectual groups, if they were unable to present the kind of new image as existed in the days of Kennedy's "New Frontier", had regained an important position. The anti-intellectualism inherent in the populist and jingoistic political movements had receded. In Europe what could be called the "ideology of the Resistance" had waned noticeably since the mid-fifties;

the dominant star was technocratic and pro-development. Myths such as that of the satisfied consumer and that the future lay not so much in the creation of new values as in the modernisation and harnessing of the possibilities of the new technico-industrial revolution — that of the microchips and biochemistry — developed into a consensus among the capitalist managerial class of the technobureaucracy.

It is true that since the Meadows Report for the Club of Rome and the Mansholt letter to the EEC Commission, the question of dwindling resources and zero growth had made their appearance; but the values of technology and the open society had not been challenged on a broad front.

With respect to the rest of the world, although decolonisation had obliged the West to accept cultural pluralism, Western criteria and political science generally (particularly the theory of development studies) were considered sufficient to explain every given situation.

To sum up, if the industrial world was not exactly what Ortega y Gasset called "abreast of the times", nor was it shrouded in that cultural uncertainty and respect for values which, according to Sorokin, characterises periods of crisis.

The March Towards Détente

Before this backdrop the two superpowers pursue their objectives which, where they coincide, can be achieved by means of a certain level of détente. The Soviet Union had launched the idea of a European Conference as far back as the Berlin Conference in 1954. A major milestone in defusing the antagonistic situation inherited from the end of the war is the Austrian State Treaty of the 15 May 1955. The Rapacki plans, in the different versions from 1958 to 1964, promoted the idea of a denuclearised zone in Central Europe. The essential objective, besides a certain reduction in tension, is to obtain recognition for frontiers resulting from the Second World War.

As far as the West was concerned, apart from Nixon's specific objective of enlisting Russion co-operation in solving his Vietnam predicament, there was increasing attraction towards the idea that détente would favour flexibility in the East with a lessening of Soviet control over the Warsaw Pact countries. The subject of human rights and freedom of cultural communication begin to develop as the counterweight to the Soviet's objective. The NATO countries reveal a certain willingness to talk in the Harmel Plan of 1967 and the declaration at the NATO meeting in Reykjavik on 25 June 1968 contains what is to be one of the mainstays of the West's negotiating position: the link between a European conference and a process of mutual and balanced reduction of forces. As from 1969 Nixon accepts the idea of global negotiation with the USSR and seeks the summit meeting as the main aim of his foreign policy.

The initiative for seeking détente in Europe belongs however, not to the Americans but to the Europeans themselves; originally during a phase of Gaullist politics, later and much more significantly as a result of Chancellor Brandt's *ostpolitik*. The treaties with the Soviet Union and with Poland and the arrangements with East Germany underpin this policy which Nixon and Kissinger view initially with concern but which they come to understand and slot into their overall strategy. When, in 1969, Finland launched the idea of a European Security Conference, the proposal, via the usual roundabout route, stayed on course until the signing of the Final Act on 1 August 1975.

The Change in Conditions

I am convinced that some profound understanding is vital to the superpowers. Consequently, after a difficult and very dangerous period of confrontation, the two powers will come to an agreement. Foreseeably, they will do so after having brought their allies to heel and after having kept up a state of tension which justifies maintaining the two blocks. This period will, nevertheless, be extremely risky because calculations based on strategic interests could be upset by reactions in individual countries provoked by hardline policies and, especially, because neither superpower will enjoy the level of security conferred by the conviction that the situation could be controlled with a high degree of precision. A crisis always produces the tendency to simplify the issues, to dramatise, to see things in black and white, to locate the blame for one's own consternation and the unfavourable situation in something that can be easily personified — the enemy. Another major source of danger is that at the moment the two powers are trying to *re-establish bipolarity when new centres of power have already made this obsolete.*

The current crisis of détente and the threat of a cold war (a new version of cold war which will not, naturally, be a carbon copy of the fifties version) are not simply the result of the Soviet intervention in Afghanistan nor the shift in American public opinion which has led to Reagan's triumph. We can trace a series of changes going back to the last years of the seventies.

Changes in the Assessment of the Strategic Situation

Shortly before the inauguration of President Carter in December of 1976 the CIA produced a report on the Soviet Union's rearmament drive. They came to the conclusion that the Russians were spending 7 per cent of the GNP on defence. Some months later a new assessment, produced by Team B, doubled the estimate, putting the figure at 13 per cent. American rearmament supporters got the maximum mileage out of this figure; they produced the rationale that said if, for a given level or armament, Soviet expenditure is greater than what the Americans would have to spend to achieve the same level, this meant reduced Soviet productivity and further difficulties for other activities. From 1976 onwards, and this report is only a symptom of a growing mood, concern about Soviet rearmament has steadily increased.

However, the reports of the International Institute for Strategic Studies in London for the years 1978 and 1979 show that parity is fundamentally intact; that there have been certain significant Russian advances in its naval forces; that the West still has superior technology; that the existence of two potential fronts — the Western and the Chinese — is a qualitative factor of inestimable importance. What the advances in the Soviet fleet and their greatly expanded airlift capacity mean, taking into account the parity existing in the central transcontinental theatre, is the possibility of long-range activity, of which Angola, Katanga and the Horn of Africa had been examples. The appearance of the Backfires and the SS-20s is interpreted as upsetting the European balance. SALT II had been viewed by the Carter Administration as being useful in itself whether or not a general movement in favour of détente came into being. But already in

1978 opponents of the treaty take the opposite view; they say that partial limitation (of the number of long-range missiles, not warheads) should be, if not the consequence, then a boundary post marking the limits of a respect for the *status quo* right across the globe.

From the Spring of 1979 onwards the circles that establish international doctrine in Washington and subsequently in the European capitals began to concentrate on an alleged inferiority. Civil defence apears on the agenda papers again. The correction of this inferiority is set as a target. A NATO armament expenditure programme appears, ear-marking 80 to 100 billion dollars to be spent over ten years on rearming. In December of 1979 it is finally decided to install the Pershing and Cruise medium-range missiles in Europe to compensate for the Russian SS-20s. Soviet intervention in Afghanistan will add weight to this logic.

On the Soviet side, the military obsession has been a constant feature. The failure of the Soviet development model in East Europe and the serious malfunctions in the USSR itself, the Chinese balance, the dissidents and those social groups who without renouncing a socialist society attack authoritarianism and sterile bureaucracy, the challenge — in 1976 and 1977 — of Eurocommunism itself; all these factors seen from the traditional viewpoint of Russian, a continental power with a "blockade complex", add to the militarisation of Soviet attitudes and concepts of its role in the world. Not even the knowledge that for the first time in its history it is no longer an encircled empire but that, thanks to its naval power, it has a global capability which is sufficient to counterbalance the defensive-aggressive complex that Russian has had right down the ages and that the USSR has added to since the days of "communism in one country".

The two superpowers militarize their attitudes, the Soviets more than the Americans; the latter do not lag far behind but although they appreciate the value of military strategy within the overall framework, their vision is not predominantly military.

The Failures of Bipolarity. The Decrease in the Relative Strength of the Superpowers

Why does this concentration on military power and, especially, on nuclear power on which the two possess a virtual monopoly stem from one crucially important historical fact: the failure of the bipolarity of power?

The reasons are numerous. In the economic field all the forecasts (the OECD reports, the Leontieff report for the United Nations, Mary Kaldor's studies, the work of Gunder Frank on the crisis, the shrewd articles by G. Barraclough, etc.) point to the fact that at the end of the century a number of centres of economic influence will have developed; one, of major importance, based on Japan and the ASEAN countries and another based on the EEC and its African system stemming initially from the Lomé agreements.

In the political field the Shi'ite-Iranian revolution brings about the downfall of a vitally important "zonal guardian". The reason for the fall is even more significant: the eruption of forces — in this, the Islamic Renaissance in its most extreme form — which cannot easily be brought into line within the ranks of pro-Western and pro-Eastern forces. Subsequent developments such as the war between Iraq and Iran are even less easy to explain in terms of the power struggle between West and East.

The Crisis Multiplies Uncertainties and Simplifies Strategies
The crisis — whose nature foreshadows the end of a system — makes the conquest of markets absolutely essential. In the boom years the industrial powers fought each other for control over the supply of raw materials, but in the crisis for markets. Today 30 per cent of American trade is conducted with the Third World. The commercial climate is one of a fight by all against all, similar to that reigning in the thirties. The tendence, unless something happens soon to correct it, is towards protectionism.

The crisis has robbed the industrial powers of their indirect, non-drastic, control measures. The loss of capacity for indirect and multi-faceted control has concentrated the efforts of leadership on direct political action.

The Struggle for Détente
Détente is not only necessary to avoid the risks of a general conflict or of local conflicts with incalculable consequences in terms of lives and destruction should it escalate into a nuclear conflict; it is also necessary to avoid a standstill of the

political situation which will prevent the synthesis of liberty and equality sought after by the peoples of the world. Tension, especially in a state of declared cold war, closes industrial societies in on themselves and favours involution. Even the non-reactionary right ought to fear the picture that seems to be taking shape, because the simplifications to which the militarization of attitudes lead prevent the possibility of integrating social demands within a capitalist but flexible system. In the case of Spain, where democracy is still in a stage of construction and thus very weak, a cold war would lead to polarisation of antagonistic attitudes, adding to the damage done by the former Franco regime and condemning the Left to a waiting stance — until the wave passes — or to shut itself up in its own ghetto in order to maintain its doctrines and cohesion, in which case it would have to renounce all pretensions to have any effective influence on the conduct of social and political life. The Left would be forced into the ghetto of absolute definitions which is precisely where the most reactionary and militant elements of the Right want to see them. The cold war and the anti-Soviet crusade would make the Communists' task of critical renovation that much more difficult. Any development towards the defence of the Socialist countries would be interpreted as a return to Stalinism. The results of the Fifth Congress of PSUC (Catalan Communist Party) and the way they have been read by the general public are proof of this.

But the neocapitalists would also find that their theses on social adaptation, on integrating social challenges within the system itself, would be seriously eroded. The struggle for détente is not, therefore, solely the task of the Left but of all the democratic forces.

From a global point of view the small and medium powers would find themselves enlisted in specific causes directed by the superpowers. The bourgeois forces of the medium powers would find none of the ideological positions which they might use to their own advantage. They would have to accept the immediate interests of the controlling nations. Tension itself, without recourse to a cold war, is a sufficient means of disciplining satellites and allies. The globalisation of local differences is more easily achieved in a climate of tension. The first task of democratic people in this part of the world —

Europe — is to *fight against the militarisation of attitudes*. Over the last two years we have been subjected to a pressure which demands that we consider all problems affecting the international community almost exclusively in terms of military power-relations. The consideration of military questions is essential because our survival depends on the balance. To that extent the Left in Europe will have to consider European defence over the next decade, with that Euro-strategic vision which will permit a certain level of autonomy in any European political project. On the other hand it would be a grave error to over-simplify (which only serves to reduce reality to the military relation between the two blocks), to fail to analyse those factors other than the military ones — the world economic order, the consequences of cultural pluralism, among others.

In the second place, the Left — and, in general, the democratic forces — must renounce *all implicitly or explicitly Euro-centrism*. The relations between the industrial world and those countries which are trying to develop are still subject to completely obsolete standards. In the first place, because they hinder rather than help the process which might permit their integration within the economic order and, from that, the stability and welfare of all parties; and also, because the will of the extra-Europeans to attain a more just order is not transitory — it will continue, despite up and downs dictated by circumstance. It is impossible to continue regarding the periphery as an object which simply reflects the state of the power struggle between the two blocks of industrialised countries. The bipolarity of power is a biased, shortsighted viewpoint which does not correspond to reality. The gravity of the situation resides in the fact that whereas this bipolarity no longer exists and the world is, and will be in the future, progressively more multipolar, there does exist a real bipolarity: that of nuclear capability and destruction. But even this nuclear oligopoly is incapable of stabilising peripheral situations. The greatest danger is that, given a peripheral conflict, the superpowers, were they to participate, and being incapable of resolving it or globalising it by indirect means, would almost inevitably have recourse to the dialectic of military power based on the nuclear oligopoly.

For the necessary adjustment to multipolarity to take place

it is necessary for there to be a reduction in tension between the superpowers, so that their weight does not blunder through the intricacies of the present world situation. It is difficult to make the imaginative leap from a cultural and political Eurocentric vision or, at least, a centric industrial vision, without there being a climate of security between what today are two blocks.

Specific Actions

Given the circumstances there are a series of objectives which the democratic forces can try and achieve directly or indirectly:

—In the first place, preventing the present *status quo,* however precarious and biased on the balance of terror it is, undergoing any radical alteration. This refers not only to military considerations, but also to the political aspects which might oblige a superpower to respond by simplifying its action and conducting itself according to purely military postulates. The amplification of the blocks, the Warsaw Pact and NATO, should be opposed. To this extent it is essential that Yugoslavia should preserve its current position, as it is also that Spain should not join NATO.

—It is equally essential that other forms of domination by the superpowers — no matter how oblique their motivation might be regarded — should not be accepted. In the case of Afghanistan, condemnation and rejection of Soviet action and support for the authentic self-determination of-the Afghan people should be a constant theme of the democratic forces.

—The undemocratic systems posed by client governments should give way to elected and truly popular governments. Today Latin America is darkened by the shadow of the so-called regimes of national security; the policy of the promotion and insistence on human rights has been abandoned.

—In Europe there must be a less rigid relationship between capitalist and socialist countries. Technological and economic co-operation could be a positive factor in promoting this flexibility. Without an Eastern Europe under a socialism with a human face and with a certain social and political pluralism, the cause of the European Left is gravely prejudiced; socialist visions are taken to task with the aim of evidence of political regimentation and although the concrete experience refutes the analogy, attempts are made, with some success, to extend it to all socialism.

— For this reason it is necessary to demand respect from the East for human rights and civil liberties; to support the people who struggle in those countries for these rights, always remembering that to convert individual fighters — whose cause is that of humanity — into instruments in an ideological cold war is to render them small service. Such action only plays into the hands of the regimes who oppress them, separating them from public opinion in their own countries and causing them acute crises of conscience. The dissidents should be understood, defended and supported, but not allowed to be manipulated for the benefit of a cold war.

— In terms of the analyses and programmes of the parties of the Left in Western Europe, these must begin to prepare an alternative for the defence of Europe which would permit this part of the world some measure of security and autonomy.

— European security and the political equilibrium require a stable economic order which avoids the diversion into smaller economic blocks prompted by protectionism. For this to happen forms of dependence on the centre must gradually disappear, the unfavourable trade terms for the Third World must be corrected and the division of world labour must not be frozen to the advantage of those countries which first attained industrialisation.

— In very concrete terms, the ESCC must be a success. Its failure would mean the public acceptance that the period of détente begun in Helsinki in 1975 had finally lapsed. The resulting dynamic of confrontation would be difficult to halt. The ensuing phase would probably end with a deal between the superpowers from positions of renewed strength, having sacrificed the local and regional interests of others. The division into two systems which are both in critical phases — late, declining capitalism and bureaucratic, authoritarian socialism — would not permit the synthesis which, beginning in Europe, the world is waiting for.

— It is true, and so it should be proclaimed, that détente is indivisible. But it is clearly unrealistic — when not an excuse — to expect that détente will appear simultaneously everywhere under the same form. Each process of détente must be taken advantage of to convert it into an element of the general détente.

Alva Myrdal, former Minister of Disarmament in Sweden, is the author of The Game of Disarmament, *described by Willy Brandt as "one of the most impressive books I have ever read about the huge problems of the worldwide arms race".*

Dynamics of European Nuclear Disarmament

Alva Myrdal

1982 will be a year of great challenges for disarmament. Several international bodies are to meet, where crossroads will be marked and ominous decisions taken. These are going to be of great importance for the whole spectrum of disarmament issues; but many are of special, indeed crucial, concern to the hopes for freedom from nuclear armaments in Europe.

The United Nations is to hold its Second Special Session for Disarmament in June 1982 and several weighty reports are now being prepared for that occasion. The Independent Commission on International Disarmament and Security (the so-called Palme Commission) has promised to present its findings in time for it. A European Conference on Disarmament is also slated to begin a first session in 1982, as recommended in several proposals at the Madrid meeting on European Security and Co-operation — or, in case agreement fails, perhaps to be organised independently without the superpowers. And for the nations of Europe, 1982 represents the year of grace before the guillotine (as to the deployment on their soil of foreign so-called euro-strategic missiles) falls in 1983. The mutual superpower negotiations, which are to be the second half of the "double track" promise by the US to NATO, must be brought about immediately.

The fateful decisions and positions to be taken are the responsibility of the chosen delegates, speaking for their respective governments. But we must all be prepared.

Public opinion has to be aroused so that it can in turn press those responsible for political decisions to stop the arms race — before it is too late. The *leaders* must by pressure from the *people* be brought to start to act, wisely and promptly, so as truly to *lead us* forward to arms control, disarmament, and peace.

The most urgent task now is to get the message across to the superpowers that they have no right to fight out their mutual hostilities and confrontations in the form of a "European war". The countries of Europe are not each others' enemies. Their peoples do not want to be used as hostages in the superpowers' gaming with each other.

Extraordinarily strong movements of public opinion are at this juncture of history astir in Europe, most immediately directed to free our part of the world from the fear of atomic weapons. My message in this essay is intended to support this awakening by strengthening the arguments it needs in reaching out. I not only admire but am also in more or less constant touch with these manifold popular movements as well as scientific pursuits. Their contributions will be heralded in my concluding section.

The fact that I am publishing this essay within the framework of END — the campaign for European Nuclear Disarmament — is partly due to the incidental circumstance that they happened to be first to ask me, but partly also because they have become a forum for the most vigorous current *debate* where the force of various arguments can be tried out. And despite all the fervour with which we have to work for that immediate goal of freeing Europe from nuclear weapons, we must never shun the duty to weigh rationally all arguments and proposals presented, in order to find out which are the best founded in reason and the most promising in practice.

This is an invitation to discuss — and then to act — with urgency.

I. Europe must speak up for itself

All right-minded people in the world are crying out with alarm for peace and all crave some steps towards disarmament. But we are well aware that it is the superpowers' arms race that bedevils the fate of our planet, potentially so rich and beautiful if we co-operate, but now, instead, politically split and economically plundered. For the illusory goal of securing an invincible stronghold over the "other side" they don't hesitate to sacrifice enormous resources that ought to be devoted to development but are instead, wasted on amassing weapons — nuclear, biological, chemical — with the power of ultimate destruction and death.

Every thinking person in Europe also knows that our countries are the prime hostages when the superpowers compete with each other to become Number One. The ceaseless arms race between them, now leaping to new technological heights, may — or may not — lead to major war. But in the way preparations for it are going on, particularly in regard to nuclear weaponry, the risks for Europe are becoming imminent.

The essay I wish to present will be an attempt to analyse as clearly and coherently as I can what I perceive to be the central issues in regard to European nuclear disarmament, focusing mainly on the problems of the smaller nations and their opportunities to take independent initiatives. In order to be pedagogical I have preferred to proceed in a rather pedantical fashion, especially so in the later, substantive sections. This might entail the risk of some repetitions, but better so than leaving loopholes.

Europe is not war prone

But let me as an introduction make some more general comments. The governing value premise for this essay, shared by a both extensively and intensively growing determination on the part of the peoples of Europe[1] is that we do not accept that we should be sacrificed in the superpowers' gaming with each other for political-military hegemony. Their bipolar struggle for an ultimate victory — the dream of one crushing the other — should not be allowed to be cloaked in any protective camouflage as being a "European interest". Their more than thirty years of posturing of mutual enmity is not of Europe's making. Any so-called "European war" would not be of European origin — this time. The "protection" the superpowers offer their allies does, in reality, only forebode death and destruction for them, and perhaps for neutral countries as well. Even an Adenauer pronounced early in his reign that a new war in Europe meant again the devastation of Europe. Other prominent political personalities have been led by sheer logic to the same conclusion. It is, however, only revealed in rare moments of candour.

I want to underline the fact that a "European war" would not be of European origin. This is not meant as a denial that tensions on political grounds and even ideological conflicts exist between countries of Europe. But that situation does not *per se,* without any extra-European prompting, call for military solutions. It would rather lead to intensifying the quest for peaceful ones, for more exchanges, more co-operation.

Persisting below the fissiparous tendencies there lives on, in Europe, a bond, grown out of a living recognition of a shared historical heritage. The European countries ought, after all their traumatic experiences, be able to work out their own future, based on partnerships of various kinds. If left to their own developments and devices — as is testified above all by what in the West is called the Ost-Politik — they would not mobilise for mutual hostility. They would not independently cause an intra-European war.

Superpowers fight each other in Europe

This is *one* fact. But there is a second one. Above the indigenous forces working for co-operation, mostly economically and culturally determined, there has been created a new superfact: Europe has become, politically and militarily, divided down the middle into two blocs of competing alliances. They are of superpower creation, demanding allegiance from so many countries to either the Soviet Union, or the United States of America, respectively. This is an artificial schism, because the European countries do not have any inherently *deeper* affinity with either of the two superpowers of today. They do not really want to be tied so closely to them, as has now become the fact which dominates our part of the world.

And worse: an additional and irrefutable truth is that Europe has without its own volition been chosen, by a kind of mutual, albeit usually tacit, agreement between the two superpowers, to become the battlefield in a potential major war of their making. It is a battlefield now over-saturated with their military threats and war preparations. And — to be well remembered — Europe is not used as a stepping stone in a superpower struggle. Since Sputnik 1957, the two have been clearly capable of fighting each other over intercontinental distances.

Saving their own homelands

Doctrines, arsenals, propaganda is all geared to make this a self-fulfilling prophesy: that if it comes to war between the two world powers they will avoid fighting it as an intercontinental duel, but preferably make it into a "European war". In *clara verba*: Europe is to be sacrificed, the European industries and farmlands destroyed, the European peoples bleeding to death or doomed to perish in painful and mutilating disease. All this in order to *save the homelands of the two big and trigger-happy nations* from experiencing such fate as it meted out for the so much more innocent ones. This "sanctuary theory" is very rarely publicly recognised by the superpowers. It is an intellectual duty to point up the falsehoods that serve to make the European peoples their hostages.[2]

On the US side there exists an abundantly rich literature and documentation, official and/or academic, on strategic problems, fed by rather enormous research and publication endeavours. But one can rarely find even a hint that the European countries might have legitimate interests of an independent character. They are treated as "objects", and evidently rather irrelevant, "dumb" objects, of superpower policies. Those are, as if by blinkers, shielded off to concentrate on their egocentric concerns. As an example might be quoted a passage from one of the most recent and most prestigious American publications, referring to the decision in 1979 to upgrade Eurostrategic nuclear weapons.[3]

There is no reason to believe that on the Soviet side the attitude would be any less cynical towards the victims of the bipolar war-gaming, although the published evidence is habitually so much more scanty.

Some readers might query an apparent over-emphasis on the possibility that Europe might become the main theatre of war between the superpowers. All news media of today tell us that the most acute dangers of such crises which might lead to a military showdown between them and, at least, a conflagration involving them, have moved *southward,* from what is habitually spoken of as "the central front" to a South-West Asian one. The Persian Gulf area, with its accent on oil, the persistent Israel-Arab conflict, the revolutionary aftermath of the Shah's downfall in Iran, the embittered divisiveness of the Moslem countries, the battles on the flanks of this area — Iran-Iraq and Lebanon where violence is even now stained with veritable bloodshed — does all this not lift the onus of war risks away from Europe?

This contains a pertinent observation: the day-to-day focusing on the area of West Asia — too often loosely labelled with the geographical misnomer "the Middle East" — gives an illustration of how storm centres shift their location. But our gaze is then — adequately enough — fixed on political tensions and military build-ups. The superpowers' involvement there, is however, not indigenous but marginal, although it may at some moment become decisive. Still, I feel it right in the context of my particular subject to leave this whole problem area aside.

Hardly anything has, as yet, made it believable that feuds and battles in that region would be fought with *nuclear* weapons. Both lavish financing and quantitative as well as qualitative competition are concentrated on what still belongs to the category of "conventional" arsenals for war making. The imagination might play with the possibility that superpower nuclear weaponry might be used for blocking a passage over mountain ranges or even on a concentration of "enemy" naval forces. But it still seems unlikely. The retaliatory strike then to be expected functions as a classical deterrent.

But if the scenario against all odds were to be played out with the actual use of nuclear weapons, the next step in escalation would bring us back to my main topic: the probability that a major superpower confrontation will take place elsewhere. This constitutes a good example of the general thesis of how the threats involved in a local conflict might be "transported" to a war risk in Europe, on its soil or in the ocean, wherever the two chose their major front.

There exists, on the other hand, a pronounced and accelerating risk that the dangers of nuclear warfare might be moving northward. We are most keenly aware of such an incipient, gradual but growing, change in the scenarios of the superpowers, with their increasing submarine activities in the North Atlantic ocean. It goes without saying that the effect this will have will not be very lenient to Europe.

For any ultimate duel between the superpowers: the most immense preparations point in no other direction than that scenarios are being envisaged for a battle over Europe. Besides the military preparedness the political motivation is also compelling: to save their own homelands from bearing the brunt of the sacrifices in destruction and death.

Thus, alas, for the foreseeable future it probably holds true that the major threat which nuclear weapons raise to the heritage of civilisation and to the greatest number masses of human beings is the amassing of weapons for *nuclear warfare in Europe*. And that is my subject.

Europe chooses nuclear disarmament

It is high time that the superpowers should begin to hear from the intended victims. Our reactions should not continue to be neglected. A more propitious time could not be chosen than the present one when one superpower, the USA, again hints at imposing a decision to deploy the abominable neutron bombs on European territory; evidently without apprehension that its counterpart on the other side would immediately follow suit. The West German and the East German territories would be most directly earmarked to be hit by ill-effects covering square kilometres around each burst. There are civilians by the million living and working in this densely populated heartland of Europe.

The *people* must be our concern — whatever their leaders are apt to say! And END — European Nuclear Disarmament — is the presently most sharp-edged instrument for opening up a movement of protest among the peoples of Europe — in the hope of awakening also the consciences of the world leaders.

Alliances force acceptance of nuclear weapons = European destruction

The peace and protest movements, already more or less potently alive in several European countries, must — and so will this essay — centre on freedom just from *nuclear* weapons. Nearly all these nations have fully understood the counter-productiveness of acquiring *atomic weapons of their own,* as any such possession would only increase the dangers to their security. Wherever decisions have been taken to renounce nuclear weapons, it has been in a very clear understanding that the acquisition of such weapons would only augment the risk of drawing nuclear fire onto them unable, as the small nations are doomed to be, to respond in equal manner and measure.

The same self-illuminatory reasoning cannot be logically blocked in regard to the *stationing of foreign nuclear weapons* on their soil. The invitation to devastating blows is the same. The neutral nations in Europe have not only been aware of the fact that possession of nuclear weapons would be counter-productive but also through sovereign political decisions drawn the practical conclusion and demonstrated their reliance on the net benefit of keeping their countries absolutely free of atomic weapons, neither planning to acquire any, nor to accept any; be they offered as "aid" or "protection".

Facts are facts also in nations tied into alliances, however bent they may be upon acquiescence and silence. The dangers speak more loudly with every day that atomic weapons are ineffective for security. That it is nothing but "absolute nonsense" to believe that nuclear weapons can secure any victory has, with both pointed realism and moving eloquence,

been expressed recently by no less authorities than Earl
Mountbatten, Lord Philip-Baker and Lord Zuckerman in
speeches, assembled in *Apocalypse Now?* [4] Their statements
are irrefutable. *To spread this message is the mission that we
should now undertake.*

From overtures to operative proposals

The supreme principles to guide any programme for disarmament measures must, in order to be realistic, focus on the
following:

1. that negotiations should always *precede* decisions, not be
   offered as a kind of *post-facto* consolation gesture after a
   unilateral commitment has already been made;
2. that a process of *graduated* steps should be initiated, as
   all-or-nothing postures have proved illusory;
3. that proposals made should be measured to find out how
   they can best be made *equitable,* foreseeing that claims will
   be raised on some parity of sacrifice.

All these points are specifically valid for planning nuclear
disarmament. And they should in each individual case be
tailored so as to relate directly to the kind of military situations which are of interest to each of the superpowers. They
must as realistically as possible serve the aim of influencing
them to overcome the immobility of their strategic thinking
and ingrown attitudes. Let me use this introductory section to
spell out in somewhat general terms some of the implications
inherent in the first principle stated above — the second and
third being treated in a more specific manner in the topical
sections to follow.

Leaving strategic nuclear systems aside

What are then, the subjects to negotiate and, possibly, decide
upon in regard to atomic weapons in Europe? The limitation
made to *European* disarmament must mean that the major
strategic systems, directly pertaining to what is perceived as
superpower mutual defence needs, must be left outside our
present concern. This would exclude our dealing here with
the ICBMs (Intercontinental Ballistic Missiles) submarines
with SLBMs (Sea-Launched Ballistic Missiles) and SLCMs
(Sea-Launched Cruise Missiles), their surface fleets,
helicopter and aircraft carriers as well as bombers and

airplanes of many descriptions with long-range capabilities, also with the related electronic and other surveillance systems and all conceivable appurtenances, insofar as and on the condition that all these are deployed *outside* the territories, territorial waters and air-space of European, i.e. non-superpower nations. Britain and France are, of course, included as per definition, but their special cases of being nuclear weapon powers, although in a minor league, will be dealt with separately towards the end.

The exclusion of strategic weaponry manifestly intended for war fighting between the superpowers themselves, is not only motivated by the desire to make the subject matter of this essay manageable and therefore concentrated on armouries intended for Europe. There is also lurking behind this selectivity what may be sensed as an ethical imperative: that nations interested in warfare ought to fight it out directly between themselves, exposing themselves to the dangers accompanying their propensity to use violence for settling conflicts. The Vikings sometimes made such rules: one of their chosen leaders was belted together with one of the enemy, to let the knifing between the two decide the outcome. Weapons are different now. But the ethical rule of not allowing the powerful to protect themselves and let the powerless suffer all the agony is still alive in the mind of many men.

Our intra-European discussion has to take charge of the subject field lying between what on one hand must be consigned to the superpowers' mutual and global affairs, partly treated in the agreements of SALT I (expired) and SALT II (non-completed), and on the other hand what relates specifically to the conventional armaments and national security of sovereign European States. That is: for nuclear weapon freedom in Europe as a whole.

Self-propelled initiatives for gradual progress

The main questions to be raised are the interrelated ones as to what *concepts* and what *structures* should be valid for Europe as a nuclear security zone, and what *process* should be utilised for achieving it. Should we be content with a loose conglomeration of nuclear weapon free States or should the aim from the beginning be one (or more) nuclear weapon free zone(s), formally established and treaty bound? Or, in other words, should we rely on a process of gradual growth, practically spontaneous, or should we draw up blueprints for a pre-planned, comprehensively structured set of agreements, topped by a multilateral convention?

The latter has been the alternative chosen for the one and only forerunner, the Tlatelolco Treaty for the prohibition of nuclear weapons in Latin America. I am personally apprehensive that many who now participate in the presently so lively debate on "nuclear free zones" are taken in by and relying too much on that specific model. It must be remembered that in that case it was able to start from scratch, there never having existed any nuclear weapons in Latin America while Europe is overfull of them!

Our over-reaching concern must be to establish a Europe, totally and lastingly free from nuclear weapons of all kinds and all provenances. We must then have a realistic appreciation of how far from the goal we are at the start. Both superpowers not only dominate the scene with enormous arsenals already deployed, but are committed to proceed with more and more irreversible decisions on new nuclear weapons systems, to be deployed in and at least targetable on European nations. They are pointed at our cities, and more or less crucial civilian installations. Even if they were only to be aimed at militarily important targets we must be aware of their unavoidable overspill on civilian victims. What they hit can never be very narrowly circumscribed, as even if it lies right within the area of the "probable error" there are *human beings* living. And more wide ranging misses do occur!

To disperse the uncertainties hovering over Europe's destinies through strategies of superpower making, I have found it necessary to try to analyse the possibilities for *self-propelled initiatives* by our nations. Our potential activities should then be viewed in regard to three different levels; let me briefly call them the unilateral, the bilateral and the multilateral ones. Of course, attention must all the time be paid to how politically varying openings to introduce action are for individual nations and, in consequence, also with rather strikingly different chances of early success. But making more dynamic efforts to set in motion the many opportunities that do exist for taking initiatives, considerable hope should be engendered that we can win and, at least, publicly vindicate our right to a nuclear weapon free Europe.

II. "To each nation the burden thereof": The freedom to take unilateral decisions

Perhaps it is necessary to underscore once more that this essay is intentionally leaving aside how the two superpowers should keep each other at bay. It is solely preoccupied with the issue that they should not drag Europe into their own mutually suicidal political-military gaming.

The freedom unilaterally to decide to abstain from producing nuclear weapons has been utilised by all European nations, except France and Great Britain. These are the only two possessing nuclear weapons by their own free will and independent decisions, thus constituting a category all to itself. They must necessarily be judged to lie furthest away from the goal of obtaining liberation from foreign nuclear weapons as well, for so long as both — or even only one of them — refuse to give up their own. In exchange they would earn the right to expect pledges of non-attack with such weapons.

All other European countries, except Albania, have solemnly underwritten the intention to forego any option of producing or otherwise acquiring nuclear weapons of their own. They have done so not just by declarations but by adhering to the internationally binding instruments of law, namely both to the Limited Test Ban Treaty (LTBT) of 1963 and the Non-Proliferation Treaty (NPT) of 1970.[5]

According to these treaties the voluntary renunciation of the nuclear weapons option by practically all European States was to be matched by Britain, the Soviet Union and the United States undertaking to proceed towards disarmament. Nearly 20 years ago they promised literally "to achieve the discontinuance of all test explosions of nuclear weapons for all time, determined to continue negotiations to this end" (LTBT) and in the famous article VI (NPT) they undertook "to pursue negotiations in good faith on effective easures relating to cessation of the nuclear arms race at an early date and to nuclear disarmament". While "effective measures" have as we all know — and they know — been technically available all the time, the political pledges to apply to them, still continue to be blatantly violated by the Soviet Union, the UK and the US — France never having promised to stop their arms race or even to negotiate.

Well, there is where we stand, in a terrifying unbalanced situation between the haves and the have-nots.

The ups and downs of protests in Europe

What has been the interplay between these two groups of nations and how should we evaluate the forces that can be brought to bear? We, the have nots, must realise that the only instrument of power which we can mobilise is *public opinion pressure on our leaders* and, through them, on the haves. The history of how *we* have used that power in order to restrain them is sometimes uplifting, sometimes depressing, while *they* have assiduously moved strength to super strength.

Nuclear weapons were introduced in Europe partly by British and French efforts to build up some independent arsenals, the first test explosions being heard in 1952 and 1960 respectively, but with the steps in that wrong direction of course having been taken much earlier. Their arsenals have remained rather insignificant in numbers in comparison with those of the superpowers but have nevertheless been of immense importance as symbolising, yes demonstrating a lack of ethical inhibitions — a dubious model for countries in other parts of the world.

But in Europe the more massive installation of nuclear weapons has been one of superpower making. It started with the introduction of such weapons through Eisenhower in 1954 and their rather solid acceptance for deployment by NATO in its crucial and at first hotly debated policy decision of 1957. That was the period when the opposition, yes fear within the European nations themselves was brought to a pitch. In our history the protest, inspired by scientists but with masses as followers, stands symbolised by the Einstein-Russell Manifesto of 1955 and the Aldermaston March in London 1960. The movement then subsided — and we must ask: Why?

The mass revolt against nuclear weapons — "ban the bomb" — did, however, set off some victories in several nations which definitely forswore nuclear weapons. Foremost among them were the neutrals who rejected both, possession of any of their own weapons or the stockpiling of foreign ones. This partial victory found its formal confirmation in the acceptance by the have-nots parties of the NPT and from 1968, not then — or later — matched by any contribution from the haves.

Why then the curious lull in audible opposition during the 'sixties and 'seventies? Public opinion in Europe apparently bowed to superpower interests and intimidations. Without more than a few murmurs of protest those powers have been able to place — as the world is now wont to hear repeated *ad nauseam* — some 10-15,000 atomic weapons in Europe, roughly divided between the USA and the USSR on a 3/5 and 2/5 basis. These have been classified as tactical, meaning theatre, weapons, ostensibly intended for and acquiesced in as belonging to a prospective European battlefield. Despite the magnitude and the somewhat different profiles of these nuclear arsenals, with American superiority in numbers and sophistication of the atomic weapons and their supporting systems, while there has been the Russian superiority in throw-weight and in the early extension of ranges to include some medium range missiles, besides the more anonymous emplacement on Soviet controlled territory. For a long time those weapons were obviously viewed by the two alliances with convenient equanimity. Probably they counted them as assuring some kind of parity and thus security through deterrence.

No hue and cry against them has been sustained in Europe with any continuity or consistency. Evidently, not much of a worry was caused by the step-wise but steep increase in their power of destruction, although the potential danger of devastation beamed at Europe had been a prominent argument in the verbal battle just before and after the main NATO decision of 1957.[6]

Against the neutron bomb

But we should know that it can pay to protest. A new wave of vociferous opposition rolled over Europe when plans became known to deploy the Enhanced Radiation Weapon — the neutron bomb — in Europe with its preference for murdering people rather than destroying armour. Its "effectiveness" to kill or at least immobilise soldiers was featured as a great plus, the number of civilians inevitably hit in the surroundings never being accounted for.

Certain facts were, however, learned by the peoples in Europe; although not willingly spread by the US military: that even a one kiloton neutron war-head would destroy all buildings and kill all people within a radius of 150 metres; that in addition to these effects, caused by a blast wave and light radiation, there would within a radius of 1,400 metres follow radiation sickness, in many cases resulting in instant death and in more with a lingering effect but fatal outcome. Within a much larger area it would entail a risk of persisting damage to its human inhabitants. The victims were to be, not material properties, but in this case, living human beings, and by far the majority would be ordinary people, civilians. The real different from other nuclear weapons is that the energy release is much slower, there being no widespread fall-out but the nuclear reactions going on, submitting people to an awful risk of a long drawnout, often terribly painful death. We, the inhabitants of European nations experienced already then in 1977 a revulsion of extraordinary poignancy.

Those who knew how to weigh and are ready honestly to report on the military effectiveness of this geographically selective but not humanely discriminating atomic killer have in some cases cooled off the belief in one side's chance of gaining advantages by just creating lethal gaps in the enemy's ranks. Helmut Schmidt, the West German Chancellor who so aptly switches between telling revealing truths and comforting half truths, recently used his most measured manner to warn other political, and not least military, leaders; as he replied to an interviewer:

"I regard as highly doubtful the opinion expressed by some Western military men and specialists, that the neutron weapon places only the defending side at an advantage and harms the aggressor."

On the previous occasion when the neutron bomb was bandied about, a forceful movement of public concern arose for European liberation from that new scourge. It was, it must be doubly underscored, a genuine revulsion and moral condemnation, not any protest engineered just on Soviet orders, as far too many ignorant people have been led to believe, particularly in America, where the mass-media have taken that purely anti-Soviet line. Was it government-inspired propaganda? Or was it that the eager Russian counter-propaganda against the bomb obtained just so much easier access to the mass-media than all the anxious European voices who spoke so loudly in their own interests?

On this occasion victory was won! By public protest abroad but also at home, President Carter was moved to cancel the plans for deployment. The power of the silent majority, when it turns out to be not so silent, was thus demonstrated — just as had been the case when his presidential predecessors had been forced to quit Vietnam because their own people no longer wanted to stand for the inhumanity of war.

The missile encirclement

In hindsight also other amazing facts become visible as to the tolerance shown in regard to some changes in military postures while other changes are able to vitalise indignation. For about two decades very little public attention was drawn to the Soviet introduction of a new generation of "improved" medium range ballistic missiles, the SS-4 and particularly the SS-5 (1959-1961) with megaton bombs and a new extensive range (2,000-3,700 kilometres) reaching over practically the entire territory of Europe. Initially, no more uproar was caused by the deployment a few years ago (from 1977 at least) of the greatly improved intermediate range missile (SS-20) with a target radius above 4,000 kilometres, precision-guided with a much smaller circular error probability (CEP) and in addition "MIRVed" with several independently targetable bombs.

It seems astonishing that neither the European countries in general nor even NATO kept a vigilant watch over this development. *It was not publicised*. Negotiations were not demanded at the early juncture when they would have been most timely. NATO would then have been in an excellent bargaining position. Instead it dallied for years until at the end of 1979 the US sprang upon its allies — and the Soviet Union — a full fledged decision, or rather command, to deploy a new generation of its nuclear weapons in Europe. The story looks even more enigmatic because of the turning down of Brezhnev's offer of negotiations — belatedly as it undeniably came (October 6, 1979) — but practically signalling an S.O.S., or at least a nervous hope to rescue détente.

We should have read the factual developments much earlier as signs of a need for negotiations to stop the spiralling of the arms race to new heights. Our error was one of negligence, not correctly assessing how that spiral was being screwed ever higher, while we were led to believe the situation was fairly safely under control in a kind of "parity" pattern. So we stood aside from demanding urgent negotiations on European "tactical" nuclear weapons, even if we were willing to let those concerning conventional forces (MBFR) proceed at their lazy pace year in and year out in Vienna. There was, to be sure, frequent mention made in the Geneva Disarmament Committee of the dangerous so-called "grey area" weapons but without any concretisation and without any following up within the European countries so directly concerned. This is *our* sin, not having unequivocally requested a SALT III set of negotiations long ago.

Their sin, the superpowers' avoidance of negotiations or even clarifications when the "grey", or now more expressly named "Eurostrategic", weapons were closing in on us, may be partly explained but not excused by their being preoccupied with SALT I and II, concerning their own major strategic weapons. The neglect is symbolised by the fact that in the course of SALT negotiations a prohibition to use cruise missiles with a range *above* 600km was debated. (ALCM = Air Launched Cruise Missiles) while of course missiles of lesser range can still constitute threats to European countries. Now, finally, in the 1980s the questions are beginning to revolve around all kind of missiles, many already on location and more in expectancy, with much longer striking ranges. And this time the surprising, yes shocking, new developments are coming from the West, specifically from the United States.

Thus Europe will be practically completely encircled by missile threats from all sides, both East and West.

Different nations, different freedom of action

There is always a greater chance to arouse public opinion when a new situation is just opening up. An opportunity of historical importance, hence not to be missed, has occurred as the period 1980-83 can be utilised for forestalling at least the *addition* of a new generation of so-called Eurostrategic

225

Figure 1. Target coverage of proposed NATO theatre nuclear weapons and the Soviet SS-5[a] and SS-20[b]

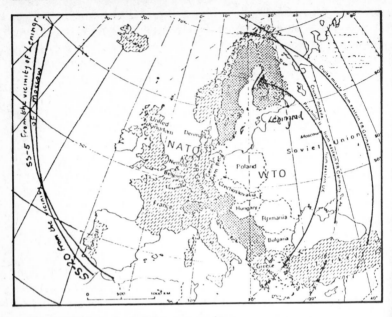

a. The SS-5 is included for comparison.
b. Deployed closer to the Polish border, for example, the SS-20 would have a considerable greater coverage than indicated. And if the range of the SS-20 is 5000km, as has been suggested, then it could be deployed well east of the Urals and still remain within reach of London.
c. The half-circle related to the range of Pershing II from a location in FR Germany should be completed so as to show coverage of large parts of Finland, Sweden and Norway. (Note by the author).

Source: From 1981 SIPRI Yearbook on World Armaments and Disarmament.

nuclear weapons.[7]

The challenge is at present being anxiously ventilated even within the few countries who have abided by the NATO decision of December 1979 and given permission to deployment of the new nuclear weapons, euphemistically referred to as "modernised" — Great Britain, Italy and West Germany, while Holland and Belgium still show some reluctance. The question is whether all or even one of these five will win political and popular support for a declaration that they do not wish to welcome such dangerous visitors. It would mean joining the greater number of countries, in the first case the non-aligned ones, who want to remain nuclear weapon free in the strictest senses and have taken unilateral decisions to that effect.

There are, if you take a closer look three categories of nations, all with their different dilemmas as well as challenging tasks. Let me briefly sign them on as the neutral, the Western allied and the Eastern allied.

The most considerable difference has to be recognised as between nations who have erected a stone wall against being drawn into the gaming net of the 'haves', and those who have not so insured themselves. The benefits of belonging to the 'have-nots' have been convincingly demonstrated by some of the major non-aligned countries who have opted for water-tight nuclear weapon free status and whose examples might be cited. One is my own country, Sweden, which in 1946, upon entering the United Nations as a member, formally declared its policy to be "non-aligned in peacetime aiming to remain neutral in case of war".

Being well advanced in industrialisation these countries have long had technological as well as financial capacity for developing nuclear weapons, if they wanted to, as they all have in operation reactors for producing nuclear energy. But they have also entered commitments against any misuse of them, their know-how and their products (chiefly plutonium), by voluntarily subscribing to the IAEA system of safeguards and accepting inspections, thus stilling any suspicions from the international community.

Among them Sweden and Yugoslavia ought to be the first to meet the test and to lead the movement for a nuclear weapon free Europe as they have for so long been vigorously outspoken members of the Geneva Disarmament Committee. There they cannot only speak in favour of European nuclear disarmament but submit specific action proposals, thus challenging their great power co-delegates in a forum that is given ample time and resources for deliberations that could enter upon near-new negotiations. Also Austria and Switzerland should be expected to become more active members of the opinion building movement and to forward concrete proposals, this on account of their neutrality, internationally so firmly recognised and respected. In this pioneer company I reckon Finland as it never tires of asserting its neutrality, inscribed in its adherence to the Finnish-Soviet Friendship and Assistance Agreement (of 1948). To reinforce the work for nuclear disarmament President Kekkonen has given his name to a far-sighted plan for a nuclear weapon free zone encompassing the Nordic countries. Also lesser nations like Malta and some others might aspire to be members of that league of double freedom: non-aligned and nuclear weapon free.

Their ranks may be widened, even from those European countries whose nuclear weapon free status is now compromised by allowing *foreign* atomic weapons and associated installations within their sovereign precincts. One cannot but sense that, deeper down, they entertain a certain envy towards the examples of those others who have doubly insured their independence by remaining both neutral and nuclear weapon free.

The conclusion in terms of recommendations for practical policy is self-evident: this is the time for all European countries who have hitherto not done so to utilise as far as possible the opportunity to take a unilateral decision at least not to accept any *further* addition of nuclear weapons. It *can* be done unilaterally.

It is no easy matter, however, to vindicate a freedom from nuclear arms for countries who have already let some such weapons into their abode. While following the letter of the law of not themselves possessing nuclear weapons, they have become fettered by allowing foreign powers, i.e. the two superpowers, to place nuclear weapons on their soverign territories, yet *under the key and command of the superpowers*. For these nations, tied to the two alliances, it would of course be a tremendous task just to persuade public opinion to forego even *future* additions of atomic weapons. But that must be a first signal, rightly calling only for a unilateral determination of the national will. For this reason the END campaign is so timely and so urgent.

The presently stirring protest does, it must be acknowledged, have the utmost direct address to members of the NATO alliance. Not to break the bonds of the alliance but to free themselves from becoming any part of nuclear war making.

Some readers may have wondered and bemoaned the fact that so little mention is made in the text of the situation in regard to nuclear weapons in East European States. The answer is not only the oft repeated acknowledgement of the regrettable fact that the outside world knows so much less about these countries than about the countries in Western Europe, and that the documentation from the Soviet Union is kept in a state of starvation in comparison with that in the United States where the risk is rather of overfeeding. But from what can be surmised there are probably no nuclear war-heads stockpiled in Eastern European countries; even the silos as well as the missile launching pads are apparently kept inside the Soviet Union. In any case, the freedom to take unilateral action to win freedom from nuclear weapons is not only politically but probably also practically non-existent in the Warsaw Pact countries.

Negotiate before commitments are locked

Immediate attention must now be given to the principle, referred to in the introduction, of negotiating before decisions — at least further decisions — are taken, lest it becomes too late. This must imply both decisions, declarations and, if necessary, negotiations as between allies and mutually between the alliance leaders. And it should hopefully be accomplished well in time before 1983 with regard to the new Eurostrategic weapons on the NATO side, as they are still only in the offing.

In hindsight, it seems astonishing that no attempts to negotiate restrictions on the medium- long-range missiles were made when, or even before, the Soviet Union started to deploy their SS-20 system; this was clearly afoot at least in 1977 and was probably known to military experts well in advance. Mutual negotiations might then have been winnable, if the US had offered its "bargaining chips" not to introduce a new generation of missiles. Instead it waited lamely and then rather abruptly pressed for them in the so-called NATO decision of December 1979. The surprise was so unpleasant to the NATO allies that they forced on the superpowers an agreement that they should start negotiations about missile *reduction* simultaneously with the missile *build-up,* the so-called "double track" procedure.

The pattern of missed opportunities to forestall tragic commitments had once more been followed, as exemplified also in the Soviet move to invade Afghanistan a few days later in that same December, instead of first proposing multilateral negotiations to achieve non-intervention in that unhappy country's internal affairs. *Negotiate first must mean negotiate in time.* This is just now urgently on the agenda for all interested in saving European nuclear disarmament.

Negotiations are now becoming facilitated, probably contrary to the intentions of the superpowers, because the whereabouts of existing and planned nuclear weapon installations are in the main becoming public knowledge. At least on the NATO side they are just now being exposed by mass-media. Maps with pin-pointed locations have been published e.g. in West Germany by *Die Stern,* and in Great Britain by the *New Statesman* (this latter is reproduced, together with a Soviet map, in Robert Neild, *How to Make Up Your Mind About The Bomb,* Andre Deutsch, 1981. The centres for launching pads and/or depots of the murderous weapons themselves have thus become verifiable, at least in peacetime.

And ordinary men and women then feel so much more keenly that the disaster-carrying gifts creep closer and closer up into their lives.

The case is not quite similar for those nuclear weapons which belong to and are probably next to exclusively deployed within the Soviet Union; its secrets being better guarded. However, technology moves forward over the whole world. Verification of the numbers, specifications and even the whereabouts of these mass-murder time-bombs raises no longer any unsurmountable difficulties. The facts are being exposed more and more fully. Subterfuges are so easily seen through by those with technical expertise and certainly by military "intelligence", even in smaller countries. For instance, the Swedish mass-media have just begun such information campaigns about the nuclear arsenals on both sides.

I hope the spread of such knowledge does not constitute exceptions, but that it will be effectively reaching all countries, so people everywhere know what lies in store for them. Also the superpowers themselves should soon recognise the value of openness. Anyway, the new publicity must serve to push the impatiently expected negotiations ahead.

Or European Participation in a New Strategy of Madness?
The newness of the situation cannot be strongly enough emphasised. It makes a special call to urgent action.

The fact — that is: the practically complete missile encirclement of Europe — should not tempt anybody to believe that what is being reached would be of better value as better "balance". That term is always a misnomer when used in regard to military postures and geopolitical realities. "Balance" of different elements can never be achieved; the weights never come out even. (The arguments are, I believe, convincingly analyzed in my book *The Game of Disarmament).* Instead it should be highlighted that more and more frightening potentialities are now rapidly building up for attacks that may hit European countries from both West and East — more or less likely for individual nations during varying phases dependent on how war operations would come to be played out. (See Fig.1).

The arch within which the Soviet Union can strike all countries — most importantly with its SS-20 missiles — will after 1983 be matched by US missiles reaching much farther out than hitherto, e.g. over a larger part of Finland as well as Sweden and several other neutral countries, not just over their "enemy allies". It means that the European countries will be more dangerously squeezed by threats from both superpower sides to suffer attack as part of any war between them. The net result of the impending changes is certainly not to our benefit. And neither is it, when realistically evaluated, called for by any danger we pose to their security.

The new situation can by no stretch of the imagination be weighed as a better balance but — on closer analysis — is seen definitely as a worse imbalance. Some readers may argue, and it is true, that we have long since learned to live in the shadow, as hostages to the two superpowers' mutual enmity. The most direct threat of being targeted has during the last twenty years originated from Soviet missiles, the SS-4 and 5, as forerunners to the SS-20s and as first in the field of weapons of Eurostrategic range. But they must all that time have been understood as threatening Western European countries not for their own sake but in their role as proxies for the Soviet Union's one and only meaningful adversary, the United States. When from that side there are deployed longer-medium range missiles with atomic war-heads, an additional risk arises for their European sites to become targets of attacks, even quite possibly pre-emptive strikes. This risk is coming to loom much larger in our consciousness. The calamity involved in some very much more probable surgical operations against well appointed localities in Britain and West Germany is rightly being experienced with a much more realistic fear than ever before. And what have the European countries done to deserve such a fate?

Still, an even more dramatically new situation is now created by the West's, i.e. the U.S. decision to acquire the capability to strike quite far *inside the Soviet Union,* from *European soil.* Are the parliaments — and the people — in Western Europe really and consciously willing to partake in such a new strategy; to forward the possibility of making one superpower the target of a direct onslaught while the other one is not? It is to be wondered if the countries in the NATO alliance will premeditatedly co-operate with this offensive princple. Here is a fundamentally new element in the game, as the Soviet Union has no comparable capacity to strike at targets within the United States territory — without making recourse to the major strategic arsenal, the "triad" of intercontinental capabilities (ICBM, SLBMs and strategic bomber aircraft).

A new lack of parity is thus introduced between the two. But, of course, their own forces in the strategic category ought to give assurance enough to the superpower combatants that they are not defenceless against each other, without using Europe as an obedient servant. So far their second strike capabilities have been — and are still — more than enough. If this situation is going to be transformed into a race for first-strike capabilities, it should not be expected to occur with the consent and co-operation of Europe.

Simultaneously with the ominous developments in NATO in 1979, an additional step towards maddening the scenarios of the future has been taken. The Carter administration in 1980, through the so-called Directive 59, demonstratively confirmed the long held suspicion that the main target which had been ostensibly held to be on population centres in enemy lands, was in reality strategically important military centres in the Soviet Union. As the previous scenario officially proffered the MAD strategy, relying on the second-strike capability, constituted a true "balance of terror", that is to say, a murderous threat towards civilians, we cannot, of course, wish it re-instated. The only humane and at the same time, rational, solution is to get rid of nuclear weapons altogether, at least in our part of the world.

In the present debate on policies for European nuclear disarmament the arguments which ought to stem from this new situation of non-parity in the scenarios for use of Eurostrategic nuclear weapons have so far gone rather unnoticed. But now their logical weight is at its most pressing. Now it is urgently necessary to protest sharply so as to demonstrate unmistakenly that European countries can hardly be counted upon as sharing the responsibility for any new facet of superpower war fighting.

If the reality were correctly perceived — that is: that the real aim of the superpowers is to crush each other — we would all understand that for any "superpower duel" between them there is no need to involve Europe.

Some argue that the US will be less able to "defend and protect" Europe if it has no nuclear weapons stationed there. But surely, US capability does not depend on land deployment of its missiles! Those which are sea-launchable from submarines are so much more invulnerable. They assure a capacity to strike even inside Soviet territory. Add the air-launchable and cruise missiles and the "US " defence of our region can certainly remain sufficiently secure.

The conclusion must be that the European countries have every interest and right to opt out of the superpowers' nuclear war preparations. But what are the chances? What replies can be expected from the superpowers? This, of course, moves the whole process into a bilateral phase, which is the one to be dealt with in the following section.

Europe must be viewed as a whole. Not only those nations in Europe which persistently follow the policies of being nuclear weapon free but all our nations would certainly, if left to their own wishes, be interested in benefiting from the freedom from nuclear weapons. Even those who, as members of military alliances acquiesce in permitting deployment of foreign atomic weapons, must be aware that they are thereby vastly increasing their own risks of being attacked, and destroyed. In the present period of ascending protest, they begin to realise that they merely serve as pawns in a super-power contest.

In conclusion I must be allowed to stress that the outcome of decisions in regard to placement and use of nuclear weapons is a matter of greatest concern, not only to the countries just now in the grip of upsetting debates and probably painful negotiations, but to all of us, as neighbours, as fellow-Europeans. We wait with bated breath.

III. The dual aspect

The pledges of abstaining from attacks with nuclear weapons
Singularly little attention has been given to the new prompters that the nuclear weapon powers have recently offered to the cause of European nuclear disarmament. They have finally come forward with carrots, where they used to treat the nuclear have-nots only with sticks, and no nation in Europe has, as yet, grasped the new opportunity!

I am referring to the pledges of non-attack, the so-called "negative guarantees" which the nuclear weapon powers have delivered after long prodding, now delivered in one form or another by all five of them. A most remarkable breakthrough was taking place at the UN Special Session on Disarmament in 1978. There two Western nations, Britain and USA, were offering far-reaching promises, as also the Soviet pledge was expressed more authoritatively than ever before; China having done it alone since entering the atom club in 1964. Why has not this event been widely publicised? It is in fact an extraordinary victory for our strivings. Who has had an interest in concealing it? As a matter of fact, the texts are hard to come by, not having been collected and published in juxtaposition, not even in SIPRI Yearbooks of 1979 or 1980 or in the UN Yearbook on disarmament.[8]

Further, to convince us that the nuclearly disarmed countries are free to interpret the promises of non-attack as a definite guarantee to them, the Soviet Union has been even more solicitous and reiterated its statement several times. Its conditions are also the most lenient, as the only requirement

234

besides our own nuclear disarmament is that we do not have any atomic weapons *on our territories.*

President Brezhnev, in his important speech on 6 October 1979, when the new NATO deployment was in the offing stated:

"I want to confirm solemnly that the Soviet union will never use nuclear weapons against those States who desist from producing and acquiring such weapons and do not have such weapons on their territory".

It is important to note that neither in these nor in more recent statements has there been any restriction to formal agreements, bilateral or otherwise.

Otherwise undertakings by the three last mentioned weapon powers remain somewhat hedged and inadequate. But they are nevertheless an indication that all nuclear weapon powers are at least becoming conscious of the need to meet the anxieties of all those States who have not followed their example of menace with weapons of mass murder.

The favourable situation now created by the conflux of events must be exploited by us, the potential beneficiaries of the "guarantees". And I definitely hold that we should proceed on independent, country-to-country courses. This corresponds to the position taken by the movement for European Nuclear Disarmament. Read, for instance, the following excerpt from its pamphlet *No Cruise Missiles — No SS-20's:*

> "*It will be the responsibility of the people of each nation to agitate for the expulsion* of nuclear weapons and bases from European soil and territorial waters, and to decide upon its own means and strategy, concerning its own territory. *These will differ from one country to another, and we do not suggest that any single strategy should be imposed."* Op.cit., p.2

Proceeding stepwise with give and take
The tactics should now begin to sort themselves out. The most unproblematic situation ought first to be tested. The non-aligned countries must be the earliest candidates, as they can already now positively meet every condition set forth by each of the five nuclear weapon powers. This means immediately challenging nations in Northern and Central

Europe to act, Austria, Sweden and Switzerland as well as Finland and Yugoslavia. As having already taken their position they cannot bargain it away by raising claims on "parity of sacrifice", but are, of course, adamant in their desire to see the nuclear powers give up some of their overkill capacity or, really, eliminate all their nuclear weapons capable of hitting goals in Europe. They have gained the right to raise demands and challenge nuclear giants by having bound themselves to nuclear weapon free status, they have all signed and ratified both the LTBT and the NPT, and — to make doubly sure — they have also placed their nuclear industrial plants and all related activities under IAEA safeguards. From a political point of view the gains of a confirmation of "non attack" could right away be "cashed in" by one, two or more of these nations and would considerably raise the publicity value of the END campaign. (On the map, Figure 2, they are indicated by their grey tone). That would be a first, minimum achievement.

An early suggestion of mine, *(Tiden,* December 1977) has been that Sweden should, as a kind of test case, take the first step, almost immediately followed by Finland, since that country is in the foreground of every debate on nuclear weapon freedom because of its advocacy of the so-called Kekkonen Plan. The other major non-aligned countries in Central Europe should then be inspired to follow suit.

So far, no nation has committed itself. The action brief is, however, the simplest conceivable. It should be taken up independently by each nation. It should consist, not in the governments of such countries entering upon any formal agreement between themselves as a group, but as one-by-one approaches by each such nation to obtain undertakings as to non-attack by each one of its nuclear weapon counterparts. Anything above a simple exchange of diplomatic notes on a bilateral basis might risk inviting additional conditions or "interpretations". I repeat: all that is needed as a start is for *one of the have-not nations to ask of the have nations for a confirmation that its pledge of non-attack is valid for its own separate case.*

Other countries who opt for nuclear disarmament would be expected rapidly to follow along this road once it is opened. Gradually, there would thus result a self-generated "zone".

Fig. 2 Nuclear Free Zone Proposals

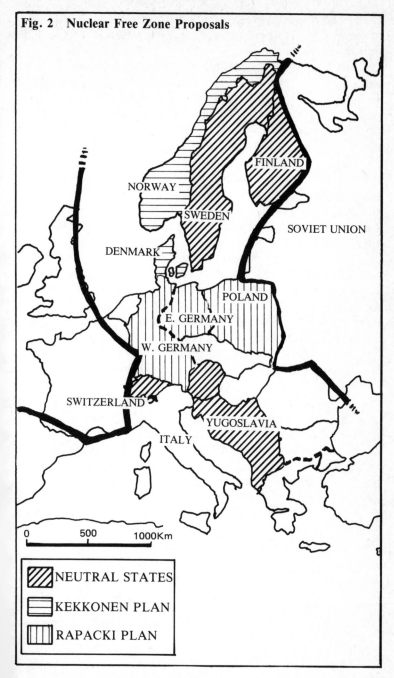

NORWAY

SWEDEN

FINLAND

DENMARK

SOVIET UNION

POLAND

E. GERMANY

W. GERMANY

SWITZERLAND

YUGOSLAVIA

ITALY

0   500   1000Km

NEUTRAL STATES

KEKKONEN PLAN

RAPACKI PLAN

(See further on the graduated process in Section V). Figure 2, at page 237, is an illustrative map where the core neutral nations are indicated.

In the case of the aforementioned nations it needs no accentuation of the self-evident: that the pledges of protection from attacks with nuclear weapons would cover the situation in both peacetime and wartime. Other countries who desire nuclear disarmament and make an explicit exchange of bilateral declarations to that effect, would share in the benefits. But countries tied into military alliances would, after an envisaged unilateral decision to achieve nuclear disarmament, have to negotiate the withdrawal of any nuclear weapons deployed within their territories with the owners of such arsenals already in peacetime, i.e. in the situation as prevailing at present. And, additionally, even more fraught with complexities, negotiations would be necessary to obtain pledges also for *wartime* freedom from being attacked with, or being utilised for temporary stationing or even for passage over their territory of any kind of atomic war-heads. Each nation then has to decide on the conditions it desires to set: NATO members would probably ask for some kind of "parity of sacrifice" from Warsaw pact members, more specifically the USA and the Soviet Union respectively.

This is exactly what the campaign for nuclear disarmament of Europe is all about. But it needs to be made quite clear that this does not *per se* raise any demand for the dissolution of the alliances. The front line attention here given to the situation of the neutral nations is intended to emphasise that theirs are the most clear-cut cases, ready for immediate action. But, more generally, the call to free Europe from nuclear arms does not constitute any advocacy for dissolution of the military blocs, neither NATO nor the Warsaw Pact.

It may be foreseen, however, that as a consequence of freeing itself from nuclear weapons, a nation may be faced with steeper demands on its own national defence. Perhaps it is worth noting that of what I have called the "core neutral nations" at least five of them — Finland, Sweden, Switzerland and Yugoslavia — are counted among those having the strongest defence organisations in Europe; and Austria having managed the best solution of security at the lowest cost level. The argument for "buying" nuclear weapon freedom with stronger demands on national defence as a preferable alternative has also been fairly explicitly made by several West Germany analysts, particularly those belonging to what may be seen as a Weizsäcker school of thought.[9]

The call on each nation to enter on new bilateral understandings with the nuclear weapon powers, if they want to achieve release from the atom weapons bondage, cannot be too strongly underscored. In my part of the world, the Nordic countries, a very heated debate has recently been engendered about the possibilities of establishing a "nuclear weapon free" zone. (See for a fuller treatment of action possibilities Section VI). I have personally advocated that we must have a clear understanding of the necessity to proceed gradually, and independently, not start by establishing a fixed zone. This is in contra-distinction to the creation of such a zone in Latin America with its very different background (see above p.219).

It is, of course, only to be regretted that the historical and cultural unity of the Nordic countries, a unity which is still so much of a conscious reality, has through the Second World War and its aftermath become politically and militarily split. The tie between Iceland and United States is so firm that I deem it as unrealistic to work on the basis of belief in the existence, at present at least, of such a common denominator as a comprehensive "Nordic zone", including the Atlantic islands, would need. A wider context, encompassing more of Europe, is required for a "zone" perspective. But individually, the various Nordic nations might take some step forward. For Denmark and Norway greater hopes may now be growing to negotiate freedom in wartime from the use of nuclear weapons over their territories, as they have already made clear reservations about non-stationing of NATO weapons in peace time. They may take steps to obtain a position to act as independently, as Finland and Sweden might already do.

The cognisance of existing political-military ties in several European nations has hitherto held the idea of a "nuclear weapon free zone" taboo. Admittedly it is a problem, but it is also a touchstone for any willingness to proceed towards European nuclear disarmament. So let us further analyse — I am certain that the obstacles can be removed and best by a more gradual approach.

IV. Nuclear weapon free zone in Europe — one or several?

The idea of a "zone" presupposes some contiguity while I have so far argued in terms of independent action by individual nations. I now want to raise the question as to if, where and when definite safety zones could be established in Europe. There is no doubt that they would be more desirable in the eyes of all those who are concerned with the security of Europe as an end in itself.

First, a rear mirror view of more of less firm plans, reflected in history, for a demilitarised or, later, denuclearised belt separating the superpowers and reducing the risks of their confrontation in Europe.

A neutral belt in Europe?

Ever since World War II plans have been appearing. From the outset the pivotal issue was how to get Germany reunited. It was a political precondition for holding Europe together.

Many efforts were made. For instance, in 1949 Moscow — in order to forestall the creation of NATO as we now know it — called for a German peace treaty, conditioned on the unification and neutralisation of Germany but also withdrawal of foreign troops. The closer West Germany was being drawn to the Atlantic course, the narrower became the margins for success for such proposals. They were, however, reiterated time after time, e.g. in March 1952 with considerable urgency by Stalin. In 1955 the issue came to the negotiating table in form of the so-called Eden plan, which did not however, meet with approval by the Western powers at their summit meeting. Evidently, they preferred a divided Europe and a militarized Germany rather than German unification, as the price was neutrality.[10]

For a long while a desire to avoid a split down the middle of Europe and to assure their own nation's unification was hopefully entertained by the Germans themselves. To facilitate a return to national unity the debate within the western part of Germany, and most emphatically the contribution to their debate by the Social Democrats, opposed plans for German re-militarisation, more specifically those developed from 1952 to move towards integration in a West European joint defence system. Due to forceful French refusal to accept, such plans were finally abandoned and i consequence West Germany was allowed into NATO in 1955.

Their opposition to the splitting up of Germany and the cleavage into two military blocks has never quite died down. As late as 1959 the Social Democrats re-vitalised their interest in non-alignment as a means to get the two Germanies to co-operate politically. With neutrality as a definite object, a plan — originating with Herbert Wehner — was tentatively launched for a so-called military zone of détente, encompassing, besides West and East Germany, also Poland, Czechoslovakia and Hungary.

Even today, the Bonn representative will, in the annual UN speech, go on record as saying that peace in Europe should make the German people "able, in free self-determination, to regain their unity". From the other German State the pronouncements have for a long time been more clouded. In a most recent speech by its chief spokesman, however, the issue of reunification was surprisingly raised again, albeit with the caveat that socialism must first become established "also" in West Germany.

The debate has never quite died down and today it seems to be awakening again. From a recent public opinion poll it can be learned that some 70 per cent of West Germans favour reunification, although about the same majority is largely pessimistic about actually achieving reunification.[11]

It may need an apology that I have spent some time on the splitting up of Europe into military and political alliances. But this is most clearly symbolised and even directly caused by "the German problem". I have dwelt upon it, not because the time has come when the superpowers might be willing to resuscitate any plans to revise history. But it is necessary, in order faithfully to render what are the true attitudes and interests of the Europeans themselves; to remind ourselves how deep down in the minds of the Europeans ideas of closer unity lie latent.

The many proposals to overcome the bloc divisions presented in the United Nations, strikingly often by the Roumanians, speak to the survivability of such a dream. It means at least that if it were to materialise, it would probably be politically-emotionally more readily acceptable by the peoples than many politicians now believe.

The achievements of the Ost-Politik: the Berlin agreement

1971 when the four victor powers agreed on a pattern for the Berlin area, West Germany's treaty with Poland in 1970 and the agreement between the two Germanies in 1972 on measures of rather considerable exchange and co-operation, are vital signs of progress towards greater intra-European co-operation.

Actually, after having lain dormant for more than twenty years — a generation — of rather rigorous faithfulness to the dominance of thinking in alliance terms, the idea of closing the ranks between the European nations themselves shows signs of revival. It is no doubt spurred on by growing awareness of, and heated debate about, the threats to European security being sharpened by the installation of Eurostrategic missiles. Thus, plans for a "security zone" encompassing all the thirty *de facto* non nuclear weapon States of Europe, are being ventilated, e.g. by a group of prominent leaders, political as well as scientific, resting on an initiative originating from Belgium.[12] The term "security zone" is meant to indicate that it is time for freeing Europe, its central as well as northern and southern parts, from *all foreign weapons,* conventional as well as nuclear. It would amount to liberating us from the present absurdity that all we now do is to take sides — and then passively wait for the holocaust.

If any of the plans mentioned as examples — and there have been, and are, many more — could have materialised, a veritable strong-belt of neutral States would have been formed, stretching all across Europe from Lapland in the north to Hellas in the south. Not only as a Swede, but for the sake of European security, I can but vividly regret that none of the plans have as yet taken off from the platform of idealistic dreams. The dilemma persists of steadily increasing military power over us and steadily decreasing national security for our peoples.

Alternative: a belt free from nuclear weapons

Failing to achieve any such comprehensive "neutral belt separating East and West", hope began to cling to the possibility of establishing at least a *de-nuclearised* zone, interposed between the superpowers and thus also gaining a greater freedom from their dominance over the smaller countries in Central Europe.[13]

The initiative was launched by the then Polish Foreign Minister, Rapacki, who in 1957 offered to the UN General Assembly a resolution with a systematic scheme providing for a nuclear weapon free zone comprising his own country, Poland, together with East Germany, on condition that West Germany accepted. (Czechoslovakia in the next version preferred its adherence). The Rapacki plan failed, as all its increasingly modest successive variations, the stumbling block constantly being West Germany's refusal to join, dictated by the US unwillingness to forego the emplacement of nuclear weapons on German soil.

At the present juncture in history the Rapacki plan is highly worthy of renewed consideration. Negotiations ought now first to focus on the three parties originally envisaged: Poland, East and West Germany. They would, if a graduated give and take formula were used, likely appear as "balancing" each other, being the most obvious arena for a new mass-slaughter, a term here used to remind us of the historic Leipzig Massenschlacht against Napoleon in that same area of Europe. An important additional argument would be that together these countries control the southern coast of the Baltic Sea, from where atomic weapons can strike far to the north, thus indicating an interest and a possibility to combine the Rapacki and the Kekkonen plans.

Politically, the hitch is, of course, the important one that the USA would have to give up more atomic weapons, both already installed, and planned for the future sites in that region. Some sacrifice must therefore be expected to be offered by, or claimed, from the Soviet Union, to reduce or remove some missiles located within its own territory, or, to be more specific, some SS 20s. A reduction in numbers and/or relocation to more distant regions must figure in the negotiations, which should be started very quickly. The countries concerned must be aware of this need for mutual "sacrifices" from the two superpowers and prepare their list of demands immediately.

The prospects for such negotiations are not too dim as at least Poland and West Germany, who carry considerable weight within their respective alliances, do show growing inclination to win greater mastery of their own affairs — the way would be clear for pressing ahead with freeing all of

Europe from nuclear weapons. A considerable measure of *détente* would also be won because the two superpowers and their military alliances would then be able to register path-breaking positive achievements of understanding.

But what if negotiations do not succeed in regard to Central Europe — the most exposed region likely to become a devastated battlefield, or before they do, other prospects must be explored.

A nuclear weapon free zone in the north?

Planning to keep a region free from nuclear weapons has been most persistently going forward in the Nordic region, once politically but even now both economically and culturally so closely knit together, a unit somewhat loosely called Scandinavia. I will follow in some detail the chronology of ideas, and worries, about the possibility of keeping nations, and most specifically their own territories, free from nuclear weapons. By this kind of analysis, more general problems will also become highlighted, of crucial importance, not only to that Viking corner of the world, but to all of Europe.

Already in 1961 no less than two resolutions were passed by the United Nations General Assembly in order to bridle the abominable nuclear weapons. Though passed on the same day, 4 December 1961 they emanated from quite different political philosophies. One, Res. 1665 (XVI), carried unanimously, had been presented by Ireland. It advocated *compulsory* abjuration of nuclear weapons by additional nations, excepting the present five' haves'. It was not aimed and did not lead to any nuclear weapon free zone but gradually to NPT. The second, proposed by the then Swedish Foreign Minister Undén, Res. 1664 (XVI) was also carried, but only with 58 votes for, 10 against and 23 abstentions, the adversaries being mostly Western ones who feared interference with NATO plans. Undén's idea was rather one not of a "zone" but of a nuclear weapon free "club", i.e. a number of nations should *voluntarily* abstain from acquiring atomic weapons, for the sake both of national and of international security.

When governments had to respond to questions posed by the UN about their willingness to adopt what has since then been called "the Undén plan" it became reformulated in the term of "zones". No such zone was, however, formally circumscribed. The Swedish Government for one, expressed its willingness to join "a nuclear weapon free zone in Northern and Central Europe of the largest possible extent". The lukewarm reception, even in the Nordic countries, was mainly due to strongly expressed Norwegian opposition, explained by its faithful allegiance to NATO.

A new beginning, which has proved to possess greater vitality, was soon tried by the "Kekkonen plan". It is somewhat younger in years, having been presented by Finland's President Kekkonen in 1963 and by the Finnish Government, but hardly anybody else, kept alive by urgent reminders, through the years. It envisages that the already nuclear weapon free Finland and Sweden, who both stand outside the NATO and WTO alliances, be joined by the other Scandinavian countries, Denmark and Norway in a "Nordic" zone.

As mentioned in the previous section, these two Scandinavian countries have, despite their allegiance to NATO, secured freedom from actual deployment of nuclear weapons on their soil. Thus in *peacetime* the four Northern countries already *de facto* constitute a zone of nuclear disarmament. (The scope of the Kekkonen plan for the Nordic countries is on the map indicated by horizontal lines, partially superimposed upon neutral Sweden and Finland).[14]

To fence off a zone from the threat of nuclear weapon attack also in *wartime* must be a matter for independent national policy decision for Denmark and Norway themselves, as well as inter-allied negotiations. A victory for any such nuclear disarmament plan as that of Kekkonen should be hailed with great satisfaction by everybody, though as a Swede I greet signs of such progress with special warmth.

Combining the Kekkonen and Rapacki plans

If the countries, envisaged in the Kekkonen and Rapacki plans — in modernised versions as they may now actually be preferred by the nations concerned — could be joined and combined in one great design with the existing area of non-aligned States who are already safely nuclear weapon free, we might finally win the right to speak realistically of a nuclear weapon free belt or a "zone", stretching "from the North

Cape to the Mediterranean''. Even if the belt would not be de-militarised as once was the dream, or neutralised as was also sometimes a political desideratum, i.e. free from foreign military installations, it would through its *nuclear disarmament* constitute an immense breakthrough, yes a watershed in world history. It would signify a gigantic gain in security for our part of the world, and — with us — for at least the whole Northern Hemisphere, leaving the superpowers to shoot out their conflicts in their own areas — including, I regret to say, the international oceans, open to all freebooters.

The hurdles which have been mounted in the way of making a reality out of the Kekkonen as well as the Rapacki plans are the same in both cases: the need to secure superpower approval.

This is also my reason for discussing them as a heuristic device in what otherwise looks like a weird time sequence. We cannot surmise where the break in the wall may become engineered. We must be open to grasp any chance. However, it would seem quite rational and, probably, politically fairly easy to expect the Nordic countries to be the precursors, lying farther out on what is seemingly a politically less sensitive flank.

But there are mini dramas playing even in that part of the world, not of their own making but because of the extent to which they have been drawn into the superpowers' gaming. While Sweden and Finland have shown considerable interest in the Kekkonen plan, Norway in particular has for a long time been less willing to accept its basic concepts, implying the construction of a separate Nordic, and perhaps even treaty-bound, zone.

Just at the present juncture, however, signs are dawning of a new opening. A lively public debate is blossoming forth in all these countries. It has occurred in conjunction with the rather unwelcome prospect of the NATO 1979 decision to introduce a new generation of Eurostrategic nuclear weapons. Even more recently and sharply the debate has followed in the wake of Norway accepting a decision to store some heavy US military equipment in order to shorten transit time in case of war. Norwegian public opinion has been ravaged by an inflammatory debate. But just at this time, several proposals favouring the nuclear weapon free idea have come forward.

This has been very much thanks to Ambassador Jens Eversen, a recent member of the Norwegian cabinet and a prominent international negotiator, together with several highly competent collaborators, who had led the way in a weighty book on "atomic weapons and the policy of insecurity".[15]

More good news: the Norwegian Labour Party has become ready to redefine the national posture, allowing a considerably more positive attitude, although tied as yet to a somewhat vague delimitation of an adequate "zone". Its programme now promises "to work for an atom weapon free zone in the Nordic region as part of the work for atom free zones in a wider European context".

In Finland the debate is also reawakened and then pursued with customary *sisu*.

The Swedish parliament has likewise moved towards more purposive work for nuclear weapon free zones in the latest decision, taken on 3 June 1981. The outcome is a formulation which can be practically juxtaposed, word for word, with that of the Norwegian Labour Party, quoted above. As a matter of fact, it is now accepted by all the Nordic Labour Parties as a minimum common denominator.

There have been some attempts, led chiefly by bourgeois parties, but also with some other discussants, to narrow the interpretation of the parliamentary decision by adding a set of "conditions". Thus, in the wording of the Swedish Foreign Minister, Ullsten (Liberal): "A prospective agreement on a nuclear weapon free zone must also include nuclear weapons which are *intended* for targets within the zone, or *stationed* close to the zone and have such range that they are predominantly fitted to be *directed* against targets within the Nordic region." (My italics).

The Nordic Labour Parties, however, have refused any preconceived setting of conditions and in a common document agreed on a recommendation with a more action oriented approach. I may use a quote from the Swedish opposition leader, Palme, recommending that the "Government should enter into contact with the other Nordic governments to explore the prerequisites for a nuclear weapon free zone in the north."

To be noted is first that none of the postures taken explicitly refer to any need for formal agreements. This is a plus. They have, however, been amiss in not mentioning at all the "negative guarantees" procured from the nuclear weapon States. They have systematically "forgotten" to enlighten the citizens about their promises of non-attack with nuclear weapons.

Most recently a new contribution in the debate has been made by Brezhnev in stating for the Soviet Union that the pledge of non-attack with nuclear weapons against the countries in a nuclear free zone is of the foremost importance, adding that the Soviet Union would not exclude the possibility of discussing measures concerning its own territories in the vicinity of such a zone.

The road to negotiations is now somewhat better paved.

Some artificial hurdles

It should go without saying that when there is debate there are also some disagreements and varying definitions.

Some voices have even persisted in demands based on exaggerated nationalistic beliefs that we have to raise considerable claims on the nuclear weapon powers before we adhere to a nuclear weapon free zone, obviously forgetting that it would represent only an advantage to us, implying a more certain protection from being a target for a nuclear strike, perhaps pre-emptive.

Such statements amount to the one great stumbling block: a totally artificial creation which should by continued clarifications be finally removed. It shows from an earlier, particularly Norwegian, insistence which has also in later years contaminated Swedish discussions, that a condition should be that the Soviet Union must, in a one-sided action, evacuate middle range nuclear missiles deployed in the Kola peninsula, sometimes even those in the Baltic Sea (where a few old nuclear submarines are stationed in the Soviet part).

The reason for my giving relatively so much space and close attention to such weird, specifically "Nordic" arguments is that they reveal a lack of both political and military rationality, which is also typical of several other geopolitical perceptions. It is of the essence that these misinterpretations be cleared up: that progress could hardly be made if only one of the superpowers is asked to relinquish its postures and even to give up freedom of action within its own territory. An effective counter-argument must be raised against this failure to appreciate the need of *equity* in whatever we suggest as *their* contribution to *our* nuclear weapon freedom: more parallel and equitable demands on co-operation from both of the superpowers.

As Nordic examples have been constantly used, such double-pronged comparisons might be made, e.g. against demands for non-deployment of nuclear weapon capabilities on the Kola peninsula would probably be posed others on the United States for non-deployment on Norwegian territory in the north, even in wartime, or even cruise missiles in the ocean space west of Narvik.

On top of it all, any such exaggerated "conditions" are not only unrealistic but unnecessary. Targets in the Nordic countries, if that is our main concern, can always be reached from any direction from which nuclear missiles — short-, medium- and, of course, long-range — are deployed, both by the Soviet Union and US-NATO, from West as well as East, from the north as well as from the south.

That Europe is and will be even more totally enclosed within the grip of the two superpowers' intermediate range ballistic missiles and possibly also cruise missiles, capable of carrying nuclear weapons to any of its corners, can be irrefutably inferred from the illustrative map. I have just put one leg of a pair of compasses at some likely launching pads of what is at present the most threatening new arsenals — the Pershing II and ground-based cruise missiles from one side, and the SS-20 and SS-5 from the other, and have then with the other leg drawn approximate half-circles corresponding to their ranges. One might notice that the Soviet missiles, even if stationed only inside its enormous land territory, would be able to reach well beyond the western most point of Norwegian land or sea territory, and to cover all of Denmark and Sweden as well. And the NATO weapons would leave no zone of safety in Sweden or Finland. From both sides, the Baltic Sea would be encompassed. So if these are the territories to worry about, the threats are parallel. For any suggestion of progress, however piecemeal, in nuclear disarmament, we must be prepared to expect that the superpowers will ask for equitable treatment, and meet any one demand for sacrifice of their freedom of action with other compensatory counter-demands.

The idea that nuclear weapons stationed in the *vicinity* of some country, like the Nordic ones, "must" be eliminated, means, of course, interfering not only with superpower strategies, for which these weapons are considered essential resources, but also infringing upon national sovereignty. And imagine the consequences if all small countries were to make their nuclear weapon freedom contingent upon such "conditions". Would it move us in any hopeful direction if a country like (for example) Holland, in order to win the benefit of freedom from nuclear weapons on its soil — which are all foreign — should require the withdrawal of NATO weapons also in West Germany? On the contrary, such a requirement would, of course, tie into an insoluble knot any prospect of progress towards such freedom. And if all small countries followed such a precedent, the result would only be a quagmire of impossible demands and counter-demands. That approach is a counter-production one.

Another far-fetched and unrealistic idea is founded on the belief that there might be short range or medium range ballistic missiles, aimed directly at and usable only for targets in the Nordic countries. By external observation we can, of course, never check what the target is. The missiles can, within a brief space of time, even be re-targetable as the to's and fro's of actual warfare might warrant! But if nuclear weapons of that category are stationed somewhere in our vicinity, whether in the East or in the West, we should expect that they would be voluntarily withdrawn as being unnecessary and extraneous to any policy planning, *once respect for nuclear weapon freedom* is established, in relation to a zone or even to a single nation.

This again, should remind everybody that the pledges of 1978 must be brought much more visibly into the foreground. The three powers which have nuclear weapons in our vicinity — Britain, Soviet Union, United States — have actually promised not to attack us with nuclear weapons when we have freed ourselves from such weapons. What a simple equation it really is! That should be our major and hopeful commentary, when thinking through the issues around which debate in Europe has in reality to evolve. Here the argument is ex emplified with an analysis of the Nordic case as it presents itself, but the same case is, of course, valid and significant for the whole of our European situation. Yet the arguments elucidated in this commentary also emphasise how completely all of Europe is now exposed to superpower weapons — a fact which we must be ready to state as being definitely not to our liking.

Without doubt, the debate now blossoming forth is a prelude which must not be underestimated. It is, at least, an invitation to intensive study. And the time is auspicious for more co-operation, for the planning of negotations and eventually agreements in more concrete details. Active steps, both within and between nations are in consequence, more and more urgent. We cannot miss the 'bus this time!

Widening the zones by matching steps

Let us try out in a purely imaginative way, what pattern a European nuclear weapon free zone might take — or, more realistically, how the circle of agreements for nuclear disarmed countries, covered by guarantees of non-attack with nuclear weapons, might grow in a rather self-generated manner.

Led on by the already thorough public discussion, well prepared proposals and perceptions, embodied in the Rapacki, Undén and Kekkonen plans, I have come to deal fairly extensively with prospective projects in a rank order from those which seem politically most feasible to the more difficult ones. Thus first the *core neutral nations:* Sweden and Finland, Yugoslavia, Austria and Switzerland; next the rather cohesive *Nordic flank nations:* Denmark and Norway in addition to the aforementioned Sweden and Finland; and finally the *crucial Central European* States which might offer themselves as "balanceable": the two Germanies and Poland, perhaps taking in also Czechoslovakia or some other East European nation.

As the interest in obtaining such added security as an acknowledged status of nuclear disarmament is probably shared by most, if not all, countries in Europe, one might dare to suggest some further extensions. For instance, *Holland* and *Belgium* might be early joiners, to judge from their own lively public debate on the issue. On the southern side, *Roumania* might perhaps be expected to follow up earlier initiatives to help establish a nuclear weapon free zone in the Balkans. If balancing is necessary, either *Greece* or *Turkey* or both, might then have to be won for a matching agreement. But perhaps Roumania might go it alone, considering its many initiatives to loosen the constraints of the military blocs, whilst preserving their political systems unaltered.[16]

The two minor nuclear weapon powers in Europe, *France* and *Great Britain,* have in this survey been relegated to another context (see the next section). Their *quid pro quo* problem is very different and much more directly concerns the superpowers' major interests.

In this essay advocating European nuclear disarmament, I have restricted the attention to those tactical and Eurostrategic weapons which, although some may be important for an overall superpower contest, are deployed by them — or intended — for use against European territories. They are definitely against our most vital interests.

Then two concluding remarks must be explicitly stressed. One is to remind us — and the superpowers — of the great positive value for the European countries attainable by buttressing *security* with their promised pledges not to attack us with nuclear weapons when we keep our own territories free from such weapons.

The second is that I have been moved to write as I do in the conviction that at bottom, not just a few, but all, people do realise the compelling need to begin now to lift the fear of doomsday which we sense in appreciating that the all-to-mighty nations in their spiralling mutual hostility use our peoples in Europe as hostages, at a time when we ourselves have become so free from aggressive impulses.

V. Graduated claims on the nuclear weapon powers

A principle of fundamental importance for European nuclear disarmament is to uphold a certain *equity* in the demands for those steps whch we expect the nuclear weapon powers to take as their share in the co-operative effort for achieving arms control and, ultimately, renunciation of nuclear weapons.

This principle is often referred to as one of maintaining the "balance" and, mistakenly, often interpreted as a rather rigid measure-for-measure parallelism in regard to reductions, or "sacrifices" of certain categories of weapons.[17] But, how is a Polaris to be counted against a Backfire? It is not their quantities or even qualities that have to be weighed and compared, but their functions and effects that have to be entered into the equation. SALT II exemplifies the complicated but still urgently necessary efforts to be made by the superpowers to obtain, in regard to their own intercontinental arsenals, a tolerable degree of "parity" — or approximate tolerable equity — through some mix of bilateral restrictions. This intricate complexity must be borne in mind also when European countries raise demands on the ruling powers to free us from the dangers of their atomic weapons. As the Soviet Union houses by far the overwhelming part of its nuclear weapons within its own territory, it is most difficult to suggest, from the outside, *specifically* which sacrifices they ought to make to achieve equitable agreements. But some must be made.

Complex linkages

The nuclear weapon powers must have found it a weakness in my presentation up to this point that I have not given sufficient attention to the complexities and, consequently, to the necessary linkage between the various security or arms control measures which have been suggested in order to enhance European safety. I have, in what may seem to be a single-minded view, stuck to those weapon systems which are slated for ground launching, and most directly to the major missile systems. For policy recommendations I do, however, without specific enumeration or even mention, include the whole scale of lower grade nuclear weapons in Europe, from landmines and artillery howitzers, from Badger to Pershing I.

But restriction in the main to the ground launched missiles is of the essence as I — and most of those participating in the END debate — want to deal with weapons over which we, the European countries, have some power, just because the superpowers need our co-operation, permission or simple acquiescence for their deployment. They demand decisions by our national, sovereign governments and parliaments. These weapons are thus the only ones for which we share a definite responsibility: the "burden whereof" I have wanted to stress with indelible emphasis.

But it is self-evident that the security of our lands is dependent not only on this category of ground-launched ballistic or cruise missiles which can take off from our territories. It finally hinges on the continued existence of a very much larger spectrum of nuclear weapon systems, all of which are capable of attacking us, or violating our neutrality, or offending our sovereignty and independence, by the unauthorised transmitting of weapons through or above our territorial or sea or air space. That applies to all weapons in the strategic category. We ought really to discuss them also, category by category, when seeking to find a pattern for the graduated process of superpower progress towards nuclear arms control. We should cry welcome with a rather greater fanfare than has so far been given to the astonishingly positive fact that all their weapons systems are covered by the pledges given by *their possessors, of non-attack upon us with nuclear weapons,* inasmuch as we are truly free of such weapons ourselves. The nuclear weapons on all kinds of carriers — the submarines and surface ships, the strike aircraft and helicopters, the launching platforms of whatever description — over which we can never pretend to gain any control because they do not need any permission from us for the take-off of their missiles and war-heads — are all still in fact to a certain extent embargoed by the promise not to use them to attack those European countries which desist from all co-operation with nuclear warfaring. Note the essential restriction, however, only to nuclear war and preparations for such war.

Graduating the responses

The method of "graduated response" is certainly not unknown, albeit too rarely practised in foreign policy as well as generally in crisis management. It wonderfully combines two distinct merits: of saving face and of probing trustworthiness when adversaries meet. A blissful example in the world political arena was given by Kennedy and Kruschev in the Cuba crisis of 1962: while the Russian ships, even with their missiles, were allowed to depart quietly, the Americans soon just as quietly withdrew the (obsolescent!) missiles from

Italy and Turkey. And already on December 19 Krushchev held out his hand to negotiate a comprehensive nuclear test ban treaty, Kennedy then grasping it within nine days.

That the alluring work plans diligently perfected by the disarmament negotiations which followed came to nothing — or rather to an aborted *Limited* Test Ban Treaty — is a different story[18]

Another demonstration of the great inherent value in the step-by-step relinquishing of hindering regulations was the politically very important syndrome of détente, called Ost-Politik in Europe. It was signalled first by a gradually more and more "benign neglect" of earlier obstructions at Checkpoint Charlie, on the border between East and West Berlin, and followed by highly important agreements between West Germany and Eastern bloc nations in the early 1970s.

But when these events took place we lived in the sunny climate of détente — how different from the frozen tundra of today's political relations between the superpowers!

The lack of a graduated trial and error effort to create understandings is nowhere exemplified in a more gaudy way than in the catastrophic obstinacy by which NATO in December 1979 took its decision to deploy new Eurostrategic weapons without any attempt at negotiations with the Soviet Union. Similarly, it is exemplified, as I have often said, in the way by which the Russians right away invaded Afghanistan, without offering any negotiation about possible joint policies of non-intervention.

In the disarmament literature we can find depicted a strategy of "Graduated and Reciprocated Initiatives in Tension reduction", called GRIT, sometimes more loosely sketched, sometimes elaborated in greater detail. This ought to be given renewed attention and strong support: proceed step by step by making first one, perhaps in itself rather insignificant, unilateral offer, expecting a matching response from the other side. And then continue the gradual process of give and take, building up confidence and recording success.[19]

A *tentative* quid pro quo *design*

We are now in the chapter where the responsibilities for action rest most decidedly with the nuclear weapon powers or, more accurately, the two superpowers as leading all others.

They must agree — but what might they be able to agree upon? Which gestures of goodwill can they immediately begin to show in order to calm our pre-occupation with threatening facts? Can one establish some kind of rank order of steps?

Obviously, the simplest moves — in fact costless — are to forget all attempts to produce those paraphernalia which are not yet in existence. The non-production, and most definitely the non-deployment, of *neutron bombs* must be most urgently assured. That is the kind of weapon that can be produced in *small* sized forms and be fitted on an aircraft, on short range ballistic missiles like the Lance in West Germany, on cruise missiles, even on howitzers: but which will wreak destruction and death on a *large* scale.

A considerable literature is available on the subject of the Enhanced Radiation Weapon (as is its technical description) from the previous occasion when the idea was broached — and happily nullified by Carter — thus stopping for the time being its use in the superpower struggle. Forebodings have now been heard that the Reagan administration intends to re-introduce plans to produce the N-bombs in order to place them in Europe. An alarm signal immediately went up in the UN Disarmament Committee in Geneva. (5 February 1981). Hope can be inspired by the fact that France, under its new president Mitterand, seems to have abandoned this gruesome road. But its recent temptation has served as a vivid reminder that such a weapon does not long remain anybody's monopoly. Many countries could soon prove capable of following the lead of the first sinner.

The neutron bomb is, in fact, a most clumsy, impractical weapon with its specific aim of annihilating human beings, not the fewest of them being civilians. It is openly destined for war making, albeit only on a battlefield.

Among the arguments most recently presented against this new-fangled mass-murder weapon belongs one brought forward by Lord Zuckerman: as in the definition of the Circular Error Probably (CEP) the chance of hitting the target can be but 50 per cent — should no thought be given to the impact of the other 50 per cent of the bombs which would miss their target but hit an area outside that intentionally targeted. More, even the planned hits are not just pinpoints; within the circumference of the N-bomb's 1 to 2km radius there will be indescribable suffering through radiation sickness, as I have indicated earlier. Death and immobilisation would come not only to the soldiers in the tanks, or military personnel inside equipment and installations, so euphemistically presented as "kill effectivity" in the description of this weapon, but death would also come with agony and burning pain also to civilians — in the buildings and in the environment. It should not be overlooked that this weapon is slated for "battlefield" use in the most densely populated areas of Europe, most probably just on both sides of the Elbe, ploughing a murderous furrow into both Germanies. Even if only one side possessed the neutron bomb to begin with, it would kill many of that side's own soldiers and have on its conscience numbers of lives of friendly allies.

The neutron bomb would function as a nuclear starter in the context of a theretofore conventional war — more widely effective killers being available to enable escalation to occur. To desist from introducing such a new terror weapon, as it literally is, would seem to be a minimal matter to agree on for the two fiendish military blocs. The nations in Europe should obstinately resist its deployment by refusing any support, and public opinion should instead arouse a storm of condemnation of the neutron bomb in the name of humanity and morality.

A next step, likewise without any real military sacrifice, should be a *freeze* at present day levels of capabilities on all weapon systems able to carry atomic bombs. This has been proposed innumerable times in the United Nations, backed by strong majorities. A standstill must at least be made effective with respect to the testing of nuclear weapons while negotiations on a CTBT are pursued — such a moratorium being a quite ridiculously minimal demand upon the superpowers, as the UN General Assembly already in 1962 decided by an overwhelming majority. Resolution 1792 A(XVII) insisted that all testing should "cease immediately and not later than January 1963"! If we now emphatically demand something as modest as a moratorium, to be most visibly marked by a cessation of nuclear weapon testing, it should at least extend (a) until the completion of a Comprehensive Test Ban Treaty, and (b) in order to cover also some wider weapons systems until a SALT II agreement is achieved, and finally (c) in order to serve even more directly Europe oriented weapons developments, be upheld for the duration of the SALT III negotiations. Negotiations were promised after the ominous NATO 1979 decision and actually began in Geneva in the autumn of 1980, but at present they are once more stalled in the political *non-possumus* doldrum. This stalemate is but one of the many tragic victims of the deterioration of the political climate and the rise of mutual apprehension, strengthened by the change of administration in the United States and the disquiet among the Soviet client States.

It should, please, be noted that the proposal for a "freeze", coupled with the expectations on SALT III, includes commitments at least not to develop, and, at least, not to deploy *new nuclear weapons*, referring especially to the European arena. It should also be underlined that what happens along the whole line of armament changes and most specifically of any additions to the nuclear arsenals can be relatively easily verified and must be monitored by us with the utmost vigilance.

But more dynamic progress than just moratoria and freezes are needed to move the world forward towards security. The two superpowers must immediately begin to initiate such moves in terms of linkage between certain weapons systems and certain geographical locations where they can most conveniently be thinned out. It seems to me that the one mutual "sacrifice" that seems most readily available is the *withdrawal of the smaller, most ineffective and in reality superfluous nuclear weapons systems*. They can gratuitously be offered for tentative unilateral steps in a graduated process, expecting a matching response. It may not even be necessary to wait for formal negotiations about their elimination, which could be begun by unilateral steps, while immediately sending signals to "the other side".

Europe is full of a galaxy of atomic weapons. Installed launching platforms are widespread, even if the nuclear warheads are piled up in more restricted areas, probably in the case of the Soviet Union concentrated within its own heartlands while in the opposite camp they are for the most part under sole US key and to a minor extent under joint US-

NATO command. In their huge number — admittedly 7,000 on the US side and it is believed perhaps about half as many on the Soviet side — they need in turn to be opted out, and that at a steadily faster rate.

A picture map of how nuclear weapon installations are strewn all over the Federal Republic of Germany was published by the magazine *Stern* on 19 February 1981, and is a conspicuous example of how irrational it is to house them in such a widespread way, how practically impossible it is to control them, and how vulnerable are their lines of communication and command. A map with corresponding revelations about Great Britain, showing "the main nuclear installations, all of which are potential nuclear targets", has been produced and is being sold by the Campaign for Nuclear Disarmament.

Now the knowledge of their presence and that of their equivalent in other countries is causing shivers of anxiety to millions of Europeans. Such arsenals ought to be swept away in as quick and as demonstrable a way as possible; experts will confirm how obsolescent many, perhaps most of them have become. Weapons of longer range and better precision are already available. And deterrence is anyway assured by the missiles which are carried on aircraft and submarines. The latter, the sea-launched or sea-launchable are the most hardened, the least vulnerable weapons and are most assuredly in themselves sufficient for second strike capability.

Reflecting the possibility of a linkage between such weapon systems and some geographical locations, some unilateral, or bilaterally matched, arrangements may be the first to be initiated. In the process of general abandonment of minor nuclear weapons systems, the easiest may be to obtain formally declared nuclear weapon freedom for *Holland and Belgium,* where strong popular movements are backing such demands, representing more than 50 per cent of people in Holland according to public opinion polls. It might possibly be reciprocated by e.g. *Hungary and Roumania.* Such moves would all be in response to the evident national ambitions of these countries and might be facilitated by their being only of marginal importance in the power relations between the two military alliances. This would establish a rather large nuclear weapon free area, by stretching out from the neutral nations both eastwards and southwards (see map Figure 2).

But it would be just a beginning. To go farther afield means, however, a more definite challenge to get the superpowers to agree between themselves. Applicable designs have their contours in what has been described as the Kekkonen and Rapacki plans and are depicted on the map by horizontal and vertical markings. The latter, encompassing at least *Poland, East Germany and West Germany,* must be the crucial one in the perception of the superpowers. It is understandably the most difficult to realise, due, not only to West German reluctance to become nuclear weapon free — a situation often falsely depicted as losing the "protection" of the US umbrella — but owing mainly to the fact that as a central issue between the superpowers it is probably the most intractable one. It would be the predominant case to be negotiated through SALT III. But East and West Germany, as well as Poland, must be expected to contribute fully through their own debates.

The *Nordic region* would seem much better tailored for the relatively early realisation of a nuclear weapon free zone. But a few complications stand in the way. An analysis of them will, as a continuation of my reasoning in the previous section, be utilised as a test case for an analysis of certain questions of principle. This selection is also motivated by the fact that I personally know their political situation better than most of the others. Such a probing of the arguments can also serve as a bridge to a closer discussion of the connections between European problems and more general superpower strategies.

The question of targeting versus deployment

As has been mentioned earlier (Section IV) some extravagent claims have been raised, particularly in regard to a Nordic nuclear weapon free zone. It has been argued that it should depend on the removal of missiles from parts of Soviet territory, the Kola peninsula and submarines in the Baltic being often mentioned, "insofar as they are targeted on points in the Nordic countries",

But this must be due to a fundamentally erroneous conception both in respect of realities and principles, first and foremost the principle of equity, but also to a neglect of the *difference between deployment and targeting.* The theme of the present debate as to European nuclear disarmament, rather concretely illustrated by the idea of nuclear weapon free zones, must be whether or not nuclear weapons are to be deployed on European territory. In a very different conceptual category belongs the question of whether or not nuclear weapons are aimed at European targets.

To demand the elimination of nuclear weapon arrangements from the vicinity of one's own land, because they might strike us from there, is ludicrously unrealistic. If Holland or Belgium, to use once more these examples, were to pose such conditions about the NATO weapons in West Germany, that would have to be deemed undue interference. And we would never be able to get out of the quagmire of criss-crossing demands of interlocking dependencies. The best *quid pro quo* to still the suspicions of the small countries is insistence upon the pledges of non-attack.

Due to the very nature of nuclear weapon systems with their missiles or aeroplanes or submarines controlling from a distance the delivery of bombs — nuclear or not — nothing short of comprehensive nuclear disarmament can hinder such weapons from being aimed at European targets. This ought to be understood as a cardinal principle, underlying any plans for European nuclear disarmament. The denuclearisation of the superpowers' own arsenals remains a moot question for "next steps". But at present we can demand only guarantees, in the form of pledges that we will not be hit by such weapons. We cannot advance by requesting for our sake the physical elimination, or immobility or even relocation of parts of the superpowers' own arsenals under their sovereign rule.

All the more is this true, as it is impossible to use any geographical delimitation of deployment to impose prohibitions because it is always possible to relocate nuclear weapons, as was pointed out already in the previous section. And the map in Figure 1 illustrates the wide reach of the SS-5 with which Europe, without any audible protestation, evidently learned to live for 20 years. Also politically, the specific ideas which propose to empty the Kola peninsula of some (or all?) short, medium or intermediary missiles is, of course unrealistic if the Soviet union is not itself willing to agree to one-sided restrictions. It would also be regarded by outsiders as unfair if it were not balanced by any request for a corresponding sacrifice on the US side.

The proposed reduction of foreign nuclear weapons in Europe, here exemplified mainly by the Kekkonen and Rapacki plans — but open to action by any individual nation — has so far *not* been made dependent on, or even mentioned as requiring, any reduction of the superpowers' own *strategic* arsenals, built up for combating each other and relying on a great number of bases of launching platforms, such as aircraft and submarines, under their own sovereignty. To this category must be referred the Kola peninsula and its Murmansk bases.

To use Norway once more as an example — offered by many of its own discussants — the present juncture, when an agreement to receive US heavy armour is in the offing, would seem an opportune one in which to solicit confirmation that this does not entail any threat — or promise! — to deploy nuclear weapons even in wartime in Norway's land, sea or air space. Such assurances, if obtained, would constitute a basis for Norway's joining the group of totally atom weapon free nations, enabling it to profit from the pledges already given by three of the powers with nuclear weapons in our region not to attack with such weapons nations which have made themselves into legitimate sanctuaries.

But the question is interesting: what kind of matching sacrifices by the two superpowers would be of particular interest to the Nordic countries as they obviously live in a very dangerous environment on the northern-most flank of Europe? A look at the map of the "encirclement", showing the very long reach of Eurostrategic missiles, might lead us to dare suggest a swap; on one hand the US renouncing the placement of cruise missiles for sea- or air-launching at locations a certain distance west of Narvik, as has been planned according to the *SIPRI Yearbook* of 1980, and, on the Russian side some determined, but to begin with, selective withdrawal, reduction or elimination of SS-5 and SS-20 missiles, wherever stationed. Of course, any other elements selected for definitive deals between the two superpowers as steps in the thinning out of their own weapons — which must be reckoned in the strategic equation — would be welcomed they are all worrying the Europeans.

Open problems relating to superpower negotiations

But there are several more moot questions which must immediately be raised, and solved, in order to complete the assurance of European security. They belong to those which have to be dealt with, at least in the process we expect from a SALT III.

Readers must have observed, and perhaps been irritated by the fact that attention has so predominantly been focused on the nations in Central and Northern Europe. The reason is, of course, that this region has been depicted as the major potential battlefield by both superpowers and has been perceived by its own peoples as directly threatening their sacrifice as victims. This has led them in turn to the most audible protests and the most visible resistance planning.

Not so in other *per se* important countries like Iceland, Ireland and even Italy, as well as practically the whole of Southern Europe. Their relative passivity and silence — hitherto — is rather remarkable. Various national considerations may have dictated their motivation. Iceland's situation at the crossroads of superpower bimodal strategies has been mentioned above. The formally neutral Ireland's embittered relations with Great Britain may have caused a hesitancy to link up with movements stemming from a country which is the seat of the most vociferous protest against nuclear weapons, although itself a nuclear weapon power. The reactions of the peoples in the NATO partner Italy are most impenetrable from my horizon, although strong protests should be expected, at least from some groups in that country, as being the only one besides West Germany which has accepted the task of providing bases for the new US Pershing II Eurostrategic missiles. All the countries in Southern Europe have been left outside the enumeration here, as their special cases would require quite a complex analysis in order to be treated with fair consideration. I am, however, hopeful that once the campaign for freedom from nuclear weapons creates an even more powerful pressure the peoples of all European countries will join in.

However, the problems evoked, it must be remembered, are to a substantial degree connected with wider ones about superpower strategies, not least in regard to the Atlantic, all the way up to the Arctic, and the Mediterranean marine environments. However close to our European borders nuclear weapon carriers wallow, I have underscored several times that strategic aircraft as well as submarines, and the whole problem field of anti-submarine warfare (AWF) with all auxiliary installations must remain outside our present concern. We have no power over them, nor any share in the responsibility for them. But as potential target victims we are definitely concerned about them. Whatever can be done at the diplomatic level or in the fora for disarmament and arms control deliberations, we must be eagerly prepared to make our voices heard.

Another, more curious than dangerous, case of oblivion is that related to *Canada*. That country does not belong to the European arena but is always, as if it were obligatory, or at least a foregone conclusion, represented in the bodies concerned with European affairs. Often it gives valuable support to efforts in the direction of more arms control, and is of course welcome to offer such support. But it would be a mistake, perhaps even one resented by the Europeans, to give Canada any determining voice in regard to the meetings, for example, in the framework of European Security and Co-operation, or any other forum as it so much serves to strengthen NATO, i.e. the US side. This is not meant to be any stricture, scaring off a very friendly nation from co-operation, but only a reminder as to what the principle of equity implies: "parallelism, yes fairness". The neutral nations meticulously refrain from any political linkage. And extra-European countries should do the same, even when they are not "neutral" in a global perspective.

Britain and France — the last Russian alibis

The most glaring omission is, of course, that no recommendation, or hardly any mention, has been made of the two smaller nuclear weapon States on Europe's own western flank, France and Great Britain. They maintain a very different perception of their roles and they create much more intricate and also more ominous problems than the rest of Europe. On the ledger of positive assets should be registered that they are absolutely free to decide on their own nuclear disarmament, not having to ask anybody for permission — although they might well want to raise some claim for reciprocation from the two superpower sides. Perhaps, as a *quid pro quo* for Russian withdrawal of SS-20 missiles and Backfire aircraft both France and Great Britain would have to stand ready, in the name of an equitable balance, to sacrifice corresponding nuclear weapon capabilities. It will be interesting to see how they are going to use, or even discuss, their "bargaining chips". To get their participation in protests now seems most likely when these are markedly directed — in the first instance — against *foreign* nuclear weapons.

Public opinion, at least in Great Britain, is readying itself by stirring up increasingly forceful movements of public protest. But France has been mute. Even with the new president, Mitterand, there seems to be no hope whatsoever of refuting the myth of the *force de frappe*. There ought to be a greater willingness, however, to suport movements to disown deployment of foreign nuclear weapons in Europe as France is not willing to accept any of these herself and should, therefore, not have any voice in welcoming them to other lands.

The prolonged stubborness of the two minor-major European powers in retaining their so-called independent, so-called retaliatory nuclear weapon forces, should be underscored as a frightening and, in fact, threatening attitude towards their smaller fellow nations — and also towards the not-so-small Germany. And worse, judged in a universal context, their unwillingness to forego their (in reality rather insignificant) nuclear arsenals, does function as a legitimation for the decision of the two great powers to remain locked in their negative attitude. The two also unquestionably serve as alibis for any other nations desirous of following their example, since they have given an aura of aggrandisement, of added "security" to the acquisition of nuclear weapons, thus encouraging proliferation.[20]

The guilt of France and Great Britain in serving as obstructionist models would, of course, not be diminished; but they will add to their respectability if they, as we truly expect, were to confirm pledges not to attack the nuclear weapon free countries of Europe with the nuclear weapons they now possess.

In conclusion: Time to act

I hope that what I have presented is a correct interpretation of how to apply the rules of the game. Taking this inventory of what looks politically feasible has led me to view European nuclear disarmament as a *gradual process,* not a programmatic, all-inclusive, one-time decision to launch once and for all a European "nuclear weapon free zone" as a fully-fledged structure.

My suggestions do not in any way run counter to, but only pave the way — by operationally designed steps — for the recommendations, so strongly underlined at the UN Special Session on Disarmament in 1978. In its Final Document it most specifically stresses in point 33 the value of establishing nuclear weapon free zones, without any attempt at delimiting them geographically, as an important feature of disarmament. Their value becomes even more evident when I make the coupling with the pledges whereby the nuclear weapon powers have promised to respect decisions by any zone, or by any individual government to remain free of atomic weapons. More States will hopefully ask that the nuclear weapon powers also act to give them such freedom. What I have wanted to emphasise more strongly than is usually the case is that "zones" can grow through independent action by sovereign nations. They can emerge — better sooner than later — either as a single or as several "zone(s)" without a contiguous shape being preset as a condition.

If the idea is accepted that European nuclear disarmament can be a process of organic growth, greater responsibility for immediate action devolves on each nation. It would be counter-productive to wait for formal agreements, manifested in pre-organised arrangements and solidified in treaty form. Indeed, any careful look at the map will make everybody see what a tangle of cumbersome negotiations would be required if we were to aim for perfection from the start.

Even more prohibitively laborious would be a realisation of the futuristic ideal of an *international convention,* a proposal supported mainly by the Soviet Union. *De facto* I am afraid that at the international level the protracted deliberations on that issue are functioning as an alibi for inaction. Regrettably it has been given special weight by many UN delegations, when placed on the agenda for the Geneva Committee on Disarmament, an agency that speaks well for arms control ambitions but has proven itself powerless when it comes to action. I personally believe that we should not be bound to any rigid formula but welcome progress towards nuclear disarmament, even if it can only be achieved through partial solutions.

My own proposal definitely favours a stepwise approach but one to be incessantly pursued at the unilateral, as well as the bilateral levels. Several occasions to apply preplanned pressure will be forthcoming in 1982, as stated already in the preface. Everywhere progress should be possible, if promoted by watchful delegates who must in time use their ability to solicit positive mandates from their governments. To see out and "work on" our national representatives, to invigorate a disarmament lobby in each country should from now on be a purposive action programme for all who are honestly interested in securing their riddance of atomic weapons.

Europe is now given a chance to negotiate — if we are prepared to take it. The two superpowers have been brought, at last, to agree that negotiations about medium range nuclear missiles for Europe should start, before the end of this year.

This is good. But it is not enough, neither in terms of timetable nor of participants. The negotiations cannot proceed above the heads of the parties mainly concerned, namely the European countries themselves. Nor can these countries passively wait until next year to discover which directions the negotiations might take.

We should make up our own minds and act, both on a schedule of more tightly planned, speedier negotiations and on building up an agenda which could produce desirable results.

How can we hasten the many-faceted pattern of negotiations? Probably we should be tentative to begin with, allowing different nations to "feel out" the possibilities of co-operation with other nations. Like-minded States like the free, non-aligned nations would be in order to open talks right away, and so would such others as the smaller and "next to nuclear free" States like those of Benelux. Members of the military alliances must begin by opening dialogues with their superpower leaders to gain insight as to how they can go forward in winning freedom from the nuclear weapon option; thus Norway and Denmark can explore how safely they can become free from being drawn into NATO's planning for using nuclear weapons in wartime.

We, the European countries — must prepare a variety of inputs for what as yet are only prospectively bilateral negotiations between the two superpowers. They should not be left alone to decide on what Germans call "Nach-Rüstung" — making some additions of new nuclear-weapon systems on European soil seem inevitable, a foregone conclusion.

Our chance to influence the decisions is the greater the sooner we start and the more decisively we act in presenting plans. Before the UN Special Session on Disarmament in 1982 something of a true agenda for nuclear disarmament must have jelled. And then the sprint should be on so as to reach the finishing line victorious, in 1983.

Within this time sequence a number of activities must be watched and others promoted, not least, a European Disarmament Conference which should not be allowed to shy away from the nuclear weapon issue.

The main locale for such high purpose lobbying will be the all-important Second Special Session on Disarmament which the United Nations organises in June 1982. All efforts must be directed — openly, bluntly or with more subtle finesse — to prepare for the success of our aims. It should not be tolerated that this session ends in empty generalities, as did the previous one five years earlier. There are so many weighty documents ready or in the works to facilitate in-depth analyses and discussions as to which road we will now choose — a race, either to oblivion, or to co-operation for peaceful development.

A basic report, with comprehensive, and to a large extent, new and crystal clear conclusions, is the one issued already in 1980; but as yet hardly noticed, the United Nations *Comprehensive Study on Nuclear Weapons* (A35/392). It reveals in more concrete details than ever before presented at the intergovernmental level, the irrefutable truths about nuclear arms, their inconceivably horrific effects and the insane race towards new technological heights. Forgive the many adjectives — but how are we going to get people to understand that atomic weapons are becoming more and more uncontrollable?

Another UN report of worldwide significance which will be on the table for intense debate is the one on *Disarmament and Development,* being prepared under the leadership of Inga Thorsson, thus upholding a legacy of Swedish specialisation on those issues. It must serve to stir up public understanding of the interconnections between unproductive expenditure on military budgets and the sacrifice of productive investments for development. It can be said to be a follow-up, both of the expert study on the same subject, chaired by me in 1972 and of the *Brandt Comission Report* of 1980, neither of which has been given the attention they deserve. Otherwise, they should have been enough to change the course of international policies on economic matters.[21]

These reports had advocated that a considerable shift from military expenditure to development for the poor of the world be undertaken, giving eloquent illustrations, even by rows of figures, of the plight that has to be overcome and the benefits which we stand to gain. The net value of the "disarmament dividend" is just waiting to be harvested by all nations, both the super-mighty which can strike out unnecessary overdrafts and overkill plans, and the less opulent ones, whose hunger can be stilled and whose lives can be spared. This by an imaginative double pronged approach to the two goals — disarmament does make possible development. This time the call for action must be listened to!

Also to be ready for the 1982 UN Special Session is the so-called Palme Commission's *Report of the Independent Commission on International Disarmament and Security.* Its objective is to make practical proposals with, I hope, arguments which will simply force nations to face the need to take action at last. Its work, with participants from both east and west, north and south, looks promising, to judge from its first publication; an analysis of the true perquisites of SALT — and the cost if it fails. It adds to our expectation that 1982 could mark a veritable turning point away from the mindlessness of the arms race.

Timed for 1982 has also been a *European Disarmament Conference.* Its fate is just about to be decided at the Madrid meeting on ESC, where three different proposals — from France, Poland and Sweden — ought to be amalgamated. If success is denied by the superpowers, or if the proposals are watered down to meaninglessness, then the European nations should be courageous enough to mount such a conference on their own responsibility. Even the presence of the nuclear superpowers is not essential, as is proven by the initiative taken by the have-nots at a conference in 1968. That time they were given only observer status, although the conference was underwritten by the United Nations. The European nations might this time forego international or outside subsidies for such a conference on their own life-and-death issue. I have been repeatedly urging the need to show more such independent courage.[22]

We are not doomed to be powerless. But the force of public opinion is the alpha and omega, if any progress is to be made.

Thus, our first order of the day is to mobilise very strong backing by the people for the goal of keeping Europe free from nuclear weapons. There are also considerable movements at work, a mounting tide of public opinion acting as the necessary counterpart, indeed, as a lobby to the official, diplomatic or expert conferences. These forces are also being fed by more and more broad-based research efforts. Peace research institutes engaged in work on armaments and disarmament are being multiplied and their publications more widely spread than ever before — although still far from enough.

Scientists have, with their unflinching respect for facts and with their international language, singular opportunities to meet on objective ground and therefore gather together colleagues from different ideological camps. An example is the Pugwash movement which, faithful to its origin in the Einstein-Russell Manifesto, has continued its series of symposia. There, American and Soviet citizens probe more and more thoroughly into the arms control issues, regardless of the cleavages which their respective governments so vehemently uphold. The international coverage of the Pubwash work remains remarkable.

That movement has lately begotten an offspring which might be able to act with even greater sensitivity in response to the most urgent issues of mixed political-military provenience. It is the Albert Einstein Peace Prize Foundation, which is just starting to seek out leading experts and politically influential high level personalities to act in a kind of "pre-crisis management" function to forestall acute conflicts in the international sphere from locking themseves into insoluble positions beyond the point of no return.

Another very recent effort to promote American-Soviet co-operation is being organised by The International Physicians for the Prevention of Nuclear War. Physicians are now making a specialised effort to arouse public opinion, so as to become in a personal manner aware of the tremendous slaughter of modern war — coming much closer to the life and death questions for all the individual human beings than is generally the cause with abstract presentations. They point out particularly, or I should say, paint up visibly, the incredibly small chances of providing medical care to victims of nuclear warfare. Just count the number of beds needed for cases of burns, and compare it with the infinitesimal availability of medical personnel to answer those needs. They have to great effect used, for example, the illustration of what happens when just a couple of giant jet planes collide, overtaxing the resources of medical care in even the richest country.

I have selected for special mention just a few organisations demonstrating hopes of mutual understanding across national and even political frontiers. There does exist an innate proneness of human beings to understand that we are all faced with one and the same risk of becoming the victims of global mass-murder. That risk has been played down by the political manipulation of information to serve nationalistic propaganda and falsify truth. But we can now see the dawn of a new insight into the realities, stirred up by a plethora of popular movements. They are certainly well-known to my readers, so many of them having already, for a long time, established their credentials to people interested in the prospects for peace. They are now gathering new strength and greater courage to speak up than they have done for a long time. We may take it as a fact that we are just now witnessing the end of what may rightly be called the "silent generation". The organisations, their marches, their petitions have found a new missionary zeal. They are too numerous to be enumerated in full and fair fashion here; only a few working effectively at the grass roots level may be mentioned as examples.

Some are directed towards universal goals, such as the prestigious International Peace Bureau, based in Geneva. It is particularly resourceful through its close contacts with all NGOs (Non-Governmental Organisations) and the United Nations' organs working for disarmament purposes. Alongside it must be mentioned the CND (Campaign for Nuclear Disarmament), based in London. It is now awakened to a new life, very much inspired by Lord Noel-Baker, as wise as tireless a fighter for peace. This movement is now engaged in amassing petitions from many lands and in many languages to increase the pressure of the people on the politicians.

Many movements are also aiming more directly at our part of the world. Perhaps I may single out the Socialist International, as it has recently established a special group on arms control and disarmament, headed by the chairman of the Finnish Labour Party, Kalevi Sorsa. In its report to a gathering in Madrid, November 1980, the International declared that "the long range objective is clear: all nuclear weapons should be withdrawn from this continent". And: "the immediate goal is to prevent a new spiral in the nuclear arms race in Europe".

The tide of protest against nuclear weapons in Europe is running higher and higher. In some countries it has taken on such a strength that governments are nervously forced to listen. This is noteworthy in the cases of Holland and Great Britain, in Belgium and Norway. The campaign for END (European Nuclear Disarmament) is spreading fast, joining hands as it should without rivalry, with all other movements which spring up in regional or national settings, and with strong support from the churches both Catholic and Protestant. What is becoming more and more articulate, is a broad and forceful movement against domination by superpowers with their nuclear weapons threatening the destiny of Europe.

But we must join forces in a more organised way than hitherto. Still, I believe it to be too early to attempt any formal co-ordination which might only as as a straitjacket — let the thousand flowers bloom! Much would be gained for a growth towards readiness for organised co-operation if all efforts at obtaining freedom from nuclear weapons were to focus sharply on one crucial event. As such a rallying point I would suggest should serve the planning for the all-European conference, to act as the indispensable follow-up of the Madrid meeting on European security. It should amount to a SALT III!

The conditions must be firmly set and maintained: even if we allow that a first session has only a reconnoitring function and centres on confidence building measures, the second one must deal with reductions of armaments and not least, nuclear ones. Possibly a third session will become necessary and should then concentrate directly on gaining European freedom from nuclear weapons. Thus should gradually grow a *joint agenda* for all public opinion movements and, gradually, also for a common front by most, if not all, European governments to safeguard their own overarching interests.

But the row of deadlines should also be borne in mind: the rare opportunity given by the UN Special Session on Disarmament in 1982, and the fateful ultimatum set for the NATO session in 1983.

And still — European nuclear disarmament cannot be a final goal, only an intermediary one. But it is an urgently necessary one. It can, and must, function as the master key to open up the process of stopping the whole insane race for more and more weapons, for greater and greater effectiveness to kill fellow human beings. What we call for is nothing less than a new and true beginning, disarming the powers who now keep us under the yoke of endless fear.

The time to act is now.

Footnotes

1. "Europe" is throughout taken to encompass the continent west of the Soviet border. It includes, of course, Great Britain and the many islands in the Atlantic and the Mediterranean, customarily counted as European, but no colonial dependencies. By definition it does not include demands relating to territories of the two superpowers or Canada, although these nations are prominent in deliberations on "European security".

2. See for an early presentation of the European case as a pre-planned vicarious theatre of a superpower war in order to preserve their own sanctuaries, together with some summaries of calculated costs of the implied destruction, my book *The Game of Disarmament,* Pantheon, New York, 1976, new edition 1978; also Manchester University Press, 1977 (paperback edition, Spokesman, 1980). This view is now further substantiated, widely shared and frankly expressed in the accelerated debate in Western Europe.

3. "The NATO decision in December 1979 to improve its long range theatre nuclear forces was coupled with a commitment to enter arms control negotiations on such forces. This offer was necessary to secure the support of some smaller members of the alliance, but did not reflect any real hope of serious negotiations, much less agreement, on such forces.

By the end of the 1970s the United States and its West European allies appeared to be drifting apart in their views of arms control . . . For some West European governments, arms control was a way of keeping the center and center-left parties interested and involved in defense issues. Nations with influential peace and disarmament constituencies were obliged to champion arms control, even when it may not have been appropriate or feasible, as a means of justifying their expenditures on defense." Joseph J. Kruzel: "Arms Control and American Defense Policy: New Alternatives and Old Realities", p.151, in *Daedalus,* Journal of the American Academy of Arts and Sciences, Winter 1981. (This issue is the second of two specialized on US Defense Policy in the 1980s).

4. *Apocalypse Now?* Spokesman, 1980.

5. Portugal has only signed but not ratified the LTBT, Spain signed but failed to ratify the NPT, according to *SIPRI Yearbook 1980.*

6. Reference might be given to the fleeting moments when Kissinger and Schmidt revealed recognition of how insecure was the so-called security umbrella of American nuclear weapon defence, held over Europe. See my book *The Game of Disarmament* (footnote 2 cited above) or the special chapter reproduced in *Protest and Survive,* ed. by E.P. Thompson and Dan Smith, Penguin Books, 1980).

7. "Eurostrategic" is the technical term employed for ground-launched missiles with a capability to strike well inside "enemy" territory, particularly missiles with a range of more than 800km, marking them as qualitively different from the tactical nuclear weapons intended for more restricted "theatre" use within a battlefield. This categorical difference from the nuclear weapons hitherto deployed in Europe makes it meaningful to concentrate the attention, as is being done in this paper as well as in the growing END campaign, on the new NATO generation of Pershing II (range 1,500-1,880km), of which 108 are intended for deployment in Western Europe and to the Ground launched Cruise missile, the so-called Tomahawk (GLCM, ranges in excess of 3,000km) with 464 in principle decided to be deployed in that same region. But not to be missed in our criticism are the Soviet IRBMs like the SS-20 (range above 4,000km), which are deployed mostly in the western part of Soviet territory but some also in the eastern part, beyond the Urals. They are gradually substituting the older SS-4 and SS-5, which are then being phased out on account of their coarse precision capabilities. See *SIPRI Yearbook, 1980,* Chapter 4, for considerably complete information.

8. I have had to extract them from their hiding places in the 1978 Conference documents and published them verbatim, with dates and names of speakers, in the Swedish *Tiden,* No. 3, 1980. The bare of the texts is also rendered in an article by William Epstein, *The Bulletin of the Atomic Scientists,* April 1979. Below I am following his presentation.

"Among the nuclear powers, only China has clearly and unequivocally declared that it would never use nuclear weapons against any non-nuclear States. The other nuclear powers have persistently refused to make such statement despite strong pressure from the non-nuclear States.

At the Special Session, however, some progress was made. The Soviet Union announced that it had signed Protocol II of the Treaty of Tlatelolco by which it undertook to respect the status of the zone and not to use nuclear weapons against any country that was also a member of the Latin-American nuclear free zone. It also declared that it would 'never use nuclear weapons against those States which renounce the production and acquisition of such weapons and d not have them on their territories,. It also announced that it was prepared to enter into bilateral agreements to that effect with any such non-nuclear States. The United States and the United Kingdom gave more limited undertakings. The U.S. declaration was: 'The United States will not use nuclear weapons against any non-nuclear weapon State party to the Non-Proliferation Treaty or to any comparable internationally binding commitment not to acquire nuclear explosive devices, except in the case of an attack on the United States, its territories or armed forces or its allies by such a State allied to a nuclear weapon State or associated with a nuclear weapon State in carrying out or sustaining the attack'.

The U.K. declaration which was similar to the American, was as follows: 'I accordingly give the following assurance, on behalf of my Government, to non-nuclear weapon States which are parties to the Non-Proliferation Treaty or to other international binding commitments not to manufacture or acquire nuclear explosive devices: Britain undertakes not to use nuclear weapons against such States except in the case of an attack on the United Kingdom, its dependent territories, its armed forces or its allies by such a State in association or alliance with a nuclear weapon State.'

France made an even more restricted pledge. It supported a ban on the use or threat of use of nuclear weapons against States that are part of a nuclear free zone, and declared that it was prepared to enter into contractual agreements with such zones for binding commitments."

9. See for example H. Afheldt, Ch. Potyoka, U.P. Reich, Ph. Sonntag, C.F. v. Weizsäcker: *Durch Kriegsverhütung zum Krieg?* Carl Hanser Verlag, München, 1972. The Max Planck Institute in Starnberg near Munich has been prominent as a centre for more independent defence analysis in West Germany. But several more experts could be quoted who have given their opinions on this somewhat sensitive question also in Denmark, Holland, Norway.

10. We are reminded by several articles and not least a recent book how prominent readers of Europe's future like Walter Lippmann and George Kennan fought for a more positive solution than the establishment of the adversary alliances. Already 1943, Lippmann prognosticated that "Eastern Europe would have to be neutral but that it all hinged on whether Russia would 'respect and support' a policy of neutralisation". And even when NATO was about to be established, Lippmann wrote to urge "the demilitarisation and neutralisation of Germany, along with the withdrawal of all foreign troops".

Ronald Steel: *Walter Lippmann and the American Century,* Little, Brown and Company, Boston 1980.

Warning voices were certainly not missing. Kennan's article in 1957 on the advisability of "disengagement" likewise made a stir.

11. The blame for the division of the common nation is divided between many takers. 15 per cent going straight to Hitler as the cause. The Soviet Union, together with East Germany, is given as the greatest share, 56 per cent; while the Western alliance has to carry 20 per cent and the two superpower blocs together 15 per cent. The Germans themselves, mostly Adenauer and the conservative Christian Democrats were only mentioned by 6 per cent.

Excerpts from *Die Welt,* 24 march 1981. Quoted from English version in *The German Tribune,* 12 April 1981.

12. Several meetings with participants from both same Western, Eastern (and Southern) countries, e.g. in Brussels on the initiative by A. De Smaele, former Belgian government member. See as example a paper "Confidence-building Measures: A New Political Deal?" presented at Pugwash Symposium, Hamburg 8-10 April 1981. Institut für Friedensforschung und Sicherheitspolitik an der Universität Hamburg.

13. See for the discussion of European zones my book *The Game of Disarmament,*

op.cit. pp.197-199, and later various studies by the United Nations, as well as debates in its Disarmament Committee in Geneva. Those many statements are, however, never precise as to the geographical framework but rather deal with "principles". So are also the pronouncements in favour of nuclear free zones in the Final Document of the UN Special Session on Disarmament 1978.

14. Iceland is also encompassed by the Kekkonen master plan, but I prefer not to include it in my operationally more realistic chain of arguments. The American bases on Iceland make it more reasonable to discuss its role in connection with superpower strategies, as we must not be oblivious of the ominous forebodings of submarine warfare in the Northern seas. But they must be regarded as lying outside the presently featured sphere of nuclear weapon free "Europe".

15. I also contributed to this book as well as to the presently very lively exchange of views by numerous articles, regrettably all available only in the Scandinavian languages. *Atomvapen og usikkerhetspolitikk,* Tiden forlag, Oslo 1980.

16. Already in 1957 Roumania, which has always been anxious to relax the rigidity of military blocs, proposed in UN an "area of peace in the Balkans, free of foreign military bases". This demand was, in 1959, clarified, also in the UN, by the Soviet Union as meaning freedom from nuclear weapons or missiles. (See AM: op.cit. p.204).

17. For exploding the logical fallacy of "balance" see my systematic rebuttal in the article "The Greatest Miscalculation: The Arms Race" in a Festschrift for Bert Röling, edited by Robert J. Akkerman, Peter J. van Krieken and Charles O. Panneberg: *Declaration on Principles — A Quest for Universal Peace,* Sijthoff, Leyden/The Netherlands, and T. Reading, Mass./USA, 1977. Or, more generally, in my book *The Game of Disarmament,* op.cit., ch. 4:2.

18. See a detailed and very instructive review in Arthur M. Schlesinger, Jr: *A Thousand Days,* André Deutsch, 1965.

19. Charles E. Osgood has written extensively on the subject of GRIT. What I have at hand is a paper originally given to the Peace Science Society in 1977 as "A Proposal for Unfreezing Force-level Postures in Europe" and quoting several instances, e.g. in regard to Berlin, where it was first called "The Policy of Mutual Exampale" and tried out by Kennedy and Krushchev in 1963. See also Osgood in *Bulletin of the Atomic Scientists,* May 1980.

20. See for a very closely reasoned argument that the independent nuclear weapon force is *not* an asset for Britain, the recent book by Robert Neild, *How To Make Your Up Mind About The Bomb,* Andre Deutsch. London 1981.

21. *Disarmament and Development:* United Nations St/ECA/174, 1972, and *North-South: A Programme for Survival,* Report of the Independent Commission on International Development Issues, Chairman Willy Brandt, Pan Books Ltd., 1980.

22. "Europe as hostage of the superpowers?" in *The Bulletin of the Atomic Scientists,* April 1980.

Conclusion

Ken Coates

At the end of April 1980, the Bertrand Russell Peace Foundation joined forces with a number of other bodies to launch an appeal for European Nuclear Disarmament at a press conference in the House of Commons. The appeal was announced by a panel consisting of Eric Heffer, MP; Tony Benn, MP; E.P. Thompson; Mary Kaldor; Monsignor Bruce Kent, the leader of the Campaign for Nuclear Disarmament and Zhores Medvedev, among others. It quickly attracted several score of parliamentary signatories in Britain, including members of the Labour and Liberal Parties, as well as Plaid Cymru, the

277

Welsh Nationalist organisation. It also gathered early support from bishops and other Church leaders, and from hundreds of academics, artists and scientists.

The text was based on a draft prepared by E.P. Thompson
in consultation with the Russell Foundation, which was
subsequently circulated by the Foundation and considered by
a wide variety of peace organisations, including the International Confederation for Disarmament and Peace (whose
secretary, Peggy Duff, played an inspiring part in the early
work, right up to the moment of her death in 1981 from a
punishingly disabling illness); the World Disarmament Campaign, whose co-founder, Lord Brockway, was among the
first signatories; and the British Campaign for Nuclear Disarmament. This draft was also modified as a result of consultations with a large number of people from other European
countries, members of a number of different political
organisations and churches. The final agreed document read
as follows:

"We are entering the most dangerous decade in human
history. A third world war is not merely possible, but increasingly likely. Economic and social difficulties in advanced industrial countries, crisis, militarism and war in
the third world compound the political tensions that fuel a
demented arms race. In Europe, the main geographical
stage for the East-West confrontation, new generations of
ever more deadly weapons are appearing.

"We do not wish to apportion guilt between the political
and military leaders of East and West. Guilt lies squarely
upon both parties. Both parties have adopted menacing
postures and committed aggressive actions in different
parts of the world.

"The remedy lies in our own hands. We must act
together to free the entire territory of Europe, from
Poland to Portugal, from nuclear weapons, air and submarine bases, and from all institutions engaged in research
into or manufacture of nuclear weapons. We ask the two
super powers to withdraw all nuclear weapons from European territory. In particular, we ask the Soviet Union to
halt production of the SS-20 medium range missile and we
ask the United States not to implement the decision to
develop cruise missiles and Pershing II missiles for deploy-

ment in Western Europe. We also urge the ratification of the SALT II agreement, as a necessary step towards the renewal of effective negotiations on general and complete disarmament.

"At the same time, we must defend and extend the right of all citizens, East or West, to take part in this common movement and to engage in every kind of exchange.

"We appeal to our friends in Europe, of every faith and persuasion, to consider urgently the ways in which we can work together for these common objectives. We envisage a European-wide campaign, in which every kind of exchange takes place; in which representatives of different nations and opinions confer and co-ordinate their activities; and in which less formal exchanges, between universities, churches, women's organisations, trade unions, youth organisations, professional groups and individuals, take place with the object of promoting a common object: to free all of Europe from nuclear weapons.

"It will be the responsibility of the people of each nation to agitate for the expulsion of nuclear weapons and bases from European soil and territorial waters, and to decide upon its own means and strategy, concerning its own territory. These will differ from one country to another, and we do not suggest that any single strategy should be imposed. But this must be part of a trans-continental movement in which every kind of exchange takes place.

"We must resist any attempt by the statesmen of East or West to manipulate this movement to their own advantage. We offer no advantage to either NATO or the Warsaw alliance. Our objectives must be to free Europe from confrontation, to enforce détente between the United States and the Soviet Union, and, ultimately, to dissolve both great power alliances.

"In appealing to fellow Europeans, we are not turning our backs on the world. In working for the peace of Europe we are working for the peace of the world. Twice in this century Europe has disgraced its claims to civilisation by engendering world war. This time we must repay our debts to the world by engendering peace.

"This appeal will achieve nothing if it is not supported by determined and inventive action, to win more people to support it. We need to mount an irresistible pressure for a Europe free of nuclear weapons.

"We do not wish to impose any uniformity on the movement nor to pre-empt the consultations and decisions of those many organisations already exercising their influence for disarmament and peace. But the situation is urgent. The dangers steadily advance. We invite your support for this common objective, and we shall welcome both your help and advice."

On the basis of this programme, the alliance which formed the movement for European Nuclear Disarmament began to find adherents in every European nation, and in an extraordinary range of national and international organisations. In some countries this statement was referred to as the "Russell Appeal", but in truth it had always represented the views of a coalition of different groupings, widely different in their origins and aims.

By contrast, we should consider another document. At the very end of December 1980, the United States' House of Representatives published a long analysis, prepared by the research staff of the Library of Congress for the Committee on Foreign Affairs. It carried the title *The Modernisation of NATO's Long Range Theatre Nuclear Forces,* and sections of it have been extensively quoted above, in one of the introductory sections of this book. In addition to the elucidation of the United States' official view of the context within which the NATO decision to install Cruise and Pershing II missiles in the European "theatre" evolved, it also carried some interesting comments on "European perspectives" on that decision. In order to situate the new movement for continental nuclear disarmament in its political environment, it is useful to cite the seven separate reports which were placed before the Committee, on the state of opinion in Federal Germany, Great Britain, Italy, the Netherlands, Belgium, Denmark and Norway. To allow the reader to distinguish between the findings of the Congress briefing, and the additional notes which arise from the experience of Europe's nuclear disarmament campaigns, we are printing the American official excerpts in small type, and the other material in our normal typeface.

Appropriately, the American document begins its round-up with an assessment of the position in West Germany:

"   A.   THE FEDERAL REPUBLIC OF GERMANY

"The West German preoccupation with the imbalance in theater forces has been instrumental in developing the TNF modernization proposal, and German political criteria have been important in establishing the essential parameters of the NATO proposal. The position adopted by the German Government is based on an effort to maintain a balance between the demands of military security and those of détente. While both defense and détente are acknowledged as equally important elements in assuring Germany security policy, they frequently present conflicting demands which require reconciliation or balancing. The NATO decision linking modernization and arms control achieves this reconciliation and it avoids, temporarily at least, the choice between military and political factors by making one dependent on the other.

"According to Chancellor Helmut Schmidt, the fundamental problem facing NATO has arisen from the rapid qualitative increases in medium range missiles on the Eastern side, plus,

" '. . . the fact that in the intercontinental strategic sector, parity has been fixed by SALT II, so that there is no longer any US "surplus" in that respect, which formerly covered the deficit in continental strategic balance and which could have compensated for this deficit now . . . Under the leadership of the United States, the alliance wants in this situation to create the option of restoring the balance in the continental strategic field by closing the arms gap.' (Speech to SPD faction, 15 Nov. 1979).

"In the Chancellor's view, the December decision was to determine first how the balance in the medium range sector could be restored through the closure of the arms gap and, second, how it could be restored through arms control negotiations. As the implementation of the first part of the decision would take 4 years, the alliance should emphasize that this implementation would depend on progress in the negotiations.

" '. . . concrete measures for closing the arms gap . . . can be kept limited to the same degree as we succeed in achieving an effective limitation of the continental strategic systems in East and West at arms control negotiations, for instance SALT III.' (Interview with German Press, 14 Oct. 1979).

"In order to emphasize the arms control potential, the Chancellor stated that, '. . . if these negotiations turn out to be successful, all that is aspired to under Part I (of the decision) need not be fully implemented, perhaps only much less, and in the ideal case, not at all. This would require, however, that the Soviet Union ideally likewise be prepared to go back to zero level with its armament which it has not only decided but in fact already produced in this field.'

"Defence Minister Apel similarly emphasized that,

" 'the necessity to modernize exists because the others have run away from us. We would prefer it if the others exerted limitation, if they negotiated with us and curtailed their arms. What we need is parity, similar chances . . . .

" 'We want to make the influx of arms that will be available in 1983-84 at the earliest dependent on the results of negotiations with the Soviet Union. It means that the Soviet Union should be brought down as close to zero as possible.' (Apel, TV discussion, 8 Nov. 1979).

"Chancellor Schmidt stated that even a result in which fewer than the proposed number of 572 NATO missiles were deployed, and in which Soviet missiles were controlled would contribute to stability. Before and after the December 12 decision, both he and Foreign Minister Genscher consistently suggested that the Soviet Union stop its present rate of modernization as a stabilising measure that would also help negotiations.

"In evolving his government's position, the Chancellor succeeded in melding the natural tendencies of a significant section of his own party which placed a higher priority on negotiations, with those of his coalition partners and elements of his party who tended to emphasize the necessity of modernization in order to achieve a balance. He achieved this by acknowledging and accommodating the strong feelings within his party that every effort be made to safeguard relations with the East. At the 1979 SPD Congress, he received a clear mandate for the Government's position supporting the NATO proposal. His personal success was demonstrated when he was elected chairman by a vote of 360 to 24 with 16 abstentions. Observers noted that for the first time he received greater support than Willy Brandt, who was re-elected deputy chairman 365 to 34 with 17 abstentions.

"Statements by leading members of the SPD indicated the preference of a substantial number of the party for a solution to the current theater nuclear problem through negotiations rather than modernization. Willy Brandt, in particular, represented this point of view. Speaking to the SPD Presidium, he said that Soviet readiness to negotiate as signified in Brezhnev's Berlin speech must be used 'for concrete and constructive talks.' He expressly opposed the idea that such negotiations should be conducted only after NATO's planned 'counter arming'. He advised that NATO and the Western governments, 'take the Soviet leaders at their word and negotiate on appropriate measures for equilibrium between the security systems'.

"The Free Democratic Party (FDP), namely through Foreign Minister Genscher, tended to place a higher priority on the necessity to modernize in order to equal the balance. In Genscher's view, Moscow bore responsibility for the arms spiral.

" 'It has become necessary because the Soviet arms lead with regard to medium range arms is endangering the balance.'

"He also stressed the importance for the alliance.

" 'I believe the important thing about the December decision is the fact that the Western Alliance will muster the political strength to make a decision that is necessary for security, it will be a sign showing that the Western democracies are prepared to stand their ground.'

"The opposition parties, the Christian Democratic Union (CDU) and the Christian Social Union (CSU) have supported the Government's position on the NATO proposal but have given a much stronger emphasis than the governing coalition to the need for NATO to modernize in response to the Eastern buildup. According to CDU Bundestag foreign policy expert Alois Mertes:

" 'There is now nothing left for the West but the bitter necessity of reestablishing the balance of strength which makes our security and peace credible.'

"The opposition was more skeptical than the Government about Brezhnev's proposals, seeing them as propagandist and designed solely to divert NATO from its course. CSU spokesmen expressed their disagreement with the non-singularity aspect of the Government's policy, arguing that the position of West Germany was too important and precarious to be made dependent on the decisions of other countries.

"The German Government continually emphasized the need for a decision in December, acknowledging that some countries, particularly the Netherlands, were having difficulties. Apel nevertheless stated,

" 'We will fully participate in supporting the NATO decision and it seems that the conditions we have named will be accepted . . . Everybody knows what important NATO political decisions are involved. A decision on the fate of NATO will also be made. In the end, democracies will be in a position to do their duty and live up to the necessary demands.' (Apel, radio interview, 14 November 1979).

"He emphasized that there could be no postponements.

" 'We cannot accept any postponements . . . We need the decision in order to negotiate with the Soviet Union. Loss of time means also loss of time in arms control negotiations with the Soviet Union in the field of medium range missiles.'

"Despite the German desire for unanimity, it was made clear that the abstention of the Netherlands or any of the other smaller countries would not be allowed to prevent a decision being taken.

"The Federal government, also stressed the role it was playing within the alliance in providing a serious initiative for disarmament and arms limitation. Speaking to the FPD Presidium, Genscher explained that the German initiative would concern three main areas:

— The proposal for stepping up the negotiations on troop reductions in Central Europe in which the West would strive for an interim agreement;
— The preparation of the Conference for Security and Cooperation in Europe review session in Madrid in 1980, where confidence-building measures in Europe are to be discussed; and
— Negotiations on medium-range weapons.

"In his speech to the SPD Bundestag faction on 13 November 1979, Chancellor Schmidt announced that a proposal pending before NATO to withdraw 1,000 nuclear warheads from Europe was a German initiative.

" 'We are presently engaged in making a new proposal for a unilateral Western announcement namely, to withdraw unilaterally 1,000 Western nuclear warheads from Europe. It is clear that this would also alleviate the FRG. I expressly promoted this suggestion in a talk with President Carter 2 weeks ago. . . . The alliance is presently dealing with it.'

"With regard to negotiations on medium-range missiles, German officials stressed that these should be between the United States and the Soviet Union and should take place as soon as possible. Consultation mechanisms would be created to allow European participation.

" '. . . (in my reply to Brezhnev) I shall express my view that negotiations should begin as soon as possible between the Soviet Union and the United States. The idea that Germany would have any part in these negotiations is well meant I think but I consider it adventurous. We must not allow the impression that we want or have to have a say at the table of the nuclear powers.' (Chancellor Schmidt speech to the SPD convention, 15 November 1979).

" 'The superpowers would negotiate . . . Naturally consultation mechanisms must be created where the Europeans would have a say because medium-range potentials in Europe are involved.' (Apel, TV discussion, 8 November 1979).

"German spokesmen also stressed that the ultimate goal must be overall parity in nuclear forces between East and West.

" 'In the end there must be an approximate parity on both sides with respect to the nuclear forces in East and West from the short to the long ranges. We must not try for intercontinental parity. Eurostrategic parity, theater weapons parity separately as this will tempt a potential aggressor to say: Well, well, we are not running the ultimate risk.' (Apel, TV interview, 8 November 1979).

"However, German officials consider the idea of trying to negotiate all nuclear issues in SALT III as impractical;

" 'The whole affair must be negotiated in stages . . . anyone setting out to negotiate in SALT III the whole worldwide problem all at once could not finish this in 3 years and would likely get bogged down. But I think if we, let's say, negotiate one stage, then 3 years is a realistic period.' (Apel, radio interview, 30 September 1979).

"In order to gain results, therefore, it was asserted that negotiations must concentrate on specific sectors.

" 'We will make the Soviet Union a concrete offer, namely negotiating on specific weapons systems, against the new systems which the Soviets have acquired.' (Apel, TV interview, 8 November 1979).

"German officials were confident that the Soviet Union had a strong incentive to negotiate and that despite Gromyko's warning at his press conference, in Brandt's words, 'this was not the last word from the Soviet side'. The Chancellor pointed to Brezhnev's use of the word 'implementation' during his October 6 speech, to suggest that Brezhnev's intimidation attempts referred to the actual deploying of NATO systems. Therefore, the Soviet leader might be willing to use the interim period for negotiations. Officials also pointed to the joint communiquè after the Gromyko visit which reaffirmed that both sides saw no reasonable alternative to the policy of dètente.

"While emphasizing their total support for the SALT II treaty, Germany officials avoided making any direct linkage between ratification and the TNF decision.

"Federal Government officials expressed general satisfaction with the December 12 decision although there was disappointment that neither Belgium nor the Netherlands had been able to give their unqualified approval. Germany spokesmen have subsequently expressed the view that they expect these countries to live up to their responsibilities.

"In the months following the invasion of Afghanistan, the German Government was placed in a difficult position. For the sake of alliance cohesion and to demonstrate solidarity with the United States, it felt obliged to support the American reaction. Yet, it was equally determined that the cooperation with the East and the stability in Europe should not be undermined. Therefore the Federal Republic of Germany gave its support to several of the American initiatives, despite considerable misgivings concerning their utility, while refusing to interfere with well-established patterns of cooperation with the East.

"The Chancellor was particularly concerned that the growing skepticism about arms control in the United States and the Carter administration's insistence that there could be no 'business as usual' until Soviet troops were out of Afghanistan, precluded the possibility of negotiations. The hostile Soviet reaction also made negotiations appear a distinctly remote contingency. Chancellor Schmidt feared that the NATO decision could become unravelled if TNF arms control, an integral part of the decision itself, did not show visible signs of progress. He needed therefore, to keep the arms control option open.

"In April 1980, the Chancellor made a series of speeches in which he reemphasized the growing disparity in medium-range systems caused by the ongoing Soviet modernization. This, he said, was increasing the problems of negotiating an acceptable balance, and he recommended that:

" 'A step in the right direction could be for both sides to simultaneously forgo the deployment of new or additional medium-range missiles for a certain number of years. I admit that the Soviet Union's presently existing lead would remain for that period of time. But that would be the case anyway, at least for the next 3 years.' (Speech by Chancellor Schmidt in Essen, 11 April 1980).

"This proposal was in fact a repeat of his pre-December suggestions that both sides agree to a freeze. In effect it would amount to a unilateral gesture on the part of the Soviet Union as NATO could not deploy its systems before 1983 anyway.

"He repeated this suggestion in another campaign speech the following day, but referred to the production rather than the deployment of new systems:

" 'A first possible step for solving this crisis could be for both sides to simultaneously renounce for a certain number of years the production of new additional or more modern medium-range missiles, so that this interim period of years can be used for negotiations on bilateral limitation — limitation to a balance on a lower level.'

"These speeches touched off a flurry of speculation both in Bonn and Washington that the Chancellor was altering his position on the December decision. His use of the phrase 'a certain number of years' led some observers to speculate that he was suggesting that the NATO deployment could be put off beyond 1983. Nor was it clear what implications his reference in his second speech to production rather than deployment had for the NATO modernization plan.

"Federal Republic of Germany Government spokesmen denied that the proposal in any way represented a change in the position adopted by NATO in December. They insisted, on the contrary, that the Chancellor was promoting NATO's offer of negotiations by urging the Soviet Union to halt its modernization program as a positive gesture to enable these negotiations to commence.

"The Chancellor clarified his position in a third speech in which he specifically referred to 1983 as the time when NATO was due to introduce its new systems. Stressing again that the Soviet's ever-increasing lead in theater nuclear systems was making negotiations more difficult he said:

"Since it will take the West until 1983 anyway to put out the first modern Western medium-range arms — we knew this when we made our decision in Brussels in December — and because these arms will by far not have the range of the Soviet missiles — they are in part still being developed and, at any rate, are not even being produced yet — since at least 3 years will pass until they will be deployed in the West, it is desirable that no deployment take place on both sides for 3 years and that one should start negotiations immediately — regardless of whether SALT II is ratified or not.' (Speech by Chancellor Schmidt in Cologne, 20 April 1980).

"Despite obvious signs of unease in Washington toward the general drift of German policy, West German officials continued to stress the importance of maintaining the option for arms control negotiations. American suspicions intensified when it was announced that the Chancellor had been invited to Moscow for discussions with Premier Brezhnev and that Schmidt was willing to accept the invitation.

"Misperceptions between Bonn and Washington multiplied. The Federal Republic of Germany Government feared that American intransigence with regard to negotiations with the Soviet Union could undermine the NATO LRTNF decision. German frustration and unease at American strategy was compounded by the apparent insensitivity and clumsiness of American tactics, much of which appeared to some to be motivated by domestic considerations. For its part, the Carter administration saw German insistence on cooperation and dialog with the East as weakening American policies and giving the Soviet Union the opportunity to divide the alliance. Some American observers alleged that the Federal Republic of Germany was moving to a more independent position within the alliance, based on accommodation with the Soviet Union.

"The American-German friction reached a climax when President Carter wrote a personal letter to the Chancellor cautioning him against making any proposal that might weaken the NATO December decision. As one of the architects of the NATO proposal and as someone who had long studied defense problems and, particularly, the problem of nuclear weapons in the alliance, Chancellor Schmidt was reportedly extremely angry over the letter. Relations between the two leaders apparently improved following their meeting at the Venice summit and the Chancellor clarified his objectives in going to Moscow.

"The Schmidt visit to Moscow has introduced a new impetus into the search for a way to begin LRTNF arms control negotiations. In a speech to the Bundestag following his return, the Chancellor reported that Brezhnev had repeated a firm Soviet stand on three issues:

"1. The Soviet Union cannot be prepared to open negotiations on SALT III before it has gained clarity about the destiny of SALT II;

"2. The negotiating offer outlined by Brezhnev on 6 October 1979 stands only if the implementation of NATO's December decision is suspended;

"3. The Soviet Union is not prepared to accept unilateral limitations of its nuclear potentials not even for a limited period of time.

"The Chancellor revealed that, despite these positions, the Soviet leadership had put forward a constructive new proposal:

" 'The Soviet leadership declared its preparedness to enter bilateral talks with the United States prior to the ratification of SALT II on the limitations of nuclear arms. In these talks, bilateral medium-range arms should be discussed and all factors bringing influence to bear on the strategic situation in this field considered. He (Brezhnev) pointed out that in this connection the so-called "forward-based systems" ought to be included. Please excuse me for using this international term of experts. I will translate it: It means those American nuclear arms which have been stationed in Europe and which can reach the Soviet Union. He added that the agreements resulting from such talks, however, could be implemented only — that is what he, the general secretary said — after the ratification and implementation of SALT II.' (Speech by Chancellor Schmidt to the Bundestag, 3 July 1980).

"The Chancellor commented that in reply to the proposal to include American forward-based systems (FBS), he had stated that in such a case, corresponding Soviet arms should be included in the talks.

"In a later interview, he confirmed that the Soviet leadership had stated that they were not at this stage interested in including British and French nuclear systems, only American FBS.

" In the Chancellor's view, a new situation had been created as a result of his visit to Moscow. The Soviet demand to suspend the NATO decision no longer hindered the talks on the mutual limitation of medium-range systems."

Having inherited this situation, the new Reagan administration, after initial hesitations, sent Mr Alexander Haig to Rome at the beginning of May 1981, to confirm with the NATO foreign ministers that the Americans would indeed negotiate with the Russians about European "theatre" nuclear armaments. Meantime it had become transparently plain that, as far as the American administration was concerned, the SALT II decisions were now in indefinite cold storage. This, and other, foreign and defence policies of the Reagan team combined to persuade European statesmen (and also a far wider public opinion) that the American government was not in the least preoccupied with détente or with the issue of arms control.

A variety of different disarmament initiatives began to develop in Germany throughout 1980. Early in the year Ulrich Albrecht, the distinguished peace researcher, took part in the London consultations which drafted the original appeal for European Nuclear Disarmament. Several other appeals, some overlapping, others different in greater or lesser degree, were soon circulating throughout Germany. During a meeting at Frankfurt at which various European Peace Groups met under END auspices, seven different German organisations began a formal liaison committee to coordinate their efforts on behalf of the END appeal. Two members of this group, Rudolf Bahro and Michael Vester, drew up a commentary on this appeal "A concept that breaks seven taboos and offers a new perspective", which was widely circulated and discussed. In 1981 it became perfectly plain that the discussion aroused in this growing agitation had secured an answering response among the members of the governing party. On May 2nd, the Baden-Wurttemburg conference of the Social Democrats took a decision to re-examine the party policy on Euro-missiles, and took it by a bone-crushing majority. Former minister, Erhard Eppler, explicitly declared in favour of reversing the policy of accepting deployment of the new missiles. At Baden-Wurttemburg the immediate rejection of the missiles was defeated narrowly, but this sharper attitude has been endorsed by the Young Socialists, who account for something near a third of their party's total membership. Meantime, the Social Democrats suffered a major reverse in West Berlin, when the local elections there revealed strong support for an alliance of "Green" and independent leftist organisations which were quite unequivocal about their opposition to nuclear weaponry. By mid-June these events had cut even deeper into Social Democratic thinking, and the party's Women' organisation went on record against the new missiles. The churches were already resounding with debate and protest and vast demonstrations began to take place. Reports of the June mobilisation at Hamburg sometimes estimated the numbers of participants around the hundred thousand mark.

The American assessment of the position in Britain is terser than its report on Germany, perhaps reflecting the importance of the two countries in United States' perceptions.

B. THE UNITED KINGDOM

The Conservative government of Mrs Thatcher has consistently adopted a hard line position toward the Soviet Union, her actions running closely parallel to current American policy. In keeping with this approach, her government fully supported the NATO proposal to respond to the Soviet build-up.

" 'By extending her own armaments efforts, the Soviet Union compels others to do likewise. We must see those who could threaten us as they are and not as we would like them to be.' (Prime Minister Thatcher, Guildhall speech, 12 November 1979).

"The United Kingdom had played an extremely active role in the work of the 'High Level Group' and in the evolution of the NATO modernization proposal. British officials were prominent in urging the importance of the December decision and in stressing the dangers of a failure by the alliance to act decisively.

"Prior to the December 12 decision, Foreign Secretary, Lord Carrington warned that Soviet appeals to talk about the limitation of Soviet arms were 'transparent'.

"According to press reports, Defense Minister Pym also argued forcefully for a unanimous decision in December. He also called for military considerations to take priority over political ones, and stressed that arms limitation talks should be negotiated from positions of strength. He rejected the Dutch request for a 2-year delay on the deployment decision as 'unrealistic'. He also pointed out that NATO's entire long-range theater nuclear force consisting of American F-111's and British Vulcans was based in the United Kingdom. The NATO plan would spread these weapons more widely throughout Europe, which would give enhanced strength to the United Kingdom and the whole alliance.

"The United Kingdom is the only one of the five prospective host countries where sitings for the deployment of the new systems have been carried out, and two main operating bases (MOB) have been selected there. Under the NATO proposal, 40 cruise launchers — 160 missiles — will be deployed in the United Kingdom. In answer to a parliamentary question, Defense Minister Pym has indicated that the United Kingdom will have a degree of say in the authorization for the use of the new systems. However, the precise implications of his statement are unclear.

"The decision to accept cruise missiles and the more recent announcement of the purchase of the Trident missile to replace the Polaris deterrent force has sparked a new wave of antinuclear feeling in the United Kingdom. Opposition to the possession of nuclear arms and the location of American nuclear bases on British soil is reported to be running higher than in the days of the 'campaign for nuclear disarmament (CND)' in the 1950's. The movement has produced a spate of literature and articles arguing for and against the Government's current position. Much of the argument has been evoked by the publication of a Government handbook on Civil Defense, 'Protect and Survive', which provoked a critical review of Government policy by Oxford historian E.P. Thompson called 'Protest and Survive'.

"Within the political parties, the anti-nuclear sentiment has been restricted largely to the left. The Labor Party, however, is split between unilateralists who want Britain to take the lead in nuclear disarmament, and the multilateralists who prefer that disarmament is carried out in the context of multilateral negotiations. The recently-elected leader Michael Foot, has declared for unilateralism and has said he would ask for the withdrawal of cruise missile bases.' "

In fact, this account underestimates the strength of feeling in Britain, even by the end of 1980. The Labour Party, at its October annual conference, opposed the new missiles by an overwhelming majority, and at the same time endorsed the goals of the new campaign for European Disarmament. Its resolution on the question read as follows;

"This Conference, alarmed at the war hysteria dominating the Tory Government's policies, and dismayed at its proposals to replace Britain's Polaris nuclear force, to increase military spending at the expense of other public spending and to welcome the deployment of Cruise and Pershing II missiles in Western Europe, applauds the National Executive Committee for launching a public campaign against these policies.

"Conference, whilst acknowledging that the safety of all people would best be served by multilateral mutual disarmament in the nuclear and conventional fields, demands that the next Labour Party manifesto — and any interim manifesto — must include a firm commitment opposing British participation in any defence policy based on the use or threatened use of nuclear weapons; a pledge to close down all nuclear bases, British or American, on British soil or in British waters; and a firm commitment to disbanding the defence sales organisation and re-organising arms industries to produce alternative products of social value.

Conference pledges its support for the European Nuclear Disarmament Campaign and calls upon the next Labour Government to take the necessary initiatives for the establishment of a European Nuclear free zone as a major step towards world wide disarmament.''

This decision was subsequently reaffirmed by one trade union after another, and even the hyper-conservative steel union endorsed a strong demand for unilateral nuclear disarmament during its 1981 Conference. By mid-1981 it was quite plain that this policy was completely irreversible, and that the Labour Party had made up its mind. Yet this was by no means all: the Liberal Party was also deeply apprehensive about the idea of limited nuclear war, while the various nationalist parties included very strong bodies of support for unilateral disarmament and a European nuclear-free zone. The Welsh and Scottish nationalists were both represented in the first British Conference on European Nuclear Disarmament, at Bradford in May 1981. Not less than 80,000 people, and very likely far more, had already participated in the London rally of the Campaign for Nuclear Disarmament in October 1980. Polls began to show that a net majority of the British people favoured unilateralism, and rejected the new missiles*. Scores of local authorities declared their areas to be nuclear-free zones, and the local elections of 1981 brought to office a Labour group which had campaigned to prohibit all movement of nuclear weapons and radioactive waste throughout the region of Greater London. By June, seventy other local authorities had given their support to this movement.

Even balder than its summary of British attitudes is the American documents' treatment of the Italian reaction:

''
C. ITALY

"To the surprise of many observers, the Christian Democrat government of Francesco Cossiga was able to adopt a favorable position on the NATO TNF modernization proposal and on the deployment of 24 cruise missile launchers (96 missiles) on Italian territory. This government position was endorsed by the Italian parliament when it approved the plan by 328 votes to 230.

"The Communist Party (PCI) found itself in a predicament as the other parties suggested that its position on the TNF issue would be an appropriate test of its independence of Moscow and its support for

---

The BBC released results showing that 56 per cent of the population opposed the deployment of cruise missiles, while 59 per cent were against the programme to equip the Navy with Trident missiles.

NATO. The PCI therefore adopted a position that, while opposed to the NATO proposal, acknowledged the existence of a problem concerning the military balance and suggested certain courses of action.

" 'The objection raised is that this is essential for restoring parity to the military balance which in Europe has allegedly been altered to the U.S.S.R's advantage. We do not have sufficient information to confirm this assumption. The problem of balance does exist and we are therefore in favor of a serious and rigorous verification of the real nuclear strength on both sides. But even admitting that this were the case, if we want to work effectively for disarmament and détente, the path we must follow is certainly not that of reestablishing parity at higher levels, but quite the opposite; that is, eliminating the cause which presumably led to the alleged unilateral alteration. And, if this cause is called SS-20, we have no hesitation in demanding that the cause be eliminated.' (PCI Foreign Section Chief Antonio Rubbi, 7 November 1979).

"The party Directorate issued the following statement on November 28 in which the PCI proposed:
1. To suspend any decision on the manufacture and deployment of new missiles, or at least postpone the question for 6 months or more.
2. To call on the U.S.S.R. to suspend the manufacture and deployment of its SS-20 missiles.
3. To open negotiations immediately on fixing a lower ceiling for the military balance which would guarantee mutual security.

"The change of coalition has not resulted in any change in the position of the Italian Government regarding the basing of cruise missiles. However, the choice of sites in Italy is expected to be made soon and it is believed that this could produce strong local reaction against government policy."

In fact, it was early in 1980 that the Italian communists began to discuss their reaction to the European movement against the new missiles. Professor Giovanni Favilli, a Pugwash member, and a municipal councillor in the Bologna commune, was the first Italian signatory of the appeal for European Nuclear Disarmament, and he secured its publication in the municipal journal. It was subsequently discussed in all the *quatieri* of the City, and then endorsed by Renato Zangheri, the mayor. The mayor of Florence soon joined him. Then other municipalities followed suit. Among these was Marzabotto, a small township famed for its Etruscan ruins, where Nazi atrocities during the war included a massacre which is always compared with that at Lidice in Czechoslovakia. For this reason all Italian peace movements since the war have found in Marzabotto their most poignant symbol, and it has more than once been the scene of mass pilgrimages for disarmament.

Early announcements of the plans for location of Cruise missiles indicated that Siena was a likely choice. Immediate local demonstrations brought a government pledge that there was no intention of installing missiles there. Later it became clear that Comiso and other sites in Sicily would be chosen, and this reinforced the view, not generally understood in Northern Europe, that Italian-based missiles might be utilised in a future Middle East conflict. Active arrangements are now being made to link the protests of the people of Comiso with similar movements in other countries. This may well assist the peoples of Europe to comprehend the mechanics by which a conflict outside our continent might easily "spill back" into it.

In 1981 the "Russell appeal" was placarded all over the holiday resort of Riccione by decision of the commune, prior to a public discussion which would determine future actions by the municipal authorities. All these actions had support from the communists, the left wing Party for Democratic Proletarian Unity, and socialist leaders like Michele Achille. At the same time, there was also from the beginning a significant body of Church interest and support. By June 1981 a committee had begun to plan demonstrations and meetings throughout Italy, and to take up formal and informal liaisons with other European groups.

The American report on the Netherlands is altogether more despondent than its forerunners on the other countries;

D. THE NETHERLANDS

"The issue of new nuclear deployments was the subject of intense public and parliamentary debate in the Netherlands. Like the proposal to introduce the ERW, it fanned the deep-rooted opposition among much of the Dutch population toward nuclear weapons. This opposition was broadly based and represented a force that the Government could not ignore.

"The present Dutch Government is a coalition of the Christian Democratic Appeal (CDA), an alliance of three parties (the Anti-Revolutionary, Catholic People, and Protestant Parties), and the Liberal Party (VVD), in fact the most conservative of the Dutch parties.

"While the political leaders, Prime Minister Van Agt, Foreign Minister Van de Klaauw, and Defence Minister Scholten, and their Liberal partners favored the NATO modernisation proposal, a substantial number of CDA members were opposed. The main opposition party, the Labor Party (PvDA), the single largest party in the Netherlands, was almost unanimously opposed to the decision and recommended that the NATO decision be postponed.

"During the party discussion before the December decision, the CDA established a number of starting points which the Government was to use in formulating its position. These included limiting the numbers of new systems (that is, less than the 572) and that the eventual decision involve production only. Under this approach, the deployment decision would be postponed for 2 years while it was determined if arms control negotiations with the Soviets were successful. This approach was presented at the November meeting of the Nuclear Planning Group, but was rejected by the other countries.

"In a nonbinding vote on December 6, the Dutch parliament rejected by 76 votes to 69 the plan for the production and deployment of new systems. The Government was thus placed in a difficult position. Acquiesence in the NATO decision risked defeat in a vote of confidence, as it possessed a majority of only 2 in the 150-member parliament. In this case, the Government's survival would depend on how many of its own CDA members voted against it. On the other hand, if the Government followed Parliament's wishes and voted against deployment, or abstained, then it risked isolation within NATO, as the other countries had declared their intention of going ahead irrespective of the Dutch position.

"In addition, the Liberals had stated that if the Government took this course of action then they would leave the coalition and thus cause the fall of the Government.

"The Government's decision to support the final communique announcing the agreement of all members for the modernization proposal, while adding a reservation that the Netherlands would not agree to participate in deploying the new systems for 2 years, was an attempt to mollify both its partners and the opposition. This compromise position was successful as the Government survived a parliamentary vote, with the CDA 'rebels' finally voting with the Government.

"The status of the SALT II Treaty makes the Dutch position even more difficult. The Foreign Minister talked of a direct link with the NATO decision, pointing out that negotiations on SALT III cannot begin unless the U.S. Senate ratifies SALT II. He reiterated that the Dutch Government cannot make 'any unconditional promises on the NATO proposal without ratification of SALT II.'

"Since the December decision, there has been no sign of a change in the mood of the country or parliament and, therefore, of the Government's position. New elections are expected next spring. A positive Dutch decision would appear likely only if the current government is returned to power with fully supportive members. In this respect a number of the CDA rebels have been given low ranking on their party list making their reelection more difficult. The election of a Labor government would almost certainly rule out a decision favoring deployment.

Two further aspects concerning the position in the Netherlands should be noted: first a number of Dutch observers believe that Dutch acceptance of deployments would have been made more possible if there

had been a clear reduction in the number of other nuclear tasks performed by Dutch forces; second, it is feared that undue NATO pressure
concerning deployments will serve to strengthen those elements who
question Dutch membership in the alliance.''

This pessimism was abundantly justified: the Dutch elections were a resounding defeat for the Euro-missiles, and the
resulting coalition, whatever shape it might ultimately take,
could in no way endorse the 1979 NATO decision.

On 29 May 1981 the *International Herald Tribune* unhap-
pily reported:

"Tuesday's Dutch general election appeared to have made
it highly unlikely that Cruise missiles would ever be
deployed on the soil of the Netherlands.

"That was the conclusion of both Dutch political
analysts and Western diplomats as they studied the con-
tradictory voting patterns that deprived Premier Andries
van Agt's center-right coalition of its majority in parliament and at the same time made his Christian Democrats
parliament's biggest single party.

"Amid all the political complexity, with no one having
any idea who would head the next government, it seemed
clear that any administration would find it impossible to
assemble the 76 or more votes necessary to win approval
for placing 48 new medium-range nuclear missiles in the
Netherlands.

"A Dutch ban on the missiles would be viewed by
Western strategic planners as a major blow to the Atlantic
alliance.''

Although Mr Van Agt won 48 seats in this contest, at least
six of his supporters were adamantly opposed to the installation of the Cruise Missiles. Democrats '66, a radical liberal
party, which had from the beginning condemned the new
weapons as provocative, more than doubled its representa-
tion to win seventeen seats; while the Labour Party lost nine
seats, some of which fell to other opponents of the new
military technology. Critics of deployment always included
more than a fringe of politicians, who lost none of their
resolve when it was learnt that the public opinion polls showed continuing strong disapproval of the NATO policy. By the
time of the election, only 8 per cent of the Dutch people were
willing to agree unconditionally with deployment, 16 per cent

were prepared to consider it only if it also involved arms control negotiations, and a further 18 per cent would accept it only if such negotiations had already been tried and completely failed. Opposition, outright opposition, was overwhelming. A leading Dutch Atlanticist told the *Herald Tribune* "for us, those figures are suicidal".

This movement even affects the armed forces. The Dutch Conscripts Union, which organises about half Holland's conscript army, has taken up the defence of two soldiers who refused guard duty over nuclear weapons, on the ground that their responsibility was to defend Holland's borders, which have nothing to do with atomic bombs.

Martin van Traa, the International Secretary of the Labour Party, pithily summed up his Party's view when he said "we are NATO's dissidents". But the Dutch were soon to be joined by many others. It was already quite clear to the American reporters by the end of 1980 that the Belgians must necessarily be among these;

E. BELGIUM

"For the past few years, Belgium has been preoccupied with a number of internal problems directly related to the friction between the Flemish and Walloon communities. This tension has been exacerbated by steadily worsening economic conditions.

"During the period of preparation and consultation that preceded the NATO December 12 decision, American officials appeared confident that the Martens coalition government would endorse the proposal and accept the deployment of Cruise missiles on the Belgian territory. This optimism was based on two factors. First, key Belgian officials, including both the Defense and the Foreign Ministers, had expressed their support for the proposal. The support of the latter, Mr Henri Simonet, was considered particularly significant, owing to his reputation and his position in the Socialist Party. Second, in comparison with Holland, domestic opposition in Belgium was relatively restrained. NATO attention and concern had thus been focused on the fierce public debate in Holland.

But domestic opposition to the deployment of cruise missiles had manifested itself in Belgium particularly among the Flemish socialists. The Belgian socialist members of the European Parliament stated in a communique that they had learned 'with concern' of the recommendation made at the NPG meeting in The Hague. They insisted that no decision should be made 'within the unduly short limits suggested by NATO'.

"Close analysis of the domestic situation and of the fragility of the Martens government might have indicated that the official optimism regarding the Belgian position was misplaced, and that despite its official leanings, the Government would have great difficulty in agreeing to such a contentious issue. Prior to the December 12 NATO ministerial meeting, the issue of Cruise missiles had scarcely been debated in the Government (then consisting of the Flemish and Walloon sections of the Christian Democrats and Socialist parties and the Francophone Front. The Cabinet met on the morning of December 12 in order to reach a decision. Their decision was presented to the NATO ministers by Foreign Minister Simonet and the official NATO minutes record that the Belgian Government, noting the consensus of the meeting, endorsed the modernization decision, but said that it would confirm the application of the decision for Belgian territory in 6 months in the light of progress on arms control. However, Belgian officials have confirmed that the Cabinet endorsed the modernization decision but said it would take its decision on the application to Belgian territory in 6 months in the light of progress on arms control. Belgian observers believe that the Foreign Minster, a strong supporter of modernization, saw this more optimistic interpretation as the best means of securing an eventual Belgian deployment decision without provoking a Government crisis. They maintain that Simonet felt his personal authority in the Cabinet would be sufficient to obtain Government confirmation after the 6-month period.

"However, following a Government crisis in April, Simonet ceased to be Foreign Minister. The coalition collapsed in April 1980. After month-long negotiations, the leaders of six political groups (the Flemish and Walloon sections of the Liberal, Christian Democrats and Socialist parties) agreed to form a new government under Mr Martens. The new Government was again totally preoccupied with the linguistic issue and the deteriorating Belgian economy. Consequently, during the meeting of the NATO Foreign Ministers in Ankara, the Foreign Minister, Mr Nothomb, said that he had not had sufficient time to make a decision and requested an extension.

"In September 1980, the Government issued a declaration which it said established its position regarding the deployment of cruise missiles on Belgian territory. The operative paragraphs of this declaration read:

" 'The Government hopes that the talks will lead to positive results and that, more especially, the balance of theater nuclear weapons will be maintained at the lowest possible level. Belgium will spare no effort to make the maximum contribution to this end.

" 'In order to facilitate the conduct of the negotiations, the Government declares that Belgium is here and now prepared to accept the outcome of the negotiations with the U.S.S.R. and to execute its role within the context of the alliance.

"Should the negotiations between the United States and the U.S.S.R. not succeed, Belgium, in concert with its allies, will take all the measures agreed upon by the NATO partners.

" 'For this purpose, the Government will examine the state and progress of the negotiations every 6 months in conjunction with its allies and draw the necessary conclusions in the context of the alliance. Parliament will be kept informed regularly'.

"The ambiguous wordings of the declaration allowed both the supporters and opponents of deployment to claim victory. The foreign press tended to interpret the declaration as a sign that Belgium would accept deployment of Cruise missiles. The domestic press was more cautious, pointing out that nowhere did the declaration explicitly say that Belgium would accept deployment. The declaration satisfied the Prime Minister's objective which was to keep Belgium's options open in order to keep faith with its NATO allies while maintaining his Cabinet intact. The top priority for Mr Martens remains the severe economic problems and in order to tackle these, he needs a united Cabinet.

"The Flemish Socialists continue to be the Cabinet group most strongly opposed to deployment. They have made opposition to deployment one of the points on which they participate in the Government and their political leaders now have considerable political investment in the issue. The French Socialists, for the most part, do not oppose deployment but would find it difficult to remain in the Government if the Flemish Socialists walked out. The latest coalition formed in October between the Flemish and French Christian Democrats and Socialists saw the departure of the Liberals who were strong supporters of deployment.

"Because of the fragility of coalition politics and the still deteriorating economic condition of the country, it is difficult to see how the Government will be in a position to take a firm decision on cruise missile deployment in the near future."

While Belgian coalitions have catwalked a no less difficult path through the first months of 1981, it is also clear that the decisive shift of policy in Holland will considerably reinforce Flemish opinion, and not only Flemish socialist opinion, against all Euro-strategic nuclear weaponry. Already in October 1980, a most interesting and positive initiative was launched by Albert de Smaele, the veteran socialist minister. Basing his proposals on the provisions of the non-proliferation treaty, Mr de Smaele called for a security zone in Europe: Europe , he said, must not become a battlefield for the great rival armies and thus be condemned to destruction.

"The extreme gravity of the situation, with the modernisation of nuclear weapons in Europe, demands strict control of our thinking; and the essential aspects must govern our reasoning. What are the *essential aspects?* The rivalry between the two great military powers has produced in thirty years the development of two nuclear arsenals for confrontation over the Atlantic. At the end of this long escalation there was a growing certainty that conflict would bring about the mutual destruction of the two countries.

"And so, immediately following the SALT II Agreements a change of strategy suddenly came to light. The transatlantic nuclear arsenals of the two powers show a clear trend towards balance and stabilisation; on the contrary their European arsenals on either side of the frontier between the two Alliances are entering into intense competition and development. The symmetry of dissuasion has disappeared between Europe and North-America; Europe becomes the potential battlefield of the great rival armies. In the event of war, the missiles lined up facing each other would strike so densely that the population would be annihilated in the operational zone.

"Not only the gravity, but also the likelihood of war is dangerously increased by new strategy, since surprise, which is impossible over the Atlantic because of radar warning systems, will now be possible on the continent due to the short ranges. With the alert period becoming insignificant, whoever fires first will have a chance of decisively weakening the enemy's retaliation. The theatre countries are going to be condemned to live in a state of permament alert, waiting for the mistake, for nerves to crack or for fanaticism to seal a tragic doom.

"It has been said: *"the search for a third way between Washington and Moscow has a flavour of absurd neutralism"*. It is sad enough that circumstances have led to two great countries to a dangerous nuclear escalation; it would be hopeless if the rest of humanity could do no better than take sides and make war and holocaust unavoidable. The real absurdity lies in the giving up of the hope that there is a role for the community of nations in the offering of better options.

"The real problem lies in the fact that the nuclear era and our millenaries old approach of international relations are incompatible. We have all been struck by that in the days of Hiroshima and Nagasaki. Then we have indulged in the illusion that we could find a compromise in balancing the terror — so much to each one — to keep everybody wise. This fiction is breaking down. However, the very aggravation of the danger through its uneven concentration — notably in the European theatre zone between the two nuclear frontiers — may offer the political stimulus for a regional negotiation, as witnessed by proposals from East and West for a European disarmament conference. On this occasion, concern to preserve military balances should go hand in hand with new basic political thought.

"In the region between the two nuclear frontiers shown on the map live 400 million people whose governments have signed the Non-Proliferation Treaty* and the Helsinki Agreements.**

"Five of the countries not members of one of the Alliances, namely Finland, Sweden, Switzerland, Austria and Yugoslavia — cover a large area and oppose a political barrier to the transit of foreign armies over ¾ of the dividing line between the two Alliances. The significant gap in this barrier extends across 600 kilometers from the Baltic Sea to the Austrian frontier. Basic treaties have already been signed between some of the countries in this gap in order to guarantee their peaceful relations. The strategic scenarios of the Alliances describe these plains as those where the decisive battle would be fought in case of war.

"Who can judge the dramatic absurdity of such an eventuality better than the nations of the continent? These nations shoulder to shoulder on a tiny territory where their common culture has developed over the centuries, these nations, whose different political regimes do not prevent exchanges and friendly relations, will they agree to play this final war? Who will impose it on them? With what right?

"The real interest for the whole world is that the theatre countries, in the context of their respective political commitments, seize the opportunity which presents itself to close the gap and to set up a barrier against the pursuit of military escalation.

"Europe is not to become a battlefield for the great rival armies and thus be condemned to destruction. European security can only be achieved by the direct political commit-

---

*except Monaco and Spain.
**North Atlantic Treaty Organisation:

North Atlantic Treaty Organisation:	11 nations	207 million
Warsaw Treaty Organisation:	6 nations	107 million
Not members of one of the Alliances:	13 nations	90 million
TOTAL:	30 nations	404 million

ment of each State of the continent in the full exercise of its sovereignty".

A considerable degree of common ground exists between this plan and the "Russell" apeal, and many of the proponents of the de Smaele scheme, including its author, have also endorsed the END call for a European Conference. These include Baron Allard; Ignaas Lindemans, of Pax Christi; and numerous academic and political leaders. During Easter 1981, the first modest international youth demonstration for a nuclear-free Europe took place in Brussels, and delivered a message to NATO headquarters.

Developments in Scandinavia have already been extensively discussed in the earlier sections of this book, so we shall cite the Danish and Norwegian sections of the Library of Congress documents together, with little additional comment:

F. DENMARK

"While the vote of Denmark, as a country which does not allow nuclear weapons on its soil, did not carry so much weight as other members, its endorsement of the decision was important in order to satisfy the German conditions of unanimity.

"As a result of pressure from a substantial number of members of the Social Democratic Party the minority Social Democratic government of Prime Minister Erhard Jorgensen was forced to review its position on the NATO proposal. The Government decided that it would not reject modernization and said it would suggest to its NATO allies that the proposal to replace existing systems with new ones should be deferred for 6 months. In the event that this deferment proposal was refused, the Government said it would reconsider its position.

"The objective of the Danish proposal was to give the Soviet union a 6-month period in which to announce its readiness to discuss the problems of medium range missiles. During these negotiations, it was hoped that the Soviet Union would halt the production and deployment of its SS-20 missiles and Backfire bomber. If this Danish initiative failed to evoke a response in the Soviet Union within the 6-month period, the Danish Government agreed that it would join the talks on NATO modernization on terms decided by the alliance.

"At the December 12 meeting, the NATO Ministers refused to accept this Danish initiative. The Danish Government then endorsed the modernization proposal. In order to seek assurances on the arms control component of the NATO proposal the Danish Foreign Minister had flown to Washington shortly before for consultations with American officials.

"The issue of new nuclear missiles provoked widespread public debate in Denmark, particularly concerning what was seen as an unnecessary escalation of nuclear arms in Europe. Public interest in the NATO proposal was particularly focused when three private American analysts were invited to Denmark to speak against the NATO decision. During elections in 1979, two right of center parties who suffered serious losses attributed their reverses to the fact that they had advocated Denmark accept nuclear weapons on its soil.

"Observers have pointed to two significant consequences of the LRTNF debate in Denmark: first, that it focused public attention on defense issues and Denmark's role in NATO to an unprecedented level; and second, that, for the first time, public and parliamentary pressure forced the Danish Government to re-assess its position.

"It should be noted that, as in the case of Belgium, Danish expenditure on defense has been affected by economic trends. The Government has announced that defense expenditure will be allowed to rise only to account for inflation.

"The Danish Government welcomed the results of the Schmidt-Brezhnev meeting stating that this was the sort of development envisaged by the Danish deferment proposal in December. At the same time the Chairman of the Labour Party went to Moscow for discussions with Soviet leaders.

G. NORWAY

"The Norwegian Government was also supportive of the NATO proposal. In his foreign policy statement to the Storting (parliament) on October 25, Foreign Minister Frydenlund said that:

" '. . . in its response to the proposal the Norwegian Government would emphasize that the proposals would not affect Norwegian policy on nuclear weapons on Norwegian soil. However, because of the self-imposed limitation inherent in this policy, Norway would have to give particular consideration to the points of view of other members of the alliance that would be directly affected by a possible decision to deploy the new medium range missiles.'

"The ensuing debate in the Storting revealed different views as to the deployment of medium-range nuclear weapons in Western Europe, but the majority of the speakers gave support to the viewpoint expressed by Mr Frydenlund.

"However, in the weeks immediately preceding the December 12 decisions a substantial number of members of the ruling Labor Party manifested a growing concern with the NATO proposal. But as the Labor Party was split on the issue and as the Conservative Party, the second largest party, was in favor of the NATO proposal, parliamentary support for the Government's position was assured.

"The dissatisfaction from within his own party was sufficient, however, for Prime Minister Odvar Nordli to fly to Washington to confer with President Carter in order to 'emphasize the importance of having real negotiations' with the Soviet Union on the reduction of missile arsenals in Europe. Any doubts on issue or arms control negotiations were presumably satisfied as Norway endorsed the NATO proposal at the December meeting.

"Foreign Minister Frydenlund welcomed Chancellor Schmidt's visit to Moscow and the possibility that arms control could begin. He has also expressed the hope that the talks would reach the so-called zero option, that is, they would make it unnecessary to deploy new missiles either in East or West.

"Both Norway and Denmark are sensitive to the views of their Nordic neighbors, Sweden and Finland. In this respect they are generally reluctant to support moves that could be interpreted as escalatory, and which could, therefore, have adverse consequences on the general stability in the northern region."

To this, much could, of course, be added, but to understand how firmly opinion in Denmark and Norway has moved since the publication of the American text, it is, perhaps, enough to cite the authoritative joint statement of the Social Democratic parties and trade unions of Scandinavia, issued on 16 May 1981:

"The Nordic Social Democratic parties and trade union movement express their concern about the accelerating rate of rearmament and about the standstill in the disarmament talks. We consider it of utmost importance that this dangerous development be reversed, and that Nordic governments take new initiatives in various international fora.

"The talks of limitation of strategic nuclear weapons must be resumed as soon as possible. It is vital to all the peoples of Europe, that a European disarmament conference be convened, and that the Soviet Union and the United States enter into negotiations on the limitation of so-called Euro-strategic nuclear weapons. The safety of all non-nuclear States must be strengthened by, among other things, effective international guarantees, anchored in the UN, against the use or threat of nuclear weapons by the nuclear powers. The disarmament talks must lead to a reduction of nuclear weapons and thereby also to the reduction of the nuclear threat to the Nordic countries.

"According to the UN disarmament session in 1978, the establishing of nuclear-free zones is an important contribution to disarmament and to regional security. The Nordic countries have contributed to stability and détente in the whole of Europe by refraining in peacetime from acquiring their own nuclear weapons or letting other countries place such weapons in any territory controlled by them. The

Nordic countries should determine what common ground there is with regard to the question of a nuclear-free zone in the Nordic countries as a link in the work for nuclear disarmament in a wider European perspective."

The following month it became clear that the Soviet Union was willing to discuss the question of whether the Kola peninsula might to some extent be included in a Nordic nuclear-free zone, although at the time of writing it is not clear precisely what is involved in this significant new development.

Meantime, on 21 June 1981, a marathon peace march for a nuclear weapon-free Europe set off from Copenhagen, to arrive in Paris on August 6th. Via Kiel, Bremen, Eindhoven and Brussels, the organizers, a group of Scandinavian women's organisations, determined in their pilgrimage to create a powerful physical link between all the separate peace movements of the Northern European countries.

These all-too-brief accounts of a growing resistance concern those countries, members of NATO, which have been scheduled to receive either Pershing II or Cruise Missiles. But although the Congress researchers did not report upon them, all the other European States are equally concerned. Two other States are apprehensively poised on the edge of incorporation in NATO, and in both Greece and Spain wide-ranging discussions on the threat of limited nuclear war in Europe have already broken out.

In Greece, Andreas Papandreou and Odysseus Elytis, the Nobel laureate, were among the earliest signatories of the END appeal. A committee was formed by Professor Dimitris Fatouros of the University of Thessalonika. Another group organised a large demonstration in memory of Lambrakis, the pioneer of the earlier movement against nuclear weapons. In Spain, numerous socialist and communist spokesmen endorsed the appeal, among whom were Enrique Baron, the secretary of the socialist group in Parliament, and Manuel Azcarate, the well-known Euro-communist theorist. A conference in Madrid, held under the auspices of the Pablo Yglesias Foundation and the Institute for Marxist Studies, brought together a representative cross-section of the spokesmen of the left-wing parties in Europe in order to consider the issues involved in the European Security Conference: this provided a platform for a lively debate on European Nuclear Disarmament. By summer 1981 there was a large rally in Madrid against joining NATO.

Among the neutral countries, Austria and Yugoslavia have provided a significant body of supporters for END. At the end of June 1981 an important demonstration took place on this theme in Vienna. It called for a nuclear-free Europe as a first step to world disarmament, advocated the dissolution of military blocs and defended the right of nations to make their own choices about their policies. It also called for the conversion of military production to peaceful purposes. In parallel with this new movement, 330 Austrian professors issued a declaration of support for any new move by Chancellor Kreisky against the arms race.

Other neutral States, like Ireland and Switzerland, also became involved. Irish neutrality had been a target of sustained undermining efforts by the Trilateral Commission, but at the Bradford Conference of British END supporters, Sean McBride was able to insist that these pressures had proved unrewarding, and that Ireland was today more committed to neutrality than ever before.

Within little more than twelve months, then, the appeal for European Nuclear Disarmament had secured an answering response from every NATO country, and all the neutrals. It had also received individual support further afield, from Finland, Hungary, Poland, Portugal and Iceland. The individuals concerned included former prime ministers and foreign secretaries, as well as trade union leaders and ordinary workers and students. Now, having assembled, we begin the difficult work of convergence upon some common forms of action. As has been true from the beginning, our only resource has remained goodwill, and that vast generosity of which people are so often capable when confronted by crisis. Our continent confronts a murderous future in which every art has been lavished on perfecting machines for killing men and women in uncountable numbers.

Tortured megadeaths now await those peoples whose previous naive visions of Hell, presented by such seers as Breughel and Bosch, had been established in the handicraft age of slaughter. Then, each dead person was the result of a personal effort by an individual hand. Today, we are all marked to share our anonymous fate equally with unknown millions of other nationals, simultaneously. Budapest and Oxford, Bologna and Oslo, each at random may be the target for sudden and final destruction on a scale unimaginable to the Lord of Hosts himself, leave alone his terrified supplicants, in previous ages. In rejecting this prospect, we shall need to liberate an alternative one, in which human warmth and affection can flood across all the frontiers to annul a truly poisonous technology and all its hateful outworks. No-one can claim that this will be easy, but just as evil is, in our modern age, inventive to unprecedented effect, so humanity is resourceful and ingenious beyond the comprehension of military strategists and armament manufacturers. There is reason, good reason, to think that European civilisation may be about to reach its highest achievement, in releasing a capacity for mutual support and solidarity which is even greater than the power of the mightiest war-machines which have ever ranged themselves against the children of the world.